"If you are starting a new business, currently own or manage a company with annual revenues of $1 million, $10 million, or $300 million . . . Michael has written this book just for *you*. Michael's unique perspective, based on his decades of experience, will provide you with the skills and insider secrets that will increase your company's profits and save you valuable time and effort.

"*Ready, Fire, Aim* asks the questions that every entrepreneur should consider prior to starting his or her own company. The challenges inherent in the business environment and pertinent to owners, CEOs, and managers are defined and explained. Michael states the problems, offers solutions, and gives you the techniques to implement the solutions to enhance customer satisfaction, growth, and profits.

"*Ready, Fire, Aim* is a great read and delivers information that, to my knowledge, is unavailable in any other format. Based on my 35 years of experience in business, Michael is on target and has shared proven techniques that work in real time to create tangible financial benefits for you and your company."

—Robert L. Cox, Author of *The Billionaire Way*

"Michael, you get it when it comes to growing a business! I have read so many 'ivory tower' books that really don't give any practical knowledge, they're just rehashed theory. I can honestly and enthusiastically say this book doesn't fall in that category. It is full of practical step-by-step advice that just makes sense. My internal 'light bulb' was going off with multiple ideas and solutions. I feel so motivated and revitalized; I am going to grow my company to over $100 million! Now, I know I can do it, I have a clear roadmap. Thanks Michael, I needed this book."

—Brent A. Jones, President of AffinityLifestyles.com, Inc.

"Wow! I just finished reading *Ready, Fire, Aim* and I'm putting the strategies to work in my business immediately! Michael Masterson's book, *Ready, Fire, Aim* has the real world, real work experience any entrepreneur can use to grow their business to the next stage of success. If you're thinking about starting a business *don't*, until you've finished reading this book—it will save you thousands of dollars and years of time and effort. *Ready, Fire, Aim* is not an academic study or esoteric theory; its real world lessons teach you how to identify where your business is right now and, most importantly, what needs to be done to grow—right now!"

—Scott Martineau, Founder and CEO of ConsciousOne.com

READY, FIRE, AIM

READY, FIRE, AIM

*Zero to $100 Million
in No Time Flat*

MICHAEL MASTERSON

John Wiley & Sons, Inc.

Published by John Wiley & Sons, Inc., Hoboken, New Jersey.
Published simultaneously in Canada.

Wiley Bicentennial Logo: Richard J. Pacifico.

For general information on our other products and services or for technical support, please contact our Customer Care Department within the United States at (800) 762-2974, outside the United States at (317) 572-3993 or fax (317) 572-4002.

Wiley also publishes its books in a variety of electronic formats. Some content that appears in print may not be available in electronic books. For more information about Wiley products, visit our website at www.wiley.com.

Library of Congress Cataloging-in-Publication Data:

Masterson, Michael.
   Ready, fire, aim : zero to $100 million in no time flat / Michael Masterson.
     p. cm.
   Includes bibliographical references and index.
   ISBN 978-0-470-18202-4 (cloth)
  1. New business enterprises—Management. 2. Entrepreneurship. 3. Small business—Management. 4. Success in business. I. Title.
   HD62.5.M3657 2008
   658.1'1–dc22   2007035350

Printed in the United States of America.

10 9 8 7 6 5 4 3 2 1

To my partners, protégés, and students

CONTENTS

FOREWORD

When Michael Masterson asked me to write this Foreword, I felt conflicted. On the one hand, I have known him for nearly 30 years and watched admiringly as he catapulted himself and the many enterprises he's been involved in to almost stratospheric levels of success and prosperity. But on the other hand, I wasn't all that certain he could readily provide a broad spectrum of entrepreneurs and business owners with a universal business growth and success strategy that would (and could) easily work for any or all who followed it.

My lifework has been identifying universal principles, laws, and tenets of business building that apply almost everywhere. So I'm quite a hard sell when it comes to endorsing any business building book.

Well, I'm delighted to prepare you for a wonderful 25-chapter journey into business building—fast-track style. Michael has produced an excellent business primer for anyone and everyone who owns or runs a business and wants more growth, profit, success, prosperity, or wealth.

I found his take on the concept of taking action quite refreshing. I'm confident you will reflect hard and long when you come to Chapters 9 through 13. Michael's unvarnished look at the agonies and ecstasies of business ownership and how to gain more of the latter and reduce or eliminate the fear is probably the best gift this book provides.

I can promise that when you put down this book when you're done reading it, you will be a far different—completely transformed— business owner than you were at the start.

I don't endorse, recommend, or write forewords for many people. Doing this for Michael's book is my great pleasure. But it'll mean a lot more to you—and your business—if you apply what you are about to learn.

JAY ABRAHAM

ACKNOWLEDGMENTS

I would like to thank the following people for their help with this book:

Judith Strauss for her efforts, for so many years, to make my sentences clean and comprehensible. Jason Holland and Suzanne Richardson for their enthusiastic work tracking down facts and conducting interviews for this book and for EarlytoRise.com. Charlie Byrne for his thoughtful comments. The folks at John Wiley & Sons for their patience and support, and Mike Ward for suggesting, once again, the title for this book.

Jay Abraham for his early mentorship in my career and for his Foreword to this book.

Porter Stansberry for his comments on mentorship, hiring, networking, and consistency. Brian Smith for his thoughts on expanding the customer base. Richard Schefren for his good ideas on management. Joe Seta and Tom Foster for introducing me to the philosophies of Elliott Jaques.

Bill Bonner for his partnership, mentorship, and specifically his contributions about running an idea-led business.

All my business mentors, to whom I will always be grateful for teaching me their best secrets and letting me go when I needed to go out on my own.

All 30 of the entrepreneurs who attended my business-building Bootcamp at the Ritz-Carlton in Manalapan last year. Preparing for that event forced me to refine my ideas about what it takes to start and grow a successful small business.

Penultimately, Christoph Amberger, Laura Davis, Justin Ford, Sandy Franks, Dave Gibson, Helmut Graf, Julia Guth, Annabelle Koffman, Erika Nolan, Myles Norin, Kathie Peddicord, Norman Rentrop, Paul Romano, Al Sears, Alan Serinsky, Brian Sodi, MaryEllen Tribby, Matt Turner, Addison Wiggin, and Katie Yeakle for allowing me to help them grow their great, multimillion-dollar businesses.

And last but not least, my beautiful wife Kathy for letting me work on the book in Chicago during our month together there last summer.

MICHAEL MASTERSON

ABOUT THE AUTHOR

Michael Masterson is not your typical businessman. An ex–Peace Corps volunteer, he never took a class in business, doesn't read the business press, and doesn't like to talk business. He spends his spare time writing, collecting fine art, and practicing Brazilian Jiu Jitsu. His neighbors call him a bohemian. But he's also an entrepreneur. He started his first business when he was 11 years old, and in the 45 years that have elapsed since then, he has played an integral part in dozens of successful businesses—public and private...local and international...retail, wholesale, and direct mail.

His entrepreneurial experience is immense, even compared to other successful entrepreneurs. At one time or another, he has consulted for multimillion-dollar businesses in all of the following areas: information publishing, investment advice, health and nutrition, bars and restaurants, retail furniture, fine art sales, painting, carpentry, pool construction, public relations, career advancement, costume jewelry, perfumes and cosmetics, personal accessories, baby products, audio-tape programs, magazines, newsletters, books, international real estate development, rental real estate management, and sports and fitness.

Richard Schefren, founder of the business coaching company Strategic Profits, says, "I consult with all of the best-known entrepreneurs in the world, and I've never known anyone who has been in more different sorts of successful businesses than has Michael Masterson."

Katie Yeakle, director of American Writers & Artists Inc., puts it this way: "You've heard of the serial entrepreneur. Michael Masterson is a polygamous entrepreneur. He is not satisfied with working on one single successful business at a time and then going on to another. If he's not having lunches with at least six CEOs a month, he's just not happy."

Michael bristles at Yeakle's assessment. "I have had a problem with entrepreneurial addiction in the past," he says. "But I've kicked the habit. When I turned 50, I promised my wife I wouldn't get involved with another start-up company. And I've kept to that promise."

Don't tell that to Dr. Al Sears, whose business, Wellness Research & Consulting Inc., was begun with Michael's help in 2006 and grew from nothing to $4 million in less than 24 months. "The pace at which we became successful was remarkable and rewarding. A good part of the credit goes to Michael," he says.

When asked about his involvement in Wellness Research, Michael blushes. "Oh, that," he says. "That doesn't count. It's not a formal client/consultant relationship. It's just a once-a-month luncheon thing."

The last business Michael admits to having helped launch is EarlytoRise.com, an Internet-based company that provides advice and training in "health, wealth, and wisdom." Started initially as an informal weekly e-mail to a handful of his protégés, it quickly morphed, under the leadership of Will Bonner and, more recently, MaryEllen Tribby, into a profitable $20 million enterprise.

Michael serves as a consultant and chief expert on entrepreneurship for EarlytoRise.com, which features dozens of business and investment experts—including, according to Michael, "lots of guys much smarter than me."

The primary focus of his business life these days, however, is split between real estate and consulting for his primary client, a $300 million, international publisher of information products with offices in England, France, Spain, Germany, South Africa, and Australia. "It's an honor to be associated with this company," Michael says, "and a pleasure to have been part of its growth."

Notwithstanding clandestine luncheons that erupt into new multimillion-dollar ventures, Michael insists that he has been spending most of his time teaching and writing since he retired, for the second time, when he turned 53. "I have wanted to be a writer since my father complimented me on the first poem I wrote. I was, I think, 12," he says. "There is nothing I like better than spending three or four hours in the morning writing, and then spending the rest of the day reading, wrestling, and going to museums and art galleries with my wife."

He writes poetry and fiction ("somewhat badly," he says), as well as books on business and wealth building (all of which have been *Wall Street Journal*, Amazon.com, or *New York Times* best sellers). "I have a readership that appreciates the way I look at things," Michael says. "And that is gratifying."

His nonfiction books include *Seven Years to Seven Figures: The Fast-Track Plan to Becoming a Millionaire, Automatic Wealth for Grads . . . and Anyone Else Just Starting Out, Automatic Wealth: The Six Steps to Financial Independence, Power and Persuasion: How to Command Success in Business and Your Personal Life*, and *Confessions of a Self-Made Millionaire*.

Michael's first business was selling his booklet, *Excuses for the Amateur*, to fellow fifth-graders when he was 11. In addition to this early entrepreneurial effort, he worked afternoons and evenings as a paperboy and in a car wash, for a silver polisher, in a warehouse, as a busboy, and as an aluminum-siding salesman. It wasn't easy growing up with seven brothers and sisters in a working-class neighborhood in New York. His father, a teacher at a private Catholic college, had an annual salary of only $12,000. Besides working in his spare time to contribute to the family's income, Michael wore hand-me-down clothes and grew up in "the poorest family on Maple Avenue"—which, he says, "wasn't on the other side of the tracks . . . it was on the tracks."

Michael doesn't complain about how difficult his childhood was. On the contrary, he says he was privileged. "It gave me good values, lifelong friends, and the impetus to go out into the world and make some money. How can I complain about that?" However, he admits that when he read Frank McCourt's memoir, *Angela's Ashes*, he thought, "So what's the big deal?"

In college, after working for $6 an hour one summer installing aboveground swimming pools, Michael and two friends started their own company doing the same thing. Working 15 hours a day for $30 an hour, he was suddenly making more money than he could spend. "That was a first for me," he says. "And I liked it."

During the winter, when it was too cold to build pools, Michael supplemented his income by tending bar and painting houses. "After that, I never relied on a single income," he says. "Having multiple incomes became a habit, one that was hard to break."

Michael continued to hold jobs and work on side businesses throughout college and graduate school. And then he quit everything and joined the Peace Corps. As a volunteer in Chad, he published his first book, taught at the university, and spent his spare time learning to speak French and play rugby.

He later landed a job in Washington, D.C., writing and producing newsletters while working on a PhD and teaching. A move to South Florida was next—and an experience he had there while he was editorial director of a financial newsletter publishing company in the early 1980s changed his life.

It happened at a Dale Carnegie success course, which he wound up in by a twist of fate. He had meant to enroll in a public-speaking course to help with some of his job responsibilities—but there he was. And though he was initially cynical, he started to work the program—beginning by critically examining his life goals, and then choosing one that would be his primary objective.

After mulling over scores of possibilities, he came to the realization that making "being wealthy" his number-one goal would put the rest of them at his fingertips. He also realized that working for other people was not going to get him there.

After making this decision, which he calls one of the most important he has ever made, Michael put all his efforts into becoming wealthy.

His first step was to learn all he could about the business he was already in—publishing and marketing newsletters. Soon he had produced an entirely new type of newsletter, with an accompanying direct-mail promotion, and convinced his boss to cut him in on the profits it brought in. He had to mortgage the equity in his home to get that cut, but Michael's stake in the newsletter was worth $1.5 million a year later. He was at the beginning of a very lucrative and successful business career.

- At the age of 33, Michael developed the Oxford Club, the most successful financial advisory ever, with an international network of thousands of investors.

- At 39, he retired for the first time, wrote fiction (including a film script that was optioned, 12 short stories that were published, and a novel that was not), and bought into an art gallery "for the fun of it."

- A year later, he joined one of his former competitors in the newsletter business and helped bring that company from $8 million to more than $300 million in 15 years.

- In the early 1990s, he began working with partners to test out ideas about small-business development. More than a dozen of the businesses they launched became multimillion-dollar ventures. Two saw revenues in excess of $20 million.

- At the same time, he began investing in real estate, both luxury home developments and apartment complexes. Within 10 years, he owned multimillion-dollar properties and projects all over the world.

- When he turned 50, he tried to retire for the second time. Unsuccessful once again at retiring, he was brought in as an adviser to the start-up of EarlytoRise.com, which has grown, in seven years, into a highly profitable, $20 million business that serves more than 200,000 customers.

These days, Michael is determined to work as little as possible. "The problem," he says, "is that I don't know the difference between work and play. If it makes me happy, I want to do it. Am I crazy?"

Ready, Fire, Aim is his tenth book and fifth with John Wiley & Sons. His next projects are a collection of poetry, a screenplay, and a book of short stories, all of which will be published next year. He continues to write about starting and developing small businesses on a weekly basis in the *Early to Rise* e-zine.

PART ONE

BEING ALL THAT YOU CAN BE

INTRODUCTION

The Very Best Job in the World

Vanessa dropped two plates of eggs and bacon on our table, a stainless steel and Formica heirloom of another generation.

"Got any hot sauce?" Harry asked.

"You gonna use it if I bring it?" she countered.

Harry looked up. Vanessa was smiling. Harry smiled back.

"You're kinda cute," he said.

"Don't kid yourself, honey," Vanessa replied. "I'm *very* cute."

She grabbed a bottle of Tabasco from a nearby table, slapped it down in front of Harry, and sauntered away. Harry watched her backside as she disappeared into the kitchen.

"I feel like I'm in an old movie," he said, salting his eggs.

"The Green Owl is old Florida," I told him. "It's not trendy, but it works."

Harry looked around. Every table was full, and every stool around the central counter was occupied. Most of the crowd was dressed in working clothes—jeans or uniforms or business suits. And everybody seemed to know everyone else.

"A local place," he said.

"That's the way I like it."

We began to eat. The eggs were good. The bacon was crisp, the coffee hot.

We talked about business. Harry, a career diplomat with the U.S. Agency for International Development (USAID),* had just begun a new post in Central America. He talked about his efforts to master Spanish, and about the challenge of motivating a staff that had been there before him, would be there after him, and was used to doing things "the old way."

"And since they are government employees, it's nearly impossible to fire them," I added sympathetically.

He asked me about my Latin American business interests—a real estate brokerage in Panama, a publishing venture in Buenos Aires, and a residential resort development in Nicaragua.

"They are all doing very well," I told him.

Then Harry leaned forward and asked the question I have been asked a hundred times in my career, the question I always have trouble answering:

"You know, I've never really understood—what exactly do you do?"

A QUESTION THEY NEVER STOP ASKING

I shook my head and smiled.

"You've known me for 25 years," I teased. "How could you *not* know what I do for a living? I know what *you* do!"

"But you ... you do so many damn things. You work with a business in Ireland that publishes a travel and retirement magazine, a business in Baltimore that sells vitamins, a business in London that sells academic books to universities—and I don't know what else!"

Harry had only scratched the surface. I have an active interest in

---

*USAID is an independent government agency that provides nonmilitary economic and humanitarian foreign aid.

> ## THE FOUR Ws OF CAREER SATISFACTION: DEMANDING THE BEST FROM YOUR JOB
>
> They say that the three most important decisions in life are:
>
> 1. What you do.
> 2. Where you do it.
> 3. With whom you do it.
>
> I think that is true. To have a great career, you must choose work that gives you satisfaction, a working environment that is pleasing, and coworkers who make it easier for you to achieve your objectives.
>
> To those three Ws, I'd add a fourth: *when*—as in *when* you work and *when* you don't. Being in charge of the hours you work and the vacations you take is an important element in the mix that makes up the perfect working lifestyle.
>
> This is a book about business, about taking your business to the next level. But it is also a book about personal power and satisfaction, about changing the way you work so that you can become increasingly in charge of the four Ws of career satisfaction and thus be able to say, "I have the greatest job in the world!"

the largest financial newsletter businesses in both the United States and England, a company that teaches people how to make career changes, about two dozen real estate businesses (including two that are at the $50+ million level), a public relations business, several health-oriented companies, and businesses in France, Australia, Germany, Spain, South Africa, and India. I have owned wholesale, retail, and direct-to-consumer businesses selling everything from perfume to televisions to horoscopes, and even a few small restaurants and hotels and oil wells.

Yet I spend most of my time writing.

Harry was right to be confused. I sometimes have trouble understanding it myself. I do know this:

I have what must be the greatest job in the world!

I work when I want, where I want, and with whom I want, doing only what I want to do. If that isn't the definition of the best job in the world, what is?

WORLD-CLASS TRAVEL PAID FOR BY MY CLIENTS

I love to travel, and my job as a consultant to the many businesses I'm involved in takes me all around the world on a regular basis. In the past year, I have spent a week in a 24-bedroom château in Normandy, as well as a week in a luxury hotel in Paris, and have spent time in Madrid and in Rome. I enjoyed several memorable days in New York, Buenos Aires, and Dublin, not to mention the time I spent in our second home overlooking the Pacific Ocean in Nicaragua.

When I travel with my wife, I spend the bulk of my day having fun visiting parks and shops and museums and going to concerts, dance performances, and the theater. When I travel by myself, I block out several hours every day to indulge myself in small museums and art galleries and take advantage of the health club and spa amenities offered by the hotels I stay in.

And because my business interests are international, travel is largely first-class and paid for by one of the companies I consult with.

My office is more a grown-up version of a boy's treehouse than it is a workplace, complete with a personal gym, Jiu Jitsu room, billiard table, movie screening room, and art studio. It is located 1.1 miles (an eight-minute jog) from my main home, which is in one of America's best cities on the Atlantic Ocean in South Florida.

So if you were to ask me "Where do you work?" my answer would be "In all the best places."

BEING IN CONTROL OF YOUR TIME

My working time used to be directed by other people and measured by a time clock.

At the Rockville Centre Car Wash back in 1962, we were penalized a half-hour's pay for each minute of tardiness. Later, as a schlepper at King Cullen's Warehouse, my high school friends and I worked whatever shift we were told to work, and we were happy to have the job. Later still, as an assistant teacher during my college and Peace Corps days and as an employee of a publishing company in Washington, D.C., I was told when to arrive at work and when I could leave. These mandates, I soon learned, were official minimums. If I wanted to advance, I had to follow the unpublished requirements that were kept in my boss's brain—which were usually an hour earlier and two hours later than the official hours.

When I went into business for myself, I began with the happy illusion that I could work the hours I wanted. But I soon discovered the truth about entrepreneurship: that the freedom it gives you is usually the freedom to work twice as long and twice as hard as you ever did, even if you thought you were working too much for someone else.

Nowadays, though, I don't work that hard. In fact, most days I don't do any "work work" until about four o'clock in the afternoon, and then I quit at about five or half past five.

You know what I mean by "work work." It's the work that you would not do unless you were getting paid to do it.

For me, "work work" is answering e-mails. Why? Because that is where and how the people I consult with get to tell me about any difficult problems they may be having. I learned, long ago, that if you refuse to help smart people solve their business problems, they solve them perfectly well themselves. But since I do like to keep tabs on the sorts of problems my clients might be experiencing at any point in time, I devote an hour a day to monitoring the progress they're making in overcoming their particular obstacles, and offering suggestions only when they really get stuck.*

What I do during the rest of my day is pretty much up to me. Most mornings I spend writing, not because writing is what I have to do, but because I like to do it. I work out every day at noon. Sometimes I lunch with business colleagues, and sometimes I lunch with friends. Once or twice a week, I'll have hour-long brainstorming sessions with creative people—again, not because I need to but because I like to. I spend 15 minutes with my personal assistant every day, and that's about it.

---

*Here is a secret to keeping your e-mail work to an hour a day: It is okay to make suggestions, but make it very clear that your suggestions are not mandates and that all decisions must be made by the people who are being paid to make decisions. If you follow the advice in this book, the decision maker will be *you* only in the early stages of a new business or project.

DOING WHAT YOU LIKE TO DO

Except for that hour a day of e-mail drudgery, my time is entirely my own and entirely enjoyable. I take off early when I want to and come in late anytime I wish. I have eliminated all the stress that used to characterize most of my workday.

The majority of my day is spent doing things I love to do:

- Writing down my thoughts and experiences.
- Having lunch with successful people.
- Reading and learning.
- Working out and playing sports.

This is, as you can see, pretty much what I always hoped my retirement years would be like, except that I'm getting paid to spend my time like this now. If you can do exactly what you want, where and when you want to do it, and get paid well for it—that's about all you can ask for.

Except for one more thing: I couldn't tell you that I have *the greatest job in the world* if I didn't also work only with people I want to work with.

HANGING OUT WITH GREAT PEOPLE

In determining *where* you want to work, *when* you want to work, and *what* you want to do, no consideration is more important than *who* you choose to work with. That's because if you fill your working life with really good people, the problems that usually hamper and plague a business at every stage of its growth will be easy to solve and will eventually seem to disappear.

Great people make all the difference.

I can't begin to tell you how many times in my career I struggled with an employee who seemed to have good potential but could never get the job done right ... and then replaced that employee with someone new who began doing everything really, really well.

Many times I have been told by an ordinary employee that certain problems were impossible to fix ... only to find another employee who went ahead and fixed them so that they were never again troublesome.

> **IS A SUCCESSFUL COMPANY LIKE A BUS?**
>
> One of the keys to making a company successful is hiring the best employees you can, the ones who are tenacious and self-motivated, and letting them set the direction of your business, allowing them to excel and adapt to change instead of forcing them toward arbitrary goals. In his book *Good to Great* (HarperBusiness, 2001), Jim Collins uses the metaphor of a bus trip to explain this principle. "If we get the right people on the bus, and the wrong people off the bus, then we'll figure out how to take it someplace great."

That's the difference between an ordinary worker and a superstar.

Have you ever wondered why some restaurants that used to have great food and service suddenly take a dip and begin offering not-so-good food served by a surly, shiftless waitstaff?

The difference is almost always the disappearance of a superstar manager.

Have you ever had a business that failed because your partner turned out to be unreliable, untrustworthy, or incompetent?

I have an interest in several good-sized, highly profitable businesses that operate without any help from me or my partners, because the individuals who are running them are so good at what they do. Once a month, for example, I have a two-hour meeting with a superstar who has created a growing business that is very profitable with only a minimum amount of input from me.

By surrounding myself with the right *who*s—lots of hardworking, problem-solving superstars like him—I've been able to master the *when*s, *where*s, and *what*s of my business life.

I really do have the world's best job. And, by the way, I make a pretty good living at it.*

---

*Since I made up my mind to surround myself with superstars and stop working hard, my income has been consistently in the top one-tenth of 1 percent in the United States. I don't need an active income anymore, but these superstars just keep handing me checks.

WHAT TO EXPECT FROM THIS BOOK

In this book—my first book that is strictly about business—I tell you all the most important things I have learned.

Some of these things are commonsense concepts that can be explained by threadbare axioms,* and some came to me as revolutionary ideas that will be new to you. All of them are equally important. All of them have been essential contributors to what I have, which is what this book can give you: *the greatest, easiest, most rewarding job in the world!*

Some of these concepts and ideas have been introduced in *Early to Rise (ETR)*, the e-zine that was accidentally started in 2000 with a memo I wrote to a colleague about the importance of getting to work before your employees. A few of them have been partially treated in my past books: *Automatic Wealth, Automatic Wealth for Grads, Seven Years to Seven Figures,* and *Confessions of a Self-Made Multimillionaire.* This is the first time I've attempted to put them together in a systematic way, however. It's the first time I've tried to create a blueprint for what I've learned how to do:

- Start a business from scratch and make it profitable quickly— usually in less than two years.
- Take a developed business that has stalled and get it moving again.
- Keep a growing business growing as annual revenues climb from a million dollars to tens of millions to hundreds of millions.
- Get other people to do almost all the hard work for you so you are free to do only the fun stuff.
- Position yourself as an indispensable business builder so you can enjoy a big share of the profits even if you are working only part-time.
- Duplicate your winning strategy in several businesses so you never have to worry about needing any one of them.
- Enjoy the very best job in the world.

This is a book about starting and growing entrepreneurial businesses. By entrepreneurial businesses, I mean businesses that create

---

*As my friend Bob Irish told me, "Just because it is common sense doesn't mean it's common practice."

their own products, do their own marketing, and determine their own destinies. This is not a book meant for professional practices, service businesses, or franchises, although the motivated owner of such an enterprise will find ideas here that can be very helpful. Nor is this book meant to be helpful to larger businesses—and by that, I mean businesses larger than, say, $500 million in revenues—although, again, a senior executive of such a business could apply some of the ideas in this book to growing a division of the company.

This is also a book about personal transformation. To become good at starting and growing businesses and getting other people to run them for you, you have to develop certain skills. I will tell you exactly what those skills are and how you can get very good at them fast.

Among other things, you will learn:

- The four stages of entrepreneurial growth and the primary problems, challenges, and opportunities that each stage presents.
- The five "magic wands" of business genius that any ambitious person can learn to wield.
- Why selling is your first business priority and the one thing you should never stop doing.
- How to become the top marketer for your business—and why it matters.
- The handful of numbers that are critical in every business. (You'll find out what those numbers are for your business and how to streamline your management by getting everyone to focus on them.)
- How to generate tipping-point ideas on a regular basis.
- When to cut your losses short and when to let your winners run.
- Why direct marketing should be part of every growing business.
- The front-end/back-end method of doubling profits easily.
- Why having a Plan B is as important as Plan A, and when and how to create it.
- How pushers, thinkers, organizers, and sellers differ from each other, and how to attract the ones you need for your business.

You will also learn why taking action matters so much in business, and why one business strategy—*Ready, Fire, Aim*—may be the single most important way to do it.

You will discover ways to develop profitable new products out of old ones, how to design powerful marketing campaigns that will regularly outsell your competitors, how to devise and integrate innovative operational procedures that will reduce costs, hassles, and customer service complaints . . .

And that's just for starters.

CHAPTER ONE

GETTING TO THE NEXT LEVEL

Ever since I started writing about business, I've had the idea of leading a very special, very high-priced retreat for entrepreneurs.*

My goal was not financial. By the time I became a business writer, I no longer needed money and could have readily come up with many easier ways to make the $300,000 that such a retreat could generate.

What inspired me was an ego challenge: All around me, self-proclaimed business experts were charging $1,000 to $5,000 for seminars, and they were getting plenty of eager people to pay up. Most of these guys were one-trick ponies—zero-down real estate gurus, direct-marketing experts, or motivational speakers. Few of them had my depth or breadth of experience. If they could get away with charging $5,000, I reasoned, I should be able to charge $10,000.

---

*I began writing about business in 2000, after a 30-year career that involved the successful start-up of several dozen multimillion-dollar businesses, including six or seven with revenues that exceeded $10 million, three or four that exceeded the $25 million mark, one that reached $135 million before it was sold (which is when I retired for the first time), and one—an ongoing business—that hit $270 million last year and is growing strongly.

So that's what I did. I spoke to MaryEllen Tribby, the superstar who runs the business advisory business EarlytoRise.com (ETR),* and she agreed to do it. Three months later, she had everything set up and 30 tickets sold.†

The only thing left was to come up with a seminar schedule that would justify an investment of four days and $10,000 by each attendee.

"Pride comes before the fall." That saying haunted me as I pondered the question: What could I do for those 30 people that would be worth so much of their time and money?

It wasn't going to be easy. Although they had all achieved a great deal in their lives, each had a different sort of business. Some were beginning new businesses. Many were growing modest-sized companies. And some had well-established $10 million to $25 million enterprises.

To make matters more challenging, their businesses ranged from professional services to publishing to manufacturing . . . even to restaurants! To make this retreat work for everyone in the time allotted, I had to come up with a format and an agenda that would identify their similarities as well as their differences.

I thought a lot about it for several days, but couldn't come up with an answer. I called in two of ETR's most powerful thinkers, senior writer Charlie Byrne and contributing business management expert Richard Schefren (both superstars in their domains), and asked them what they thought. The specific question I posed was:

What is it that all entrepreneurs and/or businesspeople—regardless of what kind of industry they are in—want for themselves and their companies?

---

*EarlytoRise.com is one of more than 10 businesses in which I have an active interest. Because it is the most recent of these businesses, it gets the greatest amount of my time. But, as you may have guessed from reading the Introduction to this book, that is a relatively modest amount—about five hours a week, on average. This is a book about how you can create and run multiple multimillion-dollar businesses without working as hard as you are working now.

†Marketing Tip: The easiest way to create profits in your business is to sell your best customers a higher-level version of something they have already bought. MaryEllen's marketers did that by sending out a special invitation to a limited number of ETR customers who had already spent $2,000 on a three-day conference with various ETR business writers. The new seminar was positioned as more (four days) and better (with me only) and sold out in a matter of weeks.

Charlie was the first to reply.

"It seems to me," he said, "that novices want to know how to start up businesses from scratch."

"And people who are already in business, (like me)," Richard added, "want to know how they can take their businesses to the next level."

Both answers sounded right—exactly right.

"So that's what we are going to do," I said. "We'll develop a program so that everybody who comes—beginners, intermediates, or even experienced entrepreneurs—will leave the seminar with a blueprint for getting to that next level."

THE FOUR STAGES OF BUSINESS DEVELOPMENT

If you look at how businesses develop over time, either from your own experience or by looking at industry statistics for entrepreneurial ventures, you will see that there are basically four stages of growth.

1. *The first stage is starting out*—taking your business from an idea to actively running and generating reasonable cash flow. For the purposes of simplicity, I delimited it by annual revenues: from zero to $1 million.
2. *The second stage is the fast-growth stage*—taking your business from the $1 million level (at which there is usually little or no profit) to a level where it is making about $1 million to $2 million a year in profits. Expressed in terms of revenues, I identified that stage as $1 million to $10 million.
3. *The third stage is the adolescent stage*—taking your business over the $10 million threshold (which is difficult for most entrepreneurs) to a substantially solid business where profits can be in the $2 million to $5 million range. The revenue parameters of this stage are from $10 million to $50 million.
4. *The fourth stage is the maturing stage*—taking your business from revenues of $50 million to $100 million or $200 million or even $300 million.

The theory that Charlie, Richard, and I developed, and that I presented to attendees at the beginning of the retreat, was that every entrepreneurial business has these four stages, and that each stage has its own unique characteristics in the form of problems, challenges, and opportunities.

I liked that theory—the simplicity of it. But what, I wondered, were those problems, challenges, and opportunities?

I spent several weeks thinking about it and came up with lots of ideas. Some of those ideas I knew were good and true. Others were true in certain cases or for certain industries but not for others. I was looking for a *unifying theory* of business growth—the problems, challenges, and opportunities that are *common to every business.*

It was difficult to find a unifying theory because of some fundamental differences between certain sorts of businesses—professional firms, franchises, nonprofits, and others. Another problem was that I have had no experience growing large companies—companies larger than $300 million—so I couldn't pretend to be able to create a theory that would be applicable to them.

But if I limited my scope to entrepreneurial businesses—businesses that create their own products, do their own marketing, and determine their own destinies—then it could work. I could come up with a list of problems, challenges, and opportunities that are common to all such businesses.*

The first task was to characterize the stages of business development. I kept it simple by limiting the number of stages to four. In human development, there are four stages of growth: infancy, childhood, adolescence, and maturity.† Thus, I labeled the four stages of business growth accordingly.

When it came time to identify the common problems, challenges, and opportunities, I also came to the conclusion that less is more. In fact, I thought it would be great if I could identify one and only

---

*Although this book is not specifically meant for professional practices, service businesses, nonprofits, or franchises, motivated owners of such enterprises will find plenty of ideas here that can grow their businesses. Likewise, senior executives of large businesses will be able to use many of the secrets and skills presented in this book to grow their divisions and/or profit centers.

†There is another stage of life, senescence; but this is not a stage of business that I will discuss in this book. Some businesses do reach a stage where they are dying and have no chance of further growth. Many, however, can be revived simply by applying the growth-giving secrets covered in these pages.

one characteristic for each category—the most important problem, challenge, and opportunity at each stage of development.

To test my new theory, I asked Jason Holland, my research assistant, to assemble the annual revenue and profit figures for the last six start-up companies I worked with. I wanted to see how fast each had grown every year, and how long it had taken them to reach certain revenue targets—$1 million, $5 million, $10 million, and so on. Perhaps that would help me identify any common characteristics.

In fact, it did. What I discovered from looking at Jason's charts and remembering the individual histories of those start-ups was that the problems, challenges, and opportunities that each faced were more or less the same at each level of growth.

The time it took to get from zero to $1 million in revenues was different for each company, ranging from one year to five, as shown in Figure 1.1. Yet there was one very revealing common aspect of this initial stage of growth. Once the business figured out how to sell its product profitably, getting to $1 million in revenues was done within a single year. The companies that took three and four and five years to hit $1 million were all struggling with the same problem—making that first profitable sale. But the moment they figured it out (indicated by having reached the $1 million revenue mark), they were up and running.

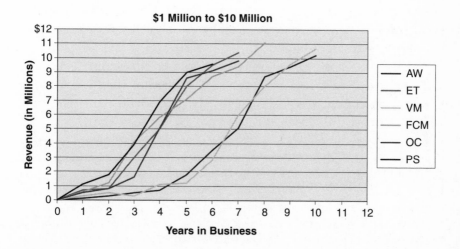

FIGURE 1.1 How Four Companies Grew from $1 Million to $10 Million

I could see from Jason's chart that once a business hit the $1 million revenue mark, it took, on average, only five years to hit the next level of $10 million in sales. And when I thought about how each of these companies achieved that next level of growth, I could see that there were two factors that mattered most: speed and innovation.

There were four companies in that group of six with revenues in excess of $10 million, as shown in Figure 1.2. Each of them experienced a year or two when problems escalated and profits dipped. To repair those problems and bring the company back to profitability, they had to implement systems and procedures that were lacking because of all the growth they had experienced.

Two of the companies reached revenues that surpassed $50 million. How they—and every other company I've worked with that has hit or exceeded $100 million—got bigger was surprisingly easy to answer.

I was excited about what we had discovered. I felt like we had come up with a unifying theory of entrepreneurial business growth. We tightened up the charts and presented them on the first night of our retreat.

Showing the graphic evidence of these growth stages evoked a pretty strong reaction from our attendees.

"I definitely can relate to your theory," one told me. "I have been stuck at the $1 million level for five years now, and can't seem to break out of it."

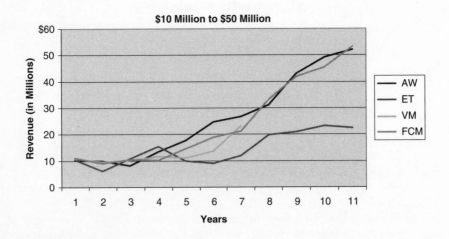

FIGURE 1.2   How Two Companies Grew from $10 Million to $50 Million

Another said, "My business is old and profitable. It did over $20 million last year, and I don't really need more money. But I would like to see it grow to $100 million in the next five or 10 years—not for me but to have something big enough to distribute to my 10 grandchildren."

Over the next four days, we made numerous references to this unifying theory—that at each of the four stages of entrepreneurial growth, you will face certain distinct problems, challenges, and opportunities, and that these problems, challenges, and opportunities depend less on what business you are in than on the size of your business.

Other issues matter as well, but if you know what to expect at each stage of the game and prepare yourself for those common problems, challenges, and opportunities, it will be much easier to reach the next level.

PROBLEMS, CHALLENGES, AND OPPORTUNITIES

I have made some improvements in my unifying theory since the retreat. Here is my updated idea about the four stages of entrepreneurial growth and the most important problem, challenge, and opportunity that presents itself at each stage:

Stage One: Infancy—zero to $1 million in revenue
Main Problem: You don't really know what you are doing.
Main Challenge: Making the first profitable sale.*
Main Opportunity: Achieving a minimum critical mass of customers.

Stage Two: Childhood—$1 million to $10 million in revenue
Main Problem: You are only breaking even or may even be losing money.
Main Challenge: Creating many additional, profitable products quickly.
Main Opportunity: Increasing cash flow and becoming profitable.

---

*By profitable, here, I mean cost-effective. The business itself will not be profitable at this point, but the cost of the sale should be such that, once you reach a critical mass of customers and generate back-end revenue, you can be profitable.

Stage Three: Adolescence—$10 million to $50 million in revenue

Main Problem: Your systems are strained, and customers are noticing.

Main Challenge: Turning the chaos into order.

Main Opportunity: Learning how to establish useful protocols and manage processes and procedures.

Stage Four: Adulthood—$50 million to $100 million in revenue and beyond

Main Problem: Sales slow down and may even stall.

Main Challenge: Becoming entrepreneurial again.

Main Opportunity: Getting the business to run itself.

Of the 30 people who attended the retreat, about six were just starting out (although several of them had completed successful careers and were beginning anew). Most were in one of the early stages of growth, and three were already closing in on $25 million in revenues.

WHAT SHOULD YOU WANT FOR YOUR BUSINESS?

Despite their differences, the retreat attendees all wanted the same thing: *to get to the next level*.

And guess what? At the end of our experience together, all of them said they knew exactly what they needed to do to achieve their individual goals.*

I was enormously gratified by their comments, hugely proud of their transformations, and immensely excited about the ideas I had gotten from them. About a third of the group said they had gotten their money's worth from the retreat "after the second day." The rest, on the final afternoon, cited specific actions they were going to take (or, in some cases, had already taken) to achieve their goals. In all,

---

*I don't want to take credit for providing all the ideas that these 30 entrepreneurs took away from the retreat. Many, if not most, of them came from the entrepreneurs themselves. The smartest thing we did in organizing the retreat was to eschew lecturing for roundtable discussions. By bringing in the questions, comments, and suggestions of 30 bright and successful people, a great deal of the hard work was done for me.

the experience was worth a great deal more than $10,000 to each and every one of them.

In the chapters that follow, you will have access to all of the ideas we talked about at that retreat,* and many more that we didn't have time to discuss during our four days of brainstorming. If you read this book actively and positively (thinking hard about how these ideas could work for you and your business, and not discarding any of them because you might have heard them before or because they just don't seem, at first glance, to be relevant to your situation), you will be able to:

- Identify where your business is now and what specific problems, challenges, and opportunities lie ahead.
- Determine a path to get your business to the next level, and then chart the next path to reach the following level.
- Continue to grow your business into the millions and tens of millions and hundreds of millions of dollars in revenue.
- Be in charge of all this growth and profit from it.
- Become a primary beneficiary of multiple multimillion-dollar businesses.
- Surround yourself with helpful, work-loving people.
- Reduce the time you spend working.
- Swap the job you have now for the very best job in the world!

In this book, I am going to give you every concept, strategy, technique, and skill you need to make your transformation. What you have to give is simply your good faith and time. Good faith and time are what every one of the 30 businesspeople gave when they came to the retreat, and those investments were enough to create for each of them a very practical plan of action that will take their businesses to the next level. It worked for them. It should work for you.

Actually, they gave something else that you haven't given: $10,000. When you put these recommendations into action and are happy with the results, I hope you'll write to me and tell me all about it. Including a check for $10,000 will be optional.

---

*It would be unfair to tell you the specific business-building plans that the attendees shared that day, but I will tell you all the principles, strategies, and concepts that led them to their plans.

CHAPTER TWO

WHY EMPLOYEE SIZE MATTERS

A Different Way of Measuring the Four Stages

Because entrepreneurs like to think about revenues when they think about growth, I have characterized the four stages of entrepreneurial growth accordingly: zero to $1 million, $1 million to $10 million, $10 million to $50 million, and $50 million to $100 million and beyond. My operating theory—that each stage has its own particular problems, challenges, and opportunities—will hold up pretty well for most people who read this book. There will be exceptions, though.

You may find that the major problem you are facing right now does not correspond to the stage you are in. That may be because I determined the stage delineations by revenue, which sometimes isn't the most important factor in corporate change. In some businesses, employee size is a better indication of growth and the problems, challenges, and opportunities that come with growth.

In *The Tipping Point* (Little, Brown, 2000), Malcolm Gladwell talks about how communication is affected by the size of the community. He presents scientific studies that suggest that communication is at its most efficient when the group is small—no more than six or seven people. And he speculates that the quality of communication breaks down as the group gets larger.

When I read that passage in *The Tipping Point*, I thought about how small businesses grow and change in terms of their population. And it occurred to me that there is a fundamental shift that occurs with each geometric progression of growth—that each time the business multiplies itself by a factor of about seven, the corporate culture changes. I have written about that phenomenon several times in *Early to Rise* over the years—and every time, I was reminded of how true it seemed.

These geometric progressions might very well correspond to the four stages of entrepreneurial growth. It may be that the number of employees you have, and not revenue, is what determines your stage of growth.

Perhaps in your company each of the four stages of entrepreneurial growth depends on how many executive-level employees you have working for you.*

The first stage starts with you and goes to seven executive employees. Why? Because you can efficiently communicate with and delegate to only seven people. Multiplying by seven, the number of executive employees grows from seven to 49 during the second stage, and during the third stage it goes from 49 to 343. The fourth stage is 344 and beyond.

THE FIRST STAGE: YOU PLUS SEVEN EXECUTIVE EMPLOYEES

When you begin your business, your initial executive employees understand exactly what you want, because they all report directly to you. With everyone on the same page, the only problem you should have (if you are paying attention to the right thing) will be figuring out how to sell your lead product.

Once you have solved that first problem and sales are coming in quickly, your business takes its first leap forward in employee growth.

---

*Since this theory is about corporate communication and growth, it makes sense to count only the employees who are responsible for creating or translating communications and, thus, rise up in the organization as the business grows—not employees who, though important to the business, merely receive information (nonmanagement workers who do customer service, data input, sales, fulfillment, accounting, etc.).

Because there are so many new demands in terms of customer service, product production and fulfillment, bookkeeping, and so forth, you generally break up the company by function, assigning each of your seven employees some specific functional responsibility. Thus one person becomes the manager for customer service, another one is put in charge of sales, and so on. Each of them then hires a team of people to execute their obligations.

Thus the first seven become functional managers, and as each additional second-tier employee is hired, your company's capacity to produce and sell more products increases too. At this stage of entrepreneurial growth, increasing production is the best way to spur growth. So you encourage it.

THE SECOND STAGE: FROM SEVEN FIRST-TIER EMPLOYEES TO 49 SECOND-TIER EMPLOYEES

Eventually, seven becomes 49. All of your first-tier and second-tier employees are fully occupied, and yet there is more work to be done. Plus, things are getting chaotic. The second stage is usually the fastest-growth stage for entrepreneurial businesses. Fast growth means new problems that have not been encountered before. Fast growth means everybody is too busy to solve them. Fast growth means some of the systems that have worked fine in the first stage are breaking down, because new employees are being hired so quickly that those systems can't be properly taught or monitored. Sales are booming, but the business feels like it is ready to burst.

You know it's time for another change, but you are not sure what it should be.

Almost everybody who is working for you is good at what they do. They work hard—usually very hard—and they have all been well trained. But the problems are mounting, and they can't keep up. Some of them, you discover, are burying their problems. Others are getting frustrated. Some are thinking of quitting.

You have given so much—figured out how to acquire new customers and then found a way to sell them more and more products so that your business is now sizable and profitable. Most of what you have learned how to do is about growth, and the growth is still occurring.

The problems—customer complaints about service and fulfillment and product quality—have to do with managing that growth. That part of the business is important, you know, but it doesn't really interest you. "Why can't someone else solve those problems?" you think. You are taking care of the most important job—and that is sales.

And you are right—sort of. Selling has been your top priority during the first two stages of growth, but now management problems threaten to endanger your company. Unless you fix them, you fear that everything you have built will start to crumble.

Because you see the problems as management issues, you decide that the change you need to make is to introduce a level of professional management.

You think about hiring a CEO from the outside. You wonder whether the person who is running your accounting department can rise to the challenge of becoming a CFO.

Right about this time, you bring in a professional consultant, who charges you a lot of money to tell you what you already know: that your business is no longer a mom-and-pop operation, and you have to get some people and systems in place to handle the problems you are now facing.

What your consultant may not tell you is that the crisis you are facing is characteristic of all businesses that are bordering on hiring a third tier of employees. And there is a good and simple reason for that.

Your first-tier employees know just about everything you know, because they have been around you, eight or 10 hours a day, since the very beginning. They not only know how to do their jobs exactly right (otherwise you would have let them go), but they also know all your ideas about how you want the business to grow. They are, in effect, extensions of your will. Since your major focus is on selling, everything they do—even if it doesn't directly involve sales—will support that primary goal.

Your second-tier employees don't answer to you directly, but they hear about you through the first-tier employees who are in direct touch with you. Sometimes those first-tier bosses will complain about you. Sometimes they will disagree with your ideas. But they will almost always communicate your wishes to their people, either directly or indirectly, so those second-tier employees will always be able to *see through* their bosses and find out what you want.

Since what you want is to increase sales by increasing production, those second-tier employees—if they are smart—will tailor their work to accommodate your ultimate goal. Even if their bosses disagree with bits and pieces of what you say, those second-tier employees recognize that their ultimate interest lies in pleasing you. So they do that, directly or indirectly, as needed.

THE THIRD STAGE: FROM 49 SECOND-TIER EMPLOYEES TO 343 THIRD-TIER EMPLOYEES

When all 49 of your executive employees are maxed out, you do what you did the last time. You allow your business to grow again—actively, by recognizing the problem and creating a new organizational structure, or passively, by allowing managers to solve problems the way they normally do: by hiring people. And thus a third tier of employees comes into the workplace.

But there is a big difference between this third tier and the second tier. And that difference is that they cannot see through their bosses to find out what you want. When these third-tier employees look through their bosses, they see your first-tier people, some of whom may harbor different ideas about running the business than you have.

This disconnect is sometimes good for growth and sometimes bad for it, but it is always bad for communication. What gets lost in the shuffle is concern for the customer. Sales are still booming, but everything else is falling apart.

As your business expands from 49 to 343 employees,* management problems will increase. At some point, everyone will turn to you for

---

*I am using exact numbers here, but I don't, of course, believe that business growth is that exact. Likewise, the idea that each tier-level employee is upgraded at each stage of development is a generalization. Some employees stay where they are. Others jump a level. Some are hired and some are fired. That said, I like this growth model because it represents an ideal. If you make it a practice to hire people with potential—the potential to do a particular job as well as or better than you can do it—your business can grow this way, with each tier being promoted to the next and each stage of growth giving rise to a new level of challenge and reward for your employees. Smart entrepreneurs will encourage their employees to hire subordinates who are as good and capable as they are. If you are not doing that, start doing it now. It will make everything easier later on.

leadership. "What are we going to become?" they will want to know. "Will we be a schlocky, fly-by-night company that is only interested in growth? Or a quality-oriented business that cares about its customers?"

If you are smart, you will answer them correctly and back up your words by taking the right actions. What you need to do is elevate the importance of customer service and product quality to make those things just as important as anything else (i.e., sales). Making that commitment will mean funding lots of nonexecutive employees—people who will not be involved directly in creating change, but rather in managing it.

To effect that change, you will have to allow your business to transform itself from the mom-and-pop sales organization it has been to a professionally run business that crosses its t's and dots its i's. As a sales-oriented entrepreneur, you won't like this change very much, because it will seem backward-moving in some way. But you will allow it because you will be sure that it is needed.

WHY 100 PERCENT EMPLOYEE RETENTION DOESN'T WORK

You may think (as many employment experts do) that the lower your employee turnover is, the stronger your business. This can be a useful indicator. If people are leaving in droves, you are probably doing something wrong. But if you subscribe to the zero-turnover mantra, which is not an achievable goal anyway, you will spend too much time making your employees happy and not enough focusing on growing your business the right way: by retaining only the key people who can make things happen.

For one thing, the hiring process is not foolproof. From time to time, everyone picks candidates who don't work out. The very best you can hope for is a 75 percent success rate, and probably only 50 percent. So out of all the new hires in a year, you'll want to keep only half or, if you're lucky, slightly more. Some of the mediocre employees will leave voluntarily, whereas some you will have to fire.

The next step is holding on to those standout employees who remain, which you do by overpaying them by at least 10 percent, giving them the resources they need to do their jobs, and, most of all, giving them your confidence, approval, and a worthy challenge that tests their abilities. They won't disappoint you.

During this stage of growth, your relationship with some of your key employees will change. Most of your first-tier employees will not welcome the change toward professional management, because it will violate everything they have learned about business—which is that growth is the only thing that really counts. Your job will be to encourage them to allow their divisions to become professionally managed. You will assure them that if they make the changes that are needed, they will be able to get back to what they like to do: stimulate growth.

You will do a very different thing with the professional managers you bring in from the outside. Since they have never been entrepreneurs themselves, you will encourage them to try to understand the value of entrepreneurship. You will caution them about bureaucratizing the business too much. You will complain about their desire to call your personnel director a human resources specialist.

By charting a middle course between growth and quality, you will—if you are smart and hardworking—achieve both. And then the business will straighten out all those terrible management problems and move back into another period of growth—slower growth than you had during the second stage, but growth.

THE FOURTH STAGE: FROM 343 THIRD-TIER EMPLOYEES TO UNLIMITED GROWTH

At some point in time, that third stage of growth may ebb and finally stop or even recede. This is likely to happen somewhere between 50 and 350 employees. When it happens, you will try to get things going by pushing on your first-tier employees, but you will find that they have already done, over and over again, everything you want them to do. You will feel frustrated.

You will once again think about hiring a consultant, remembering the last time you did so and how much money the consultant charged you to tell you what you already knew. But this time, you really don't know what to do. So, if you are smart, you will bring in someone who is good enough, and bold enough, to help you.

What you don't know is that there is a very good reason the business has stalled. And that reason is the way it is structured—the very structure that allowed it to grow from a single employee to 350.

Most entrepreneurs I know cannot make this final change. But if you can—and I will tell you one very effective way to do it in this book—you will be able to enjoy watching your business grow into maturity . . . from 350 employees to 700 and then exponentially from there.

CHAPTER THREE

BECOMING A FIVE-STAR BUSINESS GENIUS

One of the great business management theorists of all time, Elliott Jaques, believed that human potential is limited. In his seminal book *Requisite Organization*, and in others, he argued that people's inborn qualities determine their capacity to create personal wealth and succeed in business.[1]

Much of what Jaques had to say about business is invaluable.* But this idea—that we are born with limitations—is deplorable.

I recognize that certain physical limitations do present challenges for some people. Basketball players who stop growing at five feet six inches will have a hard time becoming great at that sport. But challenges are sometimes overcome and obstacles bypassed. Mugsy Bogues, at five feet three inches, was a starting guard in the National Basketball Association (NBA) for 14 years. Every time he stole the ball, dribbled it downcourt, and dunked it, it was a repudiation of everyone who ever told him he was too short to play professionally.

Creating a multimillion-dollar business is a lot easier than becoming a professional basketball player. I know. I've been a consultant for such businesses more than a dozen times, and I started out with less natural business talent than Mugsy Bogues' basketball potential.

---

*Some of his best ideas, in fact, are presented in Chapters 21 and 24 of this book.

It's easier than becoming an NBA player, but it's not easy.

In fact, it requires the development of genius.

FIVE MAGIC WANDS OF BUSINESS GENIUS

This is a book about creating and growing multimillion-dollar businesses, but it's also a book about becoming a business genius. In the following chapters, I am going to share some secrets with you—very important secrets. But I'm also going to teach you concepts and techniques that will transform you from the inside out and change the way you think about business forever.

I am going to show you how to become—there is no other way to put it—a business genius. And after I have shown you that, I will show you how to become another sort of business genius . . . and then another. In all, you will have what you need to become a business genius five times over. And when you begin to act like the genius you are, everything you are hoping for from this book—everything from making more money to having more power to working less and enjoying your life more—will come to you almost automatically.

This is the best book I've ever written, and I'm very happy to be sharing it with you. Please excuse me for speaking so unabashedly about it, but I am excited about everything you are going to be learning.

If you don't have your own business but are thinking of starting one, this book is for you. If you have a new business but can't get it to grow, you'll know how after you read this. If your business is already pretty large but has hit a plateau, don't worry. There are answers here for you. If your business is great but you are working too much, you can breathe easy. You are reading the right book.

The answers are here. Read on.

WHAT EVERY GREAT BUSINESS NEEDS

Businesses don't grow big and become profitable by accident. There are reasons why the great ones succeed.

Every marketplace is an environment where hundreds, or even thousands, of competing interests struggle to survive. Imagine a jungle of plants and ferns and flowers and trees, each one trying to get its share of the soil and water and sun. A new business is like a sapling—tender and small. If it doesn't have the ability to grow quickly, it stands no chance of growing at all. But growing quickly isn't all there is to it. For a sapling to grow into maturity and eventually become a great and dominant tree, it must be able to set its roots deep, resist pestilence and disease, and send its branches where the sun shines.

For a business to grow into a $100 million or a $300 million enterprise, it must be very good, if not great, in five areas:

1. Coming up with new and useful product ideas.
2. Selling those products profitably.
3. Managing processes and procedures efficiently.
4. Finding great employees to do the work.
5. Getting people, procedures, products, and promotions going.

To be good or great in each of these important areas, a business needs to be led by a person or people who are very good at getting the jobs done.

In the beginning, only some of these essential skills are absolutely necessary. As the business grows, more come into play. Eventually, they are all in demand. The following outline—an elaboration of the four stages of entrepreneurial growth presented in Chapter 1—isn't exact science, but it is roughly true. (For our purposes here, the alternate way of defining the stages of entrepreneurial growth in terms of number of employees that I described in Chapter 2 won't apply.)

Stage One: Infancy—zero to $1 million in revenue
Main Problem: You don't really know what you are doing.
Main Challenge: Making the first profitable sale.
Main Opportunity: Continuing to sell until you have achieved a minimum critical mass of customers.
Skills Needed: (1) Getting things going and (2) selling.

Stage Two: Childhood—$1 million to $10 million in revenue
Main Problem: You are only breaking even or may even be losing money.
Main Challenge: Creating additional, profitable products quickly.

Main Opportunity: Becoming a business of innovation, increasing cash flow, and becoming profitable.

Additional Skill Needed: Coming up with a constant stream of new and potentially tipping-point ideas.

Stage Three: Adolescence—$10 million to $50 million in revenue

Main Problem: Your systems are strained, and customers are noticing.

Main Challenge: Turning the chaos into order.

Main Opportunity: Learning how to establish useful protocols and manage processes and procedures.

Additional Skill Needed: Running your business with just three or four simple management reports.

Stage Four: Adulthood—$50 million to $100 million in revenue and beyond

Main Problem: Sales slow down and may even stall.

Main Challenge: Becoming entrepreneurial again.

Main Opportunity: Getting the business to run itself.

Additional Skill Needed: Determining the role you will play in the business's future.

As this outline indicates, you don't need to know how to create products or motivate people or manage anything to successfully start a business.* What you need are two fundamental skills:

1. You have to know how to make a sale.
2. You have to be able to put that sales process into action.

Yes, you can be dumb and foolish and incompetent and evil and still be great at starting businesses if you are good at these two skills. In Chapters 4, 5, and 6, I will prove this to you and show you how to acquire these skills—even become very good at them.

Once your business is making sales and you have achieved a minimum critical mass of customers, your problems, challenges, and opportunities change.

---

*In Chapters 4, 7, and others, I will talk about why so many top business schools, programs, books, and magazines get it wrong about what is needed to start a new business.

Now your main problem is that you are just breaking even (or even losing money), your main challenge is to add other products that are profitable, and your best chance of doing that is by changing your business into a company where innovation is a rule, not an exception. The skill you need to meet that challenge is the skill of creating, almost instantly and at will, a stream of good and profitable new ideas.

In Chapters 9, 10, and 11, I will show you how some of the companies I've worked with have done that, and how you can become a machine of innovation.

WHEN FAST GROWTH CREATES OPERATIONAL PROBLEMS

At or around the $10 million revenue mark, things often become very disorganized and stressful.* Products are imperfect. Order taking and fulfillment are sloppy, and customers are noticing and becoming unhappy.

Your challenge at that point is to solve these problems before they damage the customer relationships you've started to develop and wreck your company's chances of future growth. The way to do that is to make the company a more professional business with good systems in place. The skill you need in order to accomplish that is surprisingly simple. You don't need an MBA or a course in accounting, just an understanding of three or four critical numbers that determine a company's financial health.

In Chapters 19 and 20, I will tell you how to pinpoint those numbers and develop simple management reports that allow you and your top people to keep on top of your accounting, ensure good product quality, and keep your customers happy while you continue to grow.

The next level of business development often takes place when revenues are in the $20 million to $25 million area. At this point, the problem many companies face is a flattening of revenues and some-times, with rising costs, gradually decreasing profits.

---

*Some businesses run into this problem at the $5 million mark. It depends a lot on the industry you are in. Don't worry about recognizing this stage. When you get to it, you will know.

Since the business is generally well organized and professionally run at this time, it's not easy to point to one thing and say, "This is what we need to fix." The problem, ultimately, is a result of the changes made during the prior stage, the implementation of better systems and professional management. A business of this size often has an action-oriented CEO who focuses on protocols and procedures. Under the CEO, there is usually a group of functional managers, divided up in the traditional ways: marketing, sales, accounting, customer service, information technology/database management, and human resources.

This is a good structure for quality assurance during Stage Three growth, but at some point, growth ebbs because the genius and motivating force behind it—usually the founder and CEO of the company—has run out of innovative gas. All the founder's good ideas have been tested, implemented, and refined. The limit that the company is facing is the natural limit of one person's imagination and drive.

AFTER MUCH GROWTH, A FLATTENING

The challenge for a business with this problem is both a structural and a personal one. The structure that has made growth orderly and sustainable during the prior stage now makes further growth difficult because it does not foster innovation. Divisions are headed up by professional executives with functional responsibilities. That type of arrangement is good for order, but not so good for an entrepreneurial enterprise.

Often the last people to see this are the founders/CEOs, because they instinctively look to themselves for all the major innovations. On the company's personnel chart, they see something that makes sense: They are on top, and there are people under them who can execute every aspect of any innovations they create.

They do notice the declining growth, and they worry about rising costs. They bemoan the fact that they still have to do so much of the hard thinking themselves, and sense that their challenge is to make the business entrepreneurial again. But they can't figure out how to do that.

What they need to do is realize that they, themselves, are the problem. The business has grown as large as it can, given the fact that they are the sole or primary innovator. To break through this final barrier to growth and give the business the chance to grow to $100 million and beyond, they have to bring in new entrepreneurial talent—smart, skillful, ambitious people who understand the business—and let them create their own entrepreneurial enterprises within the context of the existing business. Finding and grooming entrepreneurial executives takes a special kind of skill. In Chapters 7 and 21, I will tell you exactly how to do it.

WHAT KIND OF GENIUS ARE YOU?

All businesspeople have skills. Some are good at selling. Others are good at managing systems. When we develop these skills over time, they feel natural to us. And because they feel natural, we use these skills reflexively whenever we confront problems, challenges, or opportunities. By using them, we become better at them. And when it becomes known that we are good at them, people come to us for help with the kind of problems we appear to have a natural genius for solving.

But is it natural? Or is it the product of practice, stimulated by intermittent positive reinforcement? Does having a special gift or expertise in one area mean that we can't develop other skills?

Some experts think so. And there are plenty of popular business books that support this notion by providing readers with self-administered quizzes that claim to be able to pinpoint their natural talents. I found one such test in a book called *If You're Clueless About Starting Your Own Business* by Seth Godin.

"The first thing you need to do is assess your own strengths and weaknesses," Godin says. "Explore your motivations and discover whether or not you have what it takes to make it all happen."[2]

The book includes a 25-question test that can determine, Godin asserts, whether you have what it takes to be an entrepreneur. A successful entrepreneur, he says, is someone who possesses certain specific traits and is willing to "expend a huge amount of energy to accomplish goals."[3]

The test is based on a set of commonly held beliefs about the natural skills and inclinations of entrepreneurs, such as these:

Natural Inclinations
- They are attracted by challenges.
- They enjoy being in leadership roles.
- They are passionate about their ideas.

Natural Skills
1. They are well organized.
2. They are good analytical thinkers.
3. They are good at sales.
4. They are good at taking the initiative.

These are all desirable inclinations and skills to have, but what if you don't have many of them? Can you still succeed in business?

I took the test and got 79 out of 100. Based on my score, here's Godin's advice to me:

> Risky business. You possess some entrepreneurial traits but probably not to the degree necessary to buck the daunting odds. If your score on the last five questions was 15 or below the risk is even greater. Keep working for someone else.[4]

My score on the last five questions was just 15. So although this book has a lot of correct and useful advice, I'm glad I didn't read it at the beginning of my business career.

Actually, Godin's test is not a bad indicator. For the most part, I think it makes sense. The truth is, I am probably not a natural entrepreneur. And yet I've been instrumental in launching dozens of multimillion-dollar businesses. I've done so by paying attention to my mentors and imitating some of their tricks.

My experiences prove that you don't need a preponderance of natural skills to start or grow a successful business. What you need is a little knowledge and a handful of tricks. The knowledge has to do with what problems, challenges, and opportunities you must pay attention to at any given moment in your business's development. The tricks are simple techniques you can use to overcome those problems, meet those challenges, and take advantage of those opportunities.

To reiterate: To start a business and keep it growing, you need to be able to correctly identify the most important problem, challenge, and opportunity you face at any given time. In addition to that, you need to become good at five basic skills:

1. Coming up with ideas
2. Selling products
3. Managing systems
4. Developing superstars
5. Taking action

I could give you a test to identify your strengths and weaknesses in each of these areas, but it wouldn't do you a lot of good—first, because you probably already know what they are, and second, because what you don't know how to do you can learn.

That's the purpose of this book: to make you a five-star business genius with expertise in each of these five areas—a five-star business genius who will always be able to do for your company what is necessary to keep it growing, while you reduce the need to work on any specific tasks yourself.

Are you ready to start?

PART TWO

STAGE ONE:

INFANCY

CHAPTER FOUR

THE SUPREMACY OF SELLING

Of the major functions of business—product development, customer service, accounting, operations, and marketing—the one that should always be given top priority in an entrepreneurial venture is marketing.

The other functions are important, but without marketing you will not have sales and without sales you will not have cash flow and without cash flow you will not be able to pay for all the other functions (except by going into debt, which is simply borrowing against the cash flow of the future). Put differently:

Without sales, it is very hard to sustain an ongoing business.

Consider this to be Rule Number One of Entrepreneurship.

Before your business makes its first sale, it is nothing more than a set of unproven ideas that you are spending money on. Some of those ideas may be good and feasible. Others may be bad and/or impractical. You can't know which are which until you test them by selling the product.

And that's why, when I consult with entrepreneurs who are still in the planning stages, I try to get them to streamline their start-up process by eliminating most of the other things they are inclined to do—such as leasing office space and buying furniture—and focusing on effecting that first, real sales transaction.

> **STAGE ONE: INFANCY—ZERO TO $1 MILLION IN REVENUE**
>
> Main Problem: You don't really know what you are doing.
> Main Challenge: Making the first profitable sale.
> Main Opportunity: Achieving a minimum critical mass of customers.
> **Main Skill Needed: Selling the product.**

An essay written by Jim Koch, founder and CEO of The Boston Beer Company, illustrates this point:

Years ago, when The Boston Beer Co. was just getting up and running, I received a phone call from my uncle, a partner at Goldman, Sachs and one of my initial financial backers. He asked me how things were going. Fine, I replied; the first batch of Samuel Adams beer was in the aging tanks and would be ready for delivery in about five weeks.

"So," my uncle continued, "what did you do today?"

I told him I'd spent the day shopping for a computer system. When he asked me why, I explained that I figured I'd need a computer to keep track of sales, payables, and the like.

"Oh yeah," he said, "sales. By the way, have you got any?" I admitted that I did not.

"So what the hell are you doing buying a computer?" he demanded. "You know, Jim, I've seen a lot more businesses go broke because they didn't have enough sales than I've seen go under from lack of computers. Why don't you work on first things first?"

That shook me up. My uncle went on to describe his early days at the investment firm—how frightened he had been then to have to make cold calls on potential customers, how he had forced himself to set a quota of at least one new account a week, no matter how many calls it took. Listening to him, I realized that somehow I had gotten the whole process backward. To make my business viable, the first thing I needed was not a computer. It wasn't even an office or a desk. What I needed was a customer.

That call really galvanized me. . . . I was determined to follow my uncle's example and go for one account a week . . . but when the morning came to go out and do it, I didn't want to get out of bed. Finally I picked out a bar near my office . . . and, wearing my usual dark pin-striped suit, walked in with six cold bottles of Samuel Adams beer in my briefcase and a lump in my throat.

There was a guy behind the bar whom I assumed was the bartender. As it turned out, not only was he merely the bar back (the guy who stacks glasses, keeps the shelves filled, and so on), but he didn't speak English. He looked at me as if I had two heads. While I stood there talking about my beer, the manager walked over and eyed me suspiciously—he probably thought I was from the IRS or something. Anyway, I went through my story one more time and asked if I could pour him a glassful. He looked at my beer, sniffed it, drank it—and immediately gave me an order for 25 cases. It was an amazing feeling. In the space of 10 minutes I went from sheer terror to ecstasy.

When I got home that evening, the vision in my head was that it's really selling that drives most businesses: the direct interface between the product and customer, the crucial feedback loop.[1]

Thanks to his uncle, Koch figured out how to sell beer before his ignorance of the process scuttled his business. Instead of wasting his valuable time and resources buying a computer, his uncle had him doing the *sine qua non* of business: selling the product.

It is amazing how many entrepreneurs make the mistake that Koch almost made. Actually, it's not so amazing when you consider what short shrift selling gets from business gurus. Koch, a product of Harvard College, Harvard Law School, and Harvard Business School (where he got an MBA) was blunt about it.

"None" of his education at Harvard, he said, prepared him for the importance of selling. In fact, there was a prejudice against it: "There, anybody who became a salesperson was considered a failure."[2]

Even at Harvard Business School, Koch said, there were a dozen courses on marketing but not a single one on selling. It was as if selling was something secondary and unappealing.

Koch found this attitude commonplace among business professionals outside of academia too: "If you go to a cocktail party and you're asked what you do for a living, and you reply, 'I'm a salesman,' people look at you like you've got crumbs on your shirt."*

---

*Reading Koch's remarks reminded me of an experience I had with academia. I was once invited to address a business club at a local university. I spent the 90 minutes allotted to me talking about the importance of selling. Afterward, the dean of the business school came up and congratulated me. "Everyone really enjoyed your

THE REAL BUSINESS EVERY BUSINESSPERSON IS IN

Every business is really two businesses says Ted Ciuba, a mail-order expert, in his book *Mail and Grow Rich*. One of those businesses has to do with the product you make or the service you provide. You make toys. You cut lawns. You fly people from city to city. That part of your business, Ciuba says, is easy to get wrapped up in. "I am a designer," the business owner thinks, "so I must spend my time designing."[3]

In fact, he says, most of a business owner's time should be spent on the real business that every business owner is in—selling.

Ciuba is right. As a business owner, selling should be your number one priority—and you must act accordingly. That means spending the lion's share of your time on marketing and sales-related activities. You don't have to do the actual selling yourself, as Koch did, but you must be very much involved in every step of the process so that you understand the problems and can sense the opportunities.

It doesn't matter what sort of expertise you bring into a new venture—whether you are a numbers person, a people person, or a systems person. To be a truly effective entrepreneur, you must become your business's first and foremost expert at selling.

There is only one way to do this: Invest most of your time, attention, and energy in the selling process. The ratio of time, creativity, and money spent on selling as opposed to other aspects of business should be something like 80/20, with 80 percent of it going toward selling and only 20 percent toward everything else.

THE BIG MISTAKE MOST WANNABE ENTREPRENEURS MAKE

In launching new businesses, many entrepreneurs do the opposite of spending 80 percent of their time on selling. They spend most of their time, attention, energy, and capital on things such as setting up an office, designing logos, printing business cards, filing forms, writing contracts, and refining the product. They have the impression that they

lecture," he said. "And I did, too. I have always thought selling was a deplorable activity. But now I am going to have to rethink my position on that."

are doing things in a logical order—getting everything just right before they open their doors. In fact, they are wasting valuable resources on secondary and tertiary endeavors.

The activities that relate to making the business look and feel like a real business (i.e., legal, accounting, operational, and image-building activities) are tertiary considerations at Stage One of a business life cycle. As tertiary considerations, they should be given little or no attention. Refining the product and establishing customer service standards are important jobs, but for most start-up businesses they should be considered secondary considerations until an effective sales program has been tested and launched.

If you are opening a restaurant, you have to get the product right from the start. So, too, if you are manufacturing cars. But for most entrepreneurial businesses, it is enough to have the product and customer service just okay at the outset. Perfecting them can be done a little later, after you have gotten feedback from your customers.

Many wannabe entrepreneurs I've spoken to over the years bridled when I told them they should be concentrating on sales. These people were proud of the new products they created and were convinced that as soon as they introduced them to the marketplace, all the selling would get done by itself. They felt that the selling process was beneath them and could easily be assigned, at some time in the future, to someone else.

There are two things wrong with this line of thinking:

1. It is arrogant. How do you know that your product idea is good? Because you think it is? Business is not and must never be about what the business owner thinks is good or right. Business is about providing value to the customer. And that value can be determined only by the customer.
2. It is foolish. If customers think your product idea is good, they will buy it, recommend it to their friends, and then buy from you again and again. If they think it is bad (or useless or too expensive and, therefore, bad), they will not buy it—or they will buy it and return it and will not recommend it to their friends. Wise business owners know that they cannot determine the goodness of an idea until they try to sell it. So they will try to sell it as soon as they can—if possible before they have spent a lot of time and money making it perfect.

Getting your product right is a very important goal, but it should not be your priority in Stage One, because it is impossible to know what "right" is until you get feedback from your customers. Money and time invested in perfecting the product before it goes to market are often wasted. What may seem like thoughtful improvements in planning may be deemed by the customer to be unnecessary or even undesirable.

I learned this lesson from my first mentor in business, JSN, a brilliant salesman and my partner in a $100+ million business. After I had my first success with a new product idea, I was in his office almost every other day with new ideas for improving it.

"How do you know the product we already have needs any improvement?" he asked.

"I just know it does," was my answer.

"Have our customers complained about it?"

"No, not yet. But maybe they will."

"Well, then, I tell you what. When they start complaining we can talk about their complaints. But right now, I don't want you thinking about that. I want you thinking about the sales we are currently making."

He paused and waited for me to ask the dumb question I was trying not to ask. Finally, I said, "Just what should I be thinking when I think about the sales we are making?"

He stood up, walked around his desk, and put his hands on my shoulders.

"You should be thinking about how to make more sales!"

"When you come in every morning, I don't want you thinking about what's wrong or right with the product. There will be a time for that later. Right now, I want you coming in wondering about how many units we sold last night and what we are doing today to improve sales. If you can make a habit of doing that, kid, then, if and when our customers tell us they want us to improve this product, we'll have the money to make all the improvements they want."

As Koch found at Harvard, most business schools don't appreciate the importance of selling at any time—in the beginning, in the middle, or at the more mature stages of a business's life span. That's the reason, he said, that so many MBAs go into business unprepared to take selling seriously.

FOUR ASPECTS OF ENTREPRENEURIAL SUCCESS

Every entrepreneurial business—regardless of what stage of growth it is in—needs four personalities at the helm:

1. A seller: someone to market the product.
2. An improver: someone to improve the product.
3. An organizer: someone to make sure things flow smoothly.
4. A pusher: someone to get people to do what they are supposed to do.

When you begin your business, if you don't have a partner, you may have to handle all of these functions. As your business grows, you will probably hire people to take on most of them—but at least during the first two stages (and probably longer), you should be in charge of one of them.

Which one should that be?

Most business experts would say that the most important role for the business leader is to be the organizer, to make sure that all the parts of the business work well together. Certainly, this was the philosophy of America's greatest business expert, Peter Drucker. In a recently published compendium of his best ideas, a book called *The Essential Drucker* (HarperCollins, 2001), he provided dozens of great tips on how to organize and manage a business more successfully.* That's probably great advice if you are running a Fortune 500 company. But if you're starting and developing an entrepreneurial business, I would focus on something else. To me, the most important job of any entrepreneur—and the one role you should *not* give up as your business grows—is to be in charge of marketing your products.

During the first two stages of growth, the priorities should be in this order:

1. Selling
2. Pushing (to make sales)
3. Improving (products and sales)
4. Organizing

*I spent a half-hour searching through *The Essential Drucker*, hoping to find something about the importance of selling. I found nothing.

(continues)

FOUR ASPECTS OF ENTREPRENEURIAL SUCCESS (Continued)

This doesn't mean you have to do the marketing and selling all by yourself. You don't have to write your own advertising copy or become your company's top salesperson. But you do have to understand how your business creates its revenues, and you have to be able to step in and stimulate more sales when they are needed.

That is the ultimate strength of an entrepreneur: the ability to stimulate sales. There are many other important skills that can help your business succeed (I would rank the ability to create great products very high on any list, for example), but there are none that will make as much difference as salesmanship.

SOME LESSONS ARE HARD TO LEARN THE FIRST TIME

Accepting the importance of selling is difficult for some would-be entrepreneurs. It certainly was for me.

Having come from an academic family, I harbored an unconscious bias against sales when I began my business career in earnest in the late 1970s.* But since I had a young family to support, I had to take a more pragmatic view of things in order to succeed.

After teaching English literature and philosophy at the University of Chad in Africa for two years, I returned to the United States and soon was working as a journalist for a small company in Washington, D.C., that produced and published newsletters related to international commerce.

By learning the ropes quickly and working long hours, I somehow managed to work my way up our little corporate ladder from assistant

---

*Although I had been working continuously since I was a teenager, I had never really enjoyed the selling process or thought highly of those people who were good at it. When I sold aluminum siding and then pots and pans as a high school student, I did it because I had to do it, but always felt it was somehow beneath my dignity. When my friends and I had a house-painting business and then a pool-installation business during my college years, we were happy to leave the selling to our customers. We told people proudly that our marketing strategy was "word of mouth."

editor to CEO in three years. My predecessor had done a pretty good job of marketing the newsletters we wrote. As a result, each one of them (there were four at the time) had several thousand subscribers who paid us about $295 a year. That was enough revenue to pay the business's expenses. And with a 90 percent renewal rate, there wasn't much pressure on me to widen our subscription base by selling more newsletters.

Despite the fact that my predecessor had discovered an effective method of selling subscriptions (direct telephone sales to corporations and embassies), I did little of that during my working hours. Instead, I spent time doing what I thought was more important: fussing around with the editorial product. I had all sorts of ideas about how to make our newsletters better. But I gave scant thought to selling them.

I probably spent 12 hours a day hiring and firing and training editors, writing editorial guidelines, brainstorming topics, outlining issues, editing copy, and so forth. I spent two hours a month reviewing new orders that mysteriously trickled in. Since we had no outbound marketing efforts, there weren't a lot of them—but our renewal rates were high, and so the bills got paid. And I had faith that if the editorial product kept improving, so would the sales.

When our industry experienced a recession in the early 1980s, our new sales—which were never great—came to a stop. Renewals were still pretty good, but the dip in new sales put the company into the red for the first time.

Since I had no experience selling our newsletters, I had no idea what to do about the decline in sales. Gradually, the company became weaker.

I left before that business collapsed, but I carried with me the humiliation of knowing that I was incapable of saving the company when it needed saving. I was showing up for work every day and I was putting in plenty of time, but I wasn't really managing that business at all. I was tweaking products that probably didn't need tweaking, while neglecting sales.

Although I didn't know any better at the time, I had been steering our little publishing ship into the ground—and feeling pretty good about myself while doing it.

Failing to Learn My First Lesson

I left that job to become the managing editor of another small newsletter publishing company that was based in Florida. In that position, I figured I didn't have to do what I should have done at my previous job—sell newsletters. So I spent my first year at the new job happily doing the same thing I had been doing for three years: namely, fooling around with editorial guidelines and style manuals. Then, one evening, I had a transforming experience: I decided to become rich.*

When I told my boss my intentions, he seemed pleased. He told me that the best way for me to achieve my goal would be to help make *him* rich—and that the best way to do that would be to start spending more of my time and energy on sales and marketing.

I continued to fuss over our newsletters—but with an entirely different perspective. I no longer cared whether our writing was clever or correct (or corresponded to *The Chicago Manual of Style*) but, instead, whether it was likely to please our subscribers and thus improve our renewal rates. I devoted every spare hour to learning the selling part of that business, which was direct-mail marketing. And after coming up with dozens of bad ideas, I finally came up with an advertising campaign that my boss liked. When it worked—and it worked extremely well—I was hooked on selling.

I further reduced the time I had been investing in tweaking the editorial quality of our newsletters, and focused even more time and energy on sales. In doing so, I became my boss's chief collaborator and eventually his partner. The result of combining our efforts dramatically increased growth and profitability. In 11 years, that business grew from practically nothing to grossing $135 million.

Learning the Lesson Once Again

The year before that business peaked, my partner had a heart attack and decided he wanted to retire. At 37, I felt that I was too young to retire, so we reinvented the structure of the business, selling off most of the equity to key employees, and stayed on as consultants. Two years later, in 1989, I decided to retire and take it easy.

---

*I've told the story of this life-changing moment in several of my previous books, including *Automatic Wealth* (John Wiley & Sons, 2005).

To fill my idle hours, I bought a half-interest in an art gallery.

But in making this investment in what I thought would be the perfect retirement business, I temporarily forgot everything I had learned.

I imagined that I would spend my days sitting in the showroom, surrounded by beautiful paintings, reading Tolstoy and occasionally being interrupted by browsing art lovers who would admire my collection, enjoy the espresso I so kindly served them, chat intelligently with me, and then insist on buying an expensive work of art.

Such was my dream. The reality was entirely different.

The fine-art business, it turned out, was just like every other business I had ever been in. Its primary activities were all—in one way or another—about selling.

Yes, my new work space was beautiful. And, yes, some of the customers were intelligent, well-spoken, and worldly. But we weren't paying rent to sit and "watch the pictures get dusty," as my partner soon reminded me.

MARKETING GENIUS TIP

My partner in the art business was extremely successful throughout his career. A former psychologist, he had—as near as I could tell—only one sales technique. When a customer was wandering through the gallery, he had a wonderful way of casually chatting them up. And when they admired a particular painting, he'd say, "You have a great eye. That one's a real beauty, isn't it?"

Of course, the customer would always agree—and, about 80 percent of the time, would then say something like, "About how much is this, anyway?"

"I'm glad you asked," my partner would say, "because a painting just like this by the same artist, but not quite as good, sold last month at Sotheby's for $25,000. But I can let you have this one for only $18,500."

It was a deceptively simple selling strategy. But it worked like gangbusters. Since then, I have seen it used in dozens of different ways by many successful sellers of art, collectibles, antiques, jewelry, and expensive watches—something to remember if you decide to go into one of those businesses.

"If you wanted to just watch the pictures get dusty," my partner explained, "you should have gotten a job as a part-time guard in a local museum."

This brings us to Rule Number Two of Entrepreneurship:

> *There is a direct relationship between the success of a business at any given time and the percentage of its capital, temporal, and intellectual resources that are devoted to selling.*

This rule is true throughout the life cycle of any business, but it is especially true in the beginning, when you are just starting out.

A TALE OF TWO START-UPS

The importance of selling during the start-up stage of business was exemplified some years ago by a profile of two entrepreneurs in *Success* magazine.

One, a New York realtor, wanted to broker surplus office space through the Internet. He spent a year and most of $10,000 he had saved to build an impressive website. He told the magazine that he believed his site would be so good that it would make him "the next Jeff Bezos."

His marketing plan was to lure customers to his website by offering free ads for a year and then renewing them at $59.95 annually. When the website was done, he was happy—until he activated it and discovered that nobody was rushing in to take advantage of his free offer.

He spent the little money he had left on a few desperate marketing schemes, but to no avail. He had exhausted all his resources building a professional-looking site with lots of bells and whistles, but he had never tested his basic sales assumption—that he could attract lots of free postings and then convert them into paid advertisers.

Meanwhile, another entrepreneur, a car repairman, had a very different business idea. He thought he could sell neon lights that attached to a car's undercarriage. He called his venture Street Glow Inc.

When he started making this toy in 1990, he had only $1,000 to invest in it. He spent about $350 installing two crude prototypes onto his own car and the car of a friend. And then he spent all of his spare time and his remaining $650 selling.

He didn't lease office space; he worked from his home. And he spent most of his time traveling to custom auto shops and automobile-themed events, trying to make sales. At first, people were curious but most were hesitant to buy. After talking to them, he made adjustments to his product, his pricing, and the way he presented it.

He worked fast. He took enough deposits to build the systems ordered, delivered them, and then reinvested the profits in selling more systems.

For months he earned nothing, because he was reinvesting his cash flow into sales. But at about the one-year mark, he was able to start pocketing profits. At that point, he began fixing up a shop, buying some new tools, and ordering inventory.

By devoting his attention to selling first and taking care of the other, secondary business concerns later, he ensured that his fledgling enterprise would not suffer the normal (and normally lethal) cash shortages most first-year businesses encounter.

By 2002 (the last year financial data was available for this privately held company), Street Glow Inc. had garnered $23 million in revenues and had shown a consistent profit, year after year.

HOW SOON SHOULD YOU START SELLING?

When beginning a new business (or launching a new product within an existing business), the sooner you can make the first sale, the better your chances are of success.

The story of Alex Tew illustrates this.

In order to earn money for college, Alex decided to join the growing trend of young people who were getting rich from Internet innovations. On a summer evening just before he was to begin classes, he stayed up late talking with friends and brainstorming moneymaking ideas.

(continues)

HOW SOON SHOULD YOU START SELLING? (*Continued*)

After rejecting dozens of ideas as impractical or unlikely, Alex seized upon one that he felt he could accomplish in the very short period of time that stood between him and his first tuition bill.

The basic idea—selling advertising space on a website—was being done by thousands of others all over the world. What made Alex's idea unique was the twist he put on it: Instead of selling website space the conventional way, through banner ads or inserts, he would sell it by the pixel.

His marketing goal was simple and challenging: to sell one million pixels at one dollar each as soon as he possibly could.

Alex had a bit of experience designing websites, but he was hardly an expert. If he'd had the time, he might have prepared himself by learning more about it or hiring someone skillful. But with his tuition bill looming, he slapped together the best site he could with the money he had—a mere hundred dollars—and activated it as MillionDollarHomePage.com.

From start to finish, it took Alex only 48 hours.

He devoted the time that remained to what he had the sense to know was his number one priority: selling those pixels. Since he knew nothing about marketing pixels and didn't have a list of potential customers, he turned to the best market for mom-and-pop start-ups: friends and relatives.

To encourage them to buy more than a single pixel to help him out, he decided to sell the pixels in bundles of 10 at $10 each. He dashed off a half-funny, half-desperate sales letter—his first effort at direct-mail marketing—and sent it out to the people on his personal e-mail list. He sold 100 bundles, and earned $1,000.

Inspired by his initial success, he wrote up a press release about his venture and sent it to local radio and television stations. The response was as good as he could have hoped for. As soon as the first small bit about him aired, he began receiving orders. In a matter of weeks, he had generated tens of thousands of dollars.

This gave him fodder for more press releases, and more publicity followed. When the story of his homespun ingenuity was picked up by regional television stations, he was flooded with orders. In less than a month, he had sold $40,000 worth of pixels—enough to cover his entire tuition.

> **HOW SOON SHOULD YOU START SELLING?** *(Continued)*
>
> Alex would have been happy with that, but the story kept getting bigger. When the national and international media got wind of his business idea, demand soared exponentially—so much so that he needed to hire people to help him fill orders from individuals and businesses in 35 countries. Within five months, Alex had achieved the goal that felt almost silly when he'd set it: a million dollars in sales.
>
> Selling is what matters most in the first stage of a start-up business.
>
> If Alex had given himself a reasonable period of time to launch his business—say, a year or two to build a great website and learn about marketing before he started selling—chances are he never would have succeeded.

PRIORITIES FOR STAGE ONE BUSINESSES

In starting a business, this is what your priorities and sequence of activities should be:

1. Get the product ready enough to sell it, but don't worry about perfecting it.
2. Sell it.
3. Then, if it sells, make it better.

That's the smart way to launch a business. But it's not the common one. Most would-be entrepreneurs do just about everything else first, such as taking care of legal requirements (forming a corporation, getting local business permits, filing DBAs, etc.), buying or leasing office space, hiring employees, or gathering the business and tax forms they will eventually have to file.

WHAT THE EXPERTS SAY

As I said, many of the would-be entrepreneurs I've met spent most of their time on secondary and tertiary business activities and too little time on selling.

There are good reasons for this. For one thing, selling is difficult. Rather than do the hard thing first, many people want to take care of easier jobs. For another thing, business schools—even the best ones, as Jim Koch pointed out—don't emphasize selling. This is also true of many small-business consultants.

One such consultant, an online company I profiled in *Early to Rise* several years ago, is a typical example. In advising potential clients about priorities for starting new businesses, the consultant gave top priority to "creating a professionally designed logo and identity system" that included "home-printed business cards with perforated edges," a corporate brochure with impressive graphics, and other material that "shows that you are committed to both your business and your clients."

Another best-selling expert on entrepreneurship (also profiled in an *Early to Rise* article several years ago) provided the following six-step to-do list for Stage One business owners:

1. Create an *instant impact message* that describes the chief benefit of your business.
2. Put it on your business cards and brochures, which you should hand out at business functions and meetings.
3. Take a field trip to discover how your product or service will satisfy people's desires.
4. Protect your "great ideas" by registering your business name, logo, and slogan.
5. Create a paper trail—tracking all meeting dates, attendees, and discussions.
6. Consult a lawyer and obtain his or her advice on how to best protect your business.

In a January 2003 article, I poked fun at a similar set of suggestions made by the writers of *More* magazine for novice female entrepreneurs. Here are the tools *More* magazine provided to help its readers get started:

- Consult with an attorney to make sure you set up the right legal structure.
- Check with your municipal authority to make sure "they permit a venture like yours to work out of the home."

- Buy business insurance and "talk to an accountant or attorney" to make sure you're not missing anything.
- Get a toll-free phone number (to give the impression that your business is much bigger than it is).
- Invest in great business cards and letterhead stationery.[4]

Yes, there are many ways to get busy with a new business, but none that is more urgent than making the first sale. Making the first sale is critical for two reasons.

1. You need to create cash flow to keep your business going.
2. You will never really know whether your big idea—what marketers call the unique selling proposition (USP) of your business—is a good one until you give it the ultimate test in the marketplace.

Think of it this way: When you begin a new business, you have no idea whether your idea is good or bad. The faster you find out, the better for you. Here's why.

THE ENTREPRENEUR'S FIRST QUESTION: HOW CAN I MAKE THE FIRST SALE?

Several years ago, an old friend referred a young man to me who was in the process of setting up an Internet counseling business. The young man (and his backers) had already spent a fortune on the website, and he wanted my advice on putting together a huge network of counselors to respond to the advertising blitz he was planning.

"What is the best way to attract these counselors?" the young man wanted to know.

I told him I thought he was making a big mistake. I told him that his primary business consideration was this: "Can you provoke (through advertising) people to log on to your website and pay for counseling online? And if so, how much would it cost you to do it?"

I tried to explain to him that his current business plan would have him spending over a million dollars before he answered this primary question. The first thing he needed to do—and the main thing he should be spending his money on at that point—was to find out how much it would cost him to acquire an online client, and how much net revenue that client would be worth. That, I said, would cost him about $50,000, not a million.

And when he was done—in 30 days—he would know with confidence if he had a viable business idea.

He thanked me for my advice, but he didn't take it. Instead, he spent two years raising a million dollars and then the third year blowing it. Oh, well.

IF I BUILD THE PRODUCT, WILL THEY COME?

A woman I have known since high school called to tell me about a cosmetics business she was starting. She had spent several years developing her own line of natural skin treatments, and had shared them with others, who raved about them. Encouraged by their reactions, she decided to go forward.

She'd spent two or three years and all of her money packaging a dozen products and producing all sorts of ancillary materials. She told me about the new labels she was designing, the contracts she was negotiating, the shopping she was doing for a retail space.

"But have you tried to sell anything yet?" I asked her.

"Everything's not about selling," she scolded me. "When the time is right, my products will sell."

Because she is a good friend, I kept pestering her, hoping she would do what she had to do to get her business going. But as far as she was concerned, her business was already up and running. She was busy day and night working on it. And she was spending all kinds of money.

Eventually, of course, we stopped talking about it. And I sometimes wonder what she could have done with those products she'd created. They were really very good.

ANOTHER WOULD-BE ENTREPRENEUR WITH AN IDEA

Just this morning, while I was working on writing this chapter, another would-be entrepreneur walked into my office. She is an employee of a company in which I have an interest, and a friend of a friend.

"I have a chance to have a business," she explained, almost breathlessly. "It's really crazy!"

She told me that she had always loved women's accessories, and had dreamed of having her own retail store selling them. Out of the blue last week, an old friend called her to say that he was starting a business selling Brazilian-made accessories in the United States, and he wanted her to be his partner.

"He's a really good guy. I've known him for years. He has lots of contacts in Brazil. And he will put up most of the money. He has another business, so he needs someone to be his partner in this new one. He said he knew I had a good feel for the kind of products he wants to offer, and that I could be an asset to him."

I asked her if he had proposed some kind of deal.

"I told him that I couldn't really talk about anything until I'd talked to you first."

"I'm glad you did. Let me ask you an important question. How do you guys plan to sell this stuff?"

She looked at me like I was speaking another language.

"What do you mean?"

"I mean, have you done any thinking or taken any actions that would help you figure out how you can sell Brazilian accessories—who might want to buy them, how much they are willing to pay, what sort of pieces they like?"

"Well," she said, her smile returning, "we have this."

She opened up a large tote bag and started laying out all sorts of things on my desk. The first one I noticed was an artist's illustration of a company logo and designs for letterhead, price tags, and shopping bags. Also in the pile was information about import regulations, a letter from a real estate agent about office space, and a DVD that she urged me to watch.

I put it in my laptop, held my breath, and pushed "play."

As I feared, it was a somewhat slick, but basically amateurish, imitation of what someone must have imagined would be a good commercial for this would-be business. It had arresting graphics, a catchy soundtrack, and lots of images of handbags, hats, and costume jewelry.

"Nice," I said, as convincingly as I could. "What were you thinking of doing with that?"

"That's what we wanted to ask you. You are the one with all the experience."

"Right," I said.

Here I was, writing this chapter on the importance of selling and, in particular, about the importance of focusing on sales at the very beginning of a business, when I am interrupted by someone with a bag full of business ideas but not a single one about sales.

"How much money are you looking to spend to start this business?" I asked.

"I don't know, but I think I will have to invest my life savings," she said.

That sounded like a very bad idea, but I knew better than to say so.

"Would you be interested in a less costly way of doing it?" I asked her.

"Sure," she said, "but what's the catch?"

"The catch is that you will have to work a little harder. To start anything new, you have to be prepared to put in both money and time. If you put in less money, you need to put in more time."

"How much more time?" she wisely asked.

"Probably all you've got," I told her.

She frowned . . . and then smiled again.

"Sure," she said. "This is my dream!"

"Okay," I said, "Here's my idea."

What I told her would apply to almost anyone interested in opening up a retail business, including any sort of store selling merchandise, as well as restaurants, hair salons, day spas, and the like.

- Don't rush out to sign a lease. Rental contracts are like marriage licenses. They feel good when you are heady in love, but after reality sets in they may feel expensive and restricting.
- Figure out how to test your basic selling proposition—that there is an active market for what you want to sell at the price you want to put on it. In this case, there are several ways our young entrepreneur can do that.

  First, she can rent booths at local flea markets and art fairs on a daily or weekly basis and peddle her merchandise there. In most parts of the country (and certainly in Florida, where she lives), there are all sorts of places to choose from: open, closed, upscale, downscale, and so on. She should begin by going to the one she thinks will be best for her merchandise, but she should try them all because her hunch may be wrong.*

Second, she should advertise on eBay, Craigslist, and other Internet-based vendor sites.

Third, she should try to wholesale her merchandise to existing retail shops and try to make distribution deals with them. This may require her to discount her merchandise so severely that there will be little profit in it. That doesn't matter. What she wants, initially, is to figure out what types of accessories will sell and at what price.

Fourth, she should sponsor office- and home-based accessory parties, where small groups of women would gather to look at her merchandise and buy what they want in a friendly, low-pressure atmosphere.

Fifth, she could make deals with local restaurants that would allow her to personally model the accessories, going from table to table in their dining rooms, in exchange for a commission on any sales she would generate. (This is done very effectively in a few of the better restaurants in my hometown.)

- If you are able to try out your product line in various venues, you will enjoy three benefits. First, you will discover which of your products sell well in what kind of selling environment and at what price. Second, you will learn how to sell your merchandise—what specific type of sales effort works best for the type of customers you want to attract. Third, and no less important than the others, you will generate cash that you will desperately need to run your business.

- Only after you have a good year of experience selling in this way will you be able to make other less critical business decisions (such as where to advertise and what type of point-of-purchase displays you should have).

---

*Marketing Tip: Never unilaterally decide what you want to sell. Find out what the market wants to buy.

- If everything goes well for that year, you will have everything you need to confidently sign a lease agreement. You will know what products to stock your store with and how to price and package them, and you will even have a good idea about where they would sell the best.

In giving this advice to our would-be entrepreneur, I mentioned that my brother-in-law and his partners started a jewelry business this way about 20 years ago. They began by selling gold "by the inch" at flea markets, graduated to discount malls, and then finally upgraded to fancy malls and shopping centers. Today, they have stores in more than two dozen locations and generate more than $10 million in annual sales.

Could she be successful faster by going directly to retail? Yes, it's possible—if she is exactly right about her products, prices, and merchandising from the get-go. But if she is wrong—even by a little bit—it could spell disaster.

In my view, it's almost always better to get into a new industry on the cheap by figuring out how to test the waters without committing yourself completely to an unproven idea. Again, here's what your priorities should be:

Start by . . .

- Identifying a way or several ways to test your basic selling idea.
- Stocking up on the merchandise you will need to make the test relevant.

Then, continue by . . .

- Selling at flea markets and art fairs.
- Doing some person-to-person wholesale selling to find out more about how the industry works and, hopefully, to establish one or two steady retail customers.
- Sponsoring some home-based party events to get immediate feedback from customers you can trust and talk to.

And finally, fine-tune by . . .

- Making adjustments to your product selection, packaging, pricing, and merchandising during the first year, when such adjustments are easy and inexpensive.

You can't test your basic selling dynamic this easily in every business. If you want to sell cars, you have to manufacture them first, and if you want to sell pharmaceuticals, you have to obtain Food and Drug Administration (FDA) approval for them. But even with such capital-intensive businesses, there is a lot you can do in the early stages to find out: "Can this business really work?"—meaning, "Can I really sell these products/services at a profit?"

CHAPTER FIVE

YOUR OPTIMUM SELLING STRATEGY AND THE FOUR FUNDAMENTAL SECRETS OF SELLING YOUR FIRST PRODUCT

I hope, by this time, I have convinced you that when you are starting a new business, selling must be your primary job.

This is true even if you don't know anything about selling, if you've never taken a course in marketing and never sold so much as a glass of lemonade on a street corner. As an entrepreneur, you have to become your company's number one salesperson—even if you fear or hate the very idea of selling.

Selling is not optional for the Stage One entrepreneur; it's *essential*.

And if selling is essential, learning to sell (i.e., developing the knowledge and skills needed to sell your company's main product) is an obligation, not a choice.

In this chapter and in Chapter 6, I will show you how to become an *expert* at selling your lead product.* Don't worry if you don't know anything about selling. Everything you are about to learn is easy. I will teach you one concept and four secrets. You will learn the concept in about five minutes. And it will take you about half an hour to understand the four secrets.

Discovering how to apply the four secrets to your particular business and your particular product—well, that will take a little time. But I am talking about days or possibly weeks, not months.†

Your educational objective during the start-up stage of your business is very narrow. All you really want to learn is how to sell one particular product to one particular market. You don't need to acquire any generalized marketing expertise or dozens of selling skills that won't apply to your situation. In essence, you are going to become a one-trick marketing pony—someone who can do one thing, and perhaps only one thing, very well: *selling the hell out of your lead product*.

If you have faith in this concept and the four secrets you are about to discover, your success at getting your business from zero to a million dollars in revenues—from Stage One to the beginning of Stage Two—will be virtually guaranteed. In fact, it's very possible that you could see your business grow well beyond the million-dollar mark to $10 million or more, simply by repeating this trick over and over again. As long as it keeps working, you should keep doing it. Later, you will acquire other selling skills. For now, this one thing is enough.

INTRODUCING: THE OPTIMUM SELLING STRATEGY

I believe that for every business at any given time there is one *best way* to acquire new customers. That best way is the way that meets the company's greatest current need. For Stage One businesses, generating

---

*By lead product, I mean the primary product that is used to acquire new customers for any business or division of a business. For start-up companies, the lead product is usually the only product.

†One of the themes of this book is that I believe most of the toughest challenges in business can be overcome with a bit of insight applied at certain strategic points. Those points are the four stages of business development I laid out in Chapter 1. And the four secrets you are about to learn will provide you with the insights you need to make success at each one of those stages not just possible but inevitable.

positive cash flow is usually—or should be—the greatest need. There-fore, Stage One entrepreneurs should be focused on that: figuring out how to acquire customers in a way that creates cash flow.*

Most entrepreneurs never stop to think about cash flow or long-term profits when they are starting out. They are so excited about their product that they imagine it selling itself. And even experienced intrapreneurs—divisional marketing executives or CEOs—often give scant attention to selling strategies when they launch new products, because they mistakenly assume that one way of selling is just about as good as another.

Nothing could be further from the truth. How you sell your pro-duct—the specific decisions you make about presenting and pricing and talking about it—has a huge impact on whether you will be suc-cessful.

The product is important but almost never sells itself. To launch the product successfully and take your new business (or product line) from zero to a million dollars (and beyond), you have to discover what I call your optimum selling strategy (OSS). This chapter and the next are devoted to teaching you how to do that.

Discovering the OSS for your product will put your business on the right track. It will make everything that happens afterward easier. Problems will be easier to solve. Obstacles will be easier to overcome. And objectives will be easier to reach. Your business will grow quickly, because you will have taken care of its biggest problem: acquiring new customers without depleting your bank account.†

Discovering the OSS for your product has other benefits too. For one thing, you will always understand the most important secret of your

---

*As the business matures and moves on to the next stage, its greatest need changes too. Once the business has a back-end marketing strategy in place, for example, it is possible to create profitable growth through negative cash flow strategies such as financing or loss-leader selling. I will cover these concepts in later chapters.

†There are businesses that are launched on the basis of a plan that requires lots of negative cash flow in the beginning. Some of these businesses can be very profitable. One of them, real estate development, has been a professional hobby of mine for more than 20 years. During that time, I have done everything I can to reduce that negative cash flow requirement, because sooner or later it bankrupts most developers, even successful ones. So, although I admit that some businesses seem to require debt and negative cash flow, I prefer to stay away from them—or, when I do dabble in them, change them as much as possible to reduce the risk of debt.

business: how to acquire new customers. This understanding will allow you to lead your employees with confidence as the business grows, and to help them fix problems if and when they arise later. There are many problems that can occur as a business grows, but there is only one that is deadly—and that is the inability to bring in new customers.

When you understand the basics of how to sell to your marketplace, nobody can fool you with cockamamie marketing strategies and idiotic sales programs. And even if you let other people take over the marketing and sales functions, you will be able to guide them as the company grows and help them take advantage of opportunities and avoid potentially damaging mistakes.

As the business grows out of its infancy—as it goes beyond the million-dollar revenue mark by selling many more products through many more channels—you can let other people do most of the day-to-day selling. But by establishing your marketing credentials during the first stage, when the selling secrets of your business are still unknown, you will gain a deep understanding of your business that will serve you well for the rest of your career.

THE FOUR SECRETS OF THE OSS

When your business is just an idea, it is impossible to know with certainty what particular selling strategy will work best for you.

Should you advertise on local radio programs or television channels? Should you buy space ads in local newspapers? Does it make sense to set up a website and try to generate business on a national or international basis with Internet strategies (such as pay-per-click advertising and search engine optimization)?

These are questions you may be asking right now. And if you look to experts for answers, you will get plenty of them. Media brokers will tout the advantages of space ads. Direct-mail marketers will try to persuade you to sell your products through the post office. Internet marketing gurus will highlight the benefits of marketing on the Web. By the time you are done gathering all this good advice, you won't have any better idea about what to do than you did when you started asking.

To determine the optimum selling strategy for your business, you need to answer four questions that will have a profound impact on how

YOUR OPTIMUM SELLING STRATEGY

Once you have determined your initial optimum selling strategy, you can start to think about how you can "test away from it." Spend some time brainstorming with your best people. Ask the key questions:

- What other products can we sell?
- How can we make the offer more enticing?
- How can we make the advertising copy more compelling?
- What other media should we test?

There are hundreds of ways a business can go bad, but only one sure way to make it better: Identify the optimum selling strategy for the stage of growth that you are in and then focus 80 percent of your resources on applying it.

New customers bring new cash, and that cash can be spent on anything your business needs, including better products, customer service, fulfillment, and so on. You name it—cash and a little time will make it happen.

That's why discovering and implementing your company's optimum selling strategy should be your top responsibility. It's that important.

successful you are at developing the positive cash flow your business needs to get to the next level. These four questions are:

1. Where are you going to find your customers?
2. What product will you sell them first?
3. How much will you charge for it?
4. How will you convince them to buy it?

Four answers to four questions—very simple, or so it seems. There is a catch, though: You need to answer all four questions, not just some of them. The optimum selling strategy for your business can unlock a padlock and open the gates of entrepreneurial success. But that padlock has four keyholes. And each of those keyholes requires a separate key.

So let's look at each of these four keys—the four secrets of the OSS—one at a time.

THE OPTIMUM SELLING STRATEGY FOR *EARLY TO RISE (ETR)*

Since its inception, EarlytoRise.com has been working hard to find its optimum selling strategy. Because we wanted the business to practice what it was preaching, it was funded with just a little bit of money—less than $10,000, I think—and I helped grow it in the beginning by contributing my consulting time for free, getting a few colleagues to kick in (in exchange for future promises), and locating it on the Internet where we could create cash flow through affiliate marketing deals with other companies that we had relationships with.

The mandate was always this: Don't spend a lot of money. We never did. After about a year of sending out e-mail messages to a gradually growing file of readers, we had about $100,000 of cash flow going from selling other people's information products. That wasn't much, but it was enough to persuade a partner of mine to invest in this new business. We didn't ask him for cash up front. Instead, we gave him 50 percent of the business in return for his promise to fund future growth up to $250,000.

He provided that, and also contributed his oldest son, just out of college, to help run the business. And that son brought a friend, who worked as a marketer. The two of them were in charge of developing EarlytoRise.com's Internet selling strategy, which at the time consisted of two very simple efforts:

1. They bought pay-per-click names and gave them each a free subscription to the daily *Early to Rise* e-zine, which then sold them all sorts of reports and home-study programs that had been created by other people.
2. Whenever one of those information products sold well, they would obtain permission to sell it directly to other websites and e-zines. People who bought those products online received the *Early to Rise* e-zine for free. Those who decided not to buy those products were given a pop-up opportunity to get the e-zine for free.

THE OPTIMUM SELLING STRATEGY FOR *EARLY TO RISE (ETR)*
(*Continued*)

It wasn't a very sophisticated strategy, but it took EarlytoRise.com from zero to more than a million dollars. Eventually, we had the answers to the four questions we needed to know:

1. *Where our customers were.* We discovered which pay-per-click lists had good names* for us, and which websites and e-zines we could profitably market to.
2. *What product(s) to sell them.* By using other people's products to test the waters, we discovered a great deal about what kind of products worked in our marketplace. Selling other people's products provided less cash flow than selling our own (because we had to split the proceeds twice—first to the affiliate on whose site or e-zine we were selling, and then to the product owner), but it reduced our risk almost to zero. Eventually, we knew enough to start creating and testing our own products successfully.
3. *What price to charge.* By tracking the spending habits of new customers, we found that those who had originally bought $20 products spent an extra $6 (net) per year, while those who initially had spent $50 were worth about $50 a year to us. Interestingly, those who had spent $100 were no more valuable, in terms of back-end buying, than those who had spent $50. So we concluded that our best strategy was to sell as many $50 reports as possible.
4. *What marketing copy to use to convince them to buy.* We were always testing copy. We tested headlines. We tested leads. We tested hard approaches against soft approaches, benefit-oriented pitches against idea-oriented ones. We tested just about anything, so long as we thought what we were testing had a reasonable chance of increasing our response rate by a substantial margin.

We learned that the highest-quality *Early to Rise* reader typically responds strongly to an offer for a product that can make him or her wealthier,

*By "good," I mean the names of people who would buy things from us and thus provide us with positive cash flow.

(continues)

THE OPTIMUM SELLING STRATEGY FOR *EARLY TO RISE (ETR)* (*Continued*)

healthier, or happier, as long as that product doesn't cost more than $50 and comes with a strong, no-questions-asked, money-back guarantee. So that's the kind of offer we construct when we test a new product in our marketplace.

Once we figured out our optimum selling strategy, cash flow increased sharply. No longer were we wasting money on worthless pay-per-click names or websites and e-zines whose customers wouldn't buy from us. We knew where our customers were, how much we could pay for them (either as pay-per-click names or by splitting revenues with affiliates), and what they were willing to spend on new products.

The products we sold them and the marketing copy we used changed as time went by. As a general rule, we found that we had to come up with a new lead product and copy about once every six months.

But that was easy to do, because we understood the most important thing: our optimum selling strategy for getting new products off the ground and running.

After about two years, when sales hit about a million dollars and EarlytoRise.com moved into Stage Two of its business development, we changed our optimum selling strategy. Our second OSS was built around a big change that it was time for us to make in the business: Instead of selling other people's products, we started selling our own.

That second-stage OSS carried us from revenues of a million dollars to $8 million in about six years. And then, once again, we changed our OSS as we changed the business. With a new CEO on board, we implemented an OSS that was perfect for the more professional nature of the business. In a single year, that new OSS took it from $8 million in sales to $20 million, and from very modest profits to very substantial ones.

In the next several years, we will have to change the business again as it moves from being a Stage Three entrepreneurial business to the final stage, which will take it from about $50 million to $100 million and beyond.

It's no longer a question of *whether* EarlytoRise.com will reach that goal. With the right OSS, it's only a matter of how soon.

Where Are Your Customers?

The first question every entrepreneur must ask is a question of location: "Where will I find my customers?"

Are the people who will be buying your products walking down Main Street? Are they listening to Howard Stern? Are they reading *The Wall Street Journal*? Are they watching Oprah? Are they surfing the Internet?

The answer may not be as easy as it sometimes seems.

Let's say you want to start a business selling a new kind of golf ball. You might think that the best place to find your customers would be in pro shops, where they are standing in line waiting to pay their greens fees and thinking about their swing. Perhaps the square foot of real estate next to the cash register would be the perfect place to reach them. If so, you might be able to lease that space and install a point-of-purchase display.

Or maybe it would be better to place an ad at the back of a golfing magazine. There are dozens of magazines to choose from, you discover, each with a different circulation and rate. Perhaps you could get started with a handful of small ads.

Or maybe you should go all out and produce a commercial that you can run on national TV during a televised golf tournament. With millions of people watching, you figure you could make a fortune with a single promotion.

And then, in a passing conversation with a friend of yours who is in the direct-marketing industry, you learn that you can rent lists with the names and addresses of amateur golfers—more than five million in total. He tells you that mailing a targeted sales letter to a portion of those names will give you the best bang for your buck.

Indeed, if you talk to the media brokers who represent each of these advertising options, you will hear good reasons why you should invest your money in theirs. You can't afford to do everything, though, so what do you do?

The Ultimate Marketing Strategies for Newbies

My best advice on this matter will not stir or inspire you. It may even disappoint you. But it is my best advice: Do what everyone else is doing.

I am a big believer in originality, but when it comes to answering most of the fundamental questions about selling your product (the four questions listed earlier), the best answer will always be this: Imitate the industry norm.

In the next chapter, I will talk about how to distinguish your sales pitch by creating a unique selling strategy. But when it comes to figuring out where to find your customers, what to sell them, how much to charge them, and the terms to offer, the answer is: Do what the competition is doing—in the beginning, at least.

As you move on and gain experience, you may be able to come up with innovative changes. You might find a new advertising medium that will deliver fresh customers, or you might develop a new offer that increases your response rates. This is what you can—and should—be doing during the second stage of your business's growth (when you go from $1 million to $10 million in revenues). But for now, at the beginning, it is smart to start by imitating success.

Locating the Best Locations

So how do you find out where successful companies in your industry are finding their customers?

That is relatively easy. Start by looking around in all the likely places.

If you were selling golf balls, for example, you would tour the pro shops looking for display ads, go to Barnes & Noble and browse all the golf magazines, and watch golf shows on TV, taking note of the advertisers. You might even stay up late and watch cable to see if anyone is selling golf paraphernalia there. You would certainly look at the major national newspapers, such as *The Wall Street Journal* and *USA Today*. And you'd spend lots of time on the Internet, for there are thousands of websites devoted to golf.

Next, talk to marketing executives. Call up your future competitors. Ask for the names of the people in charge of their marketing. Tell them that you are a marketing student eager to learn what they do (indeed, you are!) and ask for a 15-minute "informational interview." You will be surprised at how many you get, how long they last, and what wonderful, useful things they tell you.

Every industry has its own trade associations that will provide you with directories of media brokers and other industry specialists. Contact them and tell them about your plans for marketing your product. They will be interested in helping you. Everything they tell you, of course, will have a bias toward their specialty. But you can separate the wheat from the chaff.

What you are doing is assembling a master list of media placements—a map of where all the marketing activity in your industry is taking place. Your objective is to find out not just where your competitors are advertising, but also how often they are advertising and, if possible, how much they are spending. You want to know where the most popular locations are and what locations your competitors go back to time and time again.

The best locations for your competitors will probably be the best locations for you too.

None of this, by the way, should cost you any money. If you want to buy those magazines in Barnes & Noble rather than browse through them, go ahead. Yes, the telephone calls will cost you a few pennies, but all the valuable advice you will get for free.

As I said, answering this "where" question is the first thing you must do. There is nothing more important in marketing than media. You can have the world's best product and the world's best marketing copy and you can sell at the best price and with the most customer-friendly terms, but if you put your advertisement in the wrong place, it won't work—at all.

Conversely, a mediocre advertisement placed in the best location *will* work. It will make money. It's just a question of how much. So start by finding out where your customers are.

What Product Do You Sell Them First?

When you start a business, you usually do it with an idea for a particular product or product line—some sort of "better mousetrap" that will put your business on the cover of *Inc.* magazine.

Having a new product idea may be the most *common* way to start a business, but it's not always the *best* way. What if your product fails? What if it doesn't sell like crazy? What if you find out that it has already been sold, unsuccessfully, several times? What if it sells, but poorly, leaving you with financial losses?

Prudent entrepreneurs do not want to risk all their time and money on the success of a single product. If they want the best chance of having a successful business, they need to be flexible about what product they are going to sell. If their first idea doesn't sell well, they have to be able to generate a second one.

After figuring out where your customers are, selecting the right product to sell to them is the next most important task for any would-be entrepreneur. Starting with a single product in mind is usually a big mistake. You wouldn't think so from everything you see in the business media, because journalists love to tell success stories about pioneers who risked everything on a single idea. But the actual history of successful entrepreneurship tells a very different story. For every single-minded success, there are dozens of single-minded failures. You don't read about them, because their tales are so depressing. But they are the standard.

To avoid falling into that trap,* prudent entrepreneurs stay flexible about the details of their product idea. If one version doesn't work, they have several other ideas in mind that might work better.

To start a successful business, it helps to begin with a successful product. A successful product is one that captures the imagination of the marketplace. You can't know whether your product will do that until you test it—but if you are prepared to test several product ideas rather than just one, you will likely increase your chances of success.

How to Pick the Perfect Start-Up Product

There are five simple steps to creating a product that can launch a business:

1. Find out what products are currently hot in the market.
2. Determine if your product idea fits that trend.
3. If it does, you're set to go. If it doesn't, follow steps 4 and 5.
4. Come up with me-too versions of several hot products.
5. Improve them in some way by adding features or benefits the originals lack.

What Products Are Hot?

It's easy to find out what products are hot in any market. Look at the primary media that you have identified for the business you're in (or want to be in), and take note of what products are advertised the most.

---

*It is a trap of arrogance. Only arrogant people refuse to allow for the possibility that their idea might be wrong.

It's reasonable to infer that the most commonly sold products are the hot products. But it also helps to know how long they have been hot so you can gauge where you are in the trend. You don't want to launch a me-too product (with a new twist) at a time when the market is getting tired of the original product. If possible, you want to be in at the beginning.

There is no sure way to guess how long a trend will last, but you can find out how long it has been in existence by talking to people in the industry. You can do that by speaking to brokers, consultants, and even your future competitors. You can call the same people you spoke to before, when you were researching media. If they talked to you once and you thanked them for their time,* they should be happy to talk to you again.

Once you have identified the top three to five products in the market, spend some time studying them. (Again, you don't have to spend lots of money if you don't want to. You can examine the hot products in stores if they are available through retail outlets. Or you can order them, look at them, and return them for refunds.) Make a list of all their features and benefits. Compare one product to another. Try to figure out which characteristics are the most appealing. Then make a list of any shortcomings you notice.

The better acquainted you become with a product, the easier it will be to see its faults. Every fault is an opportunity for you to create a me-too version that could sell better than the original. It can be very helpful at this stage to share the product with friends and/or colleagues and get their ideas about how it could be improved. What you are looking for is an idea that will really excite you—an idea that feels like it might capture the market and create a tipping-point buying frenzy. If it feels that way, your success is not guaranteed, but your chances are much better than they would be if you weren't excited.

How Much Should You Charge?

You know where your customers are. And you have a general idea for a product that has proven itself in the market—a product that, with a few changes that are very exciting, might turn into a big seller.

---

*It is always a good idea to send a personal note of thanks for those conversations.

DISCOUNTING: THE EASIEST WAY TO BRING IN LOTS OF NEW CUSTOMERS

A powerful and reliable way to grow a small business is to market an upwardly trending product at a substantial discount to its perceived value. This observation may seem to be common sense, but it's not commonly done.

If you have the means to establish a price that is substantially less than what the competition is charging, you will likely see a very strong response to your marketing campaigns.

This is not to say that discounting is appropriate for every sales strategy. On the contrary, it is a challenging if not problematic way to grow a business. Most products should be sold by emphasizing their qualities and benefits. When you are selling back-end products to existing customers, for example, you should discount infrequently and carefully. If you overemphasize "cheapness," you will encourage them to think of you as a provider of cheap and therefore inferior products. Holding a position of discounted quality is hard to do.

That said, nothing will grow a customer base faster than drastically underpricing the competition. The ideal pricing mix for me is one lead product that is promoted at a heavy discount and all other products sold by emphasizing quality.

The purpose of marketing a heavy discount is to attract as many qualified customers as possible. After those customers come in, they should be "pummeled" with lots of back-end buying opportunities, which will result in a very high lifetime value for each customer.

The higher the lifetime value, the more you can afford to spend on each acquired customer. Most of the businesses I work with are happy to spend between 30 percent and 100 percent of the price of the new product to acquire a customer.

If you don't have a price-driven offer among your front-end marketing efforts, you should try one. You may be surprised at the results.

The next question you must answer is: How much should it cost?

The price you charge for your product has a major impact on sales—an impact that is third only to the media you use and the appeal of the product itself. Choosing the price, like choosing the media or the product, is a fairly easy thing to do. You should start—as you did with media and product—by finding out what the competition is doing.

If your competitors' widgets are selling for $19.95, you should consider selling yours for $19.95 too. That is almost certainly where the market is—the soft spot where you get the greatest number of profitable new customers. You can safely assume that any product that has been selling well at $19.95 has been tested by your competitors at other prices—higher and lower—and that $19.95 is where the money is.

Optimal Selling Price

For every product, there is an optimal selling price—a price at which the selling campaign will yield the greatest profits. This optimal price can change during the life cycle of the product (being higher when the product is hot, for example), but it is always important to know. If you deviate from it significantly, you will reduce profits or even create losses where profits should have been.

In the newsletter business, for example, I found that consumer health publications are best sold at $39 a year. If you sell them for less—at $19 or even $29—it is hard to cover fulfillment costs and thus remain profitable. If you price them higher—$50 or more—response rates drop dramatically, which also results in reduced or negative profits. In my 15 years of experience with that industry, I've seen half a dozen prices tested in dozens of clever ways, but none has been able to beat the control price of $39 for any significant length of time.

So if I were launching a new health-related newsletter, I would want to start at the optimal price and only later test against it.

Cheaper Can Sometimes Be Better

Testing a higher-than-average price for your product is a good thing to do, but only after you have first sold it at the industry standard—the optimal price—and have a good handle on response rates, cross sales, upgrades, and the cost of product fulfillment and customer service. If you test a higher price and it brings in the same number of responses as the lower price, you immediately and automatically increase your profits.

THE THEORY OF MARKET ELASTICITY

Except for certain products for which the demand is required and not optional (like fuel for factories), market elasticity describes what happens when most businesses raise or lower their prices. The theory is that there is an indirect relationship between the price of a product and (1) supply (the amount of it that is produced by the manufacturer) and (2) consumer demand.

A company should always take into account this concept of elasticity when raising or lowering prices. If consumer demand for the product is elastic, a price cut could persuade them to buy more, whereas too much of an increase could cause sales to fall dramatically and/or drive consumers to buy similar products instead. However, if demand for the product is inelastic, a price increase or decrease would not necessarily lead to an increase or decrease in sales.

Generally speaking, the higher price should reduce the number of sales. (The theory of market elasticity says that the number of sales will go down when the price goes up, and vice versa.) The question is: by how much? If it is only a modest decrease, you might do better with the higher price because you initially will generate more gross profit and possibly bring in a higher-quality customer who will spend more money with you later.

If you jack the price up too high, though, sales will drop precipitously to a point where you are bringing in too few new customers to maintain cash flow. This is usually easy to notice and fix.

I have had little success with selling lead (front-end) products at prices that are higher than the market, but I've enjoyed some great successes by undercutting the market. When you enter an existing market selling a popular me-too product at a discount, you can sometimes enjoy a very strong response.

When consumers see multiple promotions for popular products, they eventually figure out what the appropriate price is. That price is—from the marketer's point of view—the optimal selling price. If you can sell into that kind of market at a discount, you will definitely see a good response. The question is: Can you afford to fulfill the product and run your business like that?

The answer is probably not, unless you have a way to manufacture and/or deliver the product to the customer at a cost that is significantly below the competition. With so many products being made in China these days, that possibility exists. Information publishing also lends itself to steep discounting.

HOW TO PRICE PRODUCTS FOR NEW CUSTOMER ACQUISITION

For most of the products you sell, pricing is not difficult to determine. You have to charge enough to cover all your costs and give you an acceptable profit.

If, for example, you are in the restaurant business, you have to price your hamburgers high enough so that the price of each burger pays for the cost of the meat, the labor to prepare and serve it, a reasonable portion of your overhead (rent, taxes, etc.), and another 20 percent or so for profit.

If you are in the retail business, it's likely that the price you will be charging for most of your goods will be roughly equal to twice the cost of the products. That calculation is relatively easy.

The challenge is to figure out how much to charge for a product that you are selling with the main purpose of bringing in new customers.

In the restaurant business, you might want to discount some menu items either periodically or permanently. Most restaurants do this by offering nightly specials. If you wanted to break into a new market, you would want to do something more aggressive to catch your customers' attention.

When I was in the restaurant business many years ago, we offered a $2 all-you-can-eat steak special on Thursday nights. Two dollars was considerably less than it cost us to acquire and serve the food, but we found that customers spent so much money on beer and soft drinks that we were able to break even. Breaking even is not a good business strategy unless there is a point to it. For us, the object was to get the word out about our restaurant and encourage people to return on other nights when food was priced normally (i.e., at twice the cost). And that strategy worked very well. When the restaurant got to the point where it was busy

(continues)

HOW TO PRICE PRODUCTS FOR NEW CUSTOMER ACQUISITION
(*Continued*)

all the time, we gradually reduced the $2 offer to a single hour, and eventually dropped it completely.

We established the $2 price without any idea about whether it made sense economically. All we knew—or believed we knew—was that lots of people would come in if they heard about the deal. Since then, I have learned a lot more about establishing prices for the purpose of attracting new customers. I have even learned the term *allowable acquisition cost (AAC)*, which is, admittedly, sort of haughty—but it conveys the idea. I have learned, for example, that if you discount your lead product too much, you may bring in the wrong type of customer—bargain hunters who will patronize you only when they are getting the better side of the deal.*

So how do you figure the allowable acquisition cost?

The formula is very simple. Figure out how much a customer will spend with you, on average, over a lifetime. Deduct the cost of goods from that. Then deduct a percentage of your overhead. And then figure out and deduct how much you want to profit from that customer. The final number is your allowable acquisition cost—the amount of money you can "spend" (i.e., lose) to attract a first-time buyer.

Step One: Determine Your Lifetime Gross Profit

Let's say you are in the pet supply business and you have found (from your own experience or from industry data, which is based on someone else's experience) that the average customer will stay with you for four years and spend $60 per year with you. That's a total of $240 in purchases. If you are paying wholesale for the pet supplies you're selling, your cost of goods will be half of that $240 or $120, leaving you with $120 in gross profit over the four-year "lifetime" of your average customer.

$240 lifetime gross sales after first purchase − $120 cost of goods sold

= $120 lifetime gross profit

---

*I learned that lesson when I was in the bar business. Nickel Beer Night was a smashing success in terms of the number of people who came to the Right Track Inn. The problem was that they were all rowdies who would drink cheap, get drunk, and then get in fights and wreck the place. And they never returned on other nights, sober and willing to pay the regular price for their beer.

HOW TO PRICE PRODUCTS FOR NEW CUSTOMER ACQUISITION
(*Continued*)

Step Two: Determine Your Lifetime Net Value

The $120 that is your lifetime gross profit does not take into consideration all your overhead expenses, such as rent, utilities, payroll, and so on. Before you can decide what your allowable acquisition cost is, you have to figure in those expenses. You have to deduct them from your gross profit. In this case, since we are talking about a retail business, let's assume that your overhead is pretty high—equal to half of your gross profit.

$120 lifetime gross profit − $60 lifetime overhead = $60 lifetime net value

Step Three: Determine a Reasonable Profit

Now you have to account for the profit you want to make and deduct that from the lifetime net value. As a general rule, healthy retail businesses yield 10 percent net profits. But I don't like making plans based on 10 percent; it leaves too little room for error. I prefer figuring in at least 20 percent of gross sales for profit. If you did that in our example, you'd have:

$60 lifetime net value − $48 lifetime net profit (20 percent of $240)

= $12 allowable acquisition cost

In other words, you could lose $12 on every first-time sale and still have a business that generates a 20 percent profit over your average customer's lifetime.

That information could give you a significant advantage over your competitors. It could, for example, allow you to advertise and sell (to first-time customers only) flea collars for a nickel apiece or giant bags of birdseed for $5 or pooper-scoopers for 99 cents.

Discounting isn't the only way to bring in new customers, but it is certainly one of the most common. If you know your allowable acquisition cost, you can try all sorts of different discounts without ever taking much risk.

Figuring Lifetime Value—Quick and Easy

When you are in your first year of business, you can't know with certainty how valuable your customers will be over the period of time they will be

(continues)

HOW TO PRICE PRODUCTS FOR NEW CUSTOMER ACQUISITION
(*Continued*)

spending money with you. But if you did your homework before starting your business, you will have a pretty good dollar amount in mind: They should be worth to you what they are worth to other similar businesses in your industry. Of course, you will try to increase that lifetime value by following the suggestions in this book. But when you are figuring out how much you can spend to acquire new customers, using a number that's standard for your industry is a good start.

If, for whatever reason, you can't find out what the industry standard is, you can make the following assumption: Depending on the nature of your industry and how good you are at customer service, after their initial purchase your customers will spend, on average, between 100 percent and 500 percent of their original purchase price with you over time. That means—and this is more important—that they will be worth, on a gross profit basis (after the cost of goods sold), between 50 percent and 100 percent of what they spent on their first purchase.

If you are in the business of selling frozen steaks through a catalog, for example, and your average first order is $82, you can expect your average customer to spend an additional $200 to $300 with you—which will leave you, after deducting the cost of products and shipping, about $82 in gross profits. If you are in the business of selling fancy soaps at a chain of flea markets and the average first-time purchase is $19, you can expect your average customer to spend another $19 with you, which will net out to about $10.

An important part of what you will learn in this book is about ratcheting up that lifetime value. By following some of the suggestions I have given you here, you could increase your customers' average lifetime value significantly—easily to three to five times their initial purchase. But when you are starting out and don't have any experience behind you, it would be prudent to run your projections based on two assumptions:

1. A lifetime value of 50 percent of the initial purchase price (conservative).
2. A lifetime value of 100 percent of the initial purchase price (realistic).

Back-End Pricing

This idea of optimal pricing and discounting applies to front-end marketing only—to bringing in first-time customers. Once you have acquired a customer, you add that name to your customer file. What you want to do then is develop your relationship with your customers as much as you can so you can sell them products that are similar to the products they first bought from you, but at much higher prices. I will talk more about this later in the book.

How Will You Persuade Them to Buy Your New Product?

The optimum selling strategy includes the media you choose to advertise in, the product you decide to sell, the pricing of the product, and also the copy platform—the big idea behind your advertising campaign, along with all the words and images you will use to sell your product.

As with the other components of selling, the best copy platform can change over time, But at any given moment in a product's history, there is one best way to present your offer to your prospective customer—and your job as a Stage One entrepreneur is to find out what that is for your new product.

Marketing copy matters. The difference between a good copy concept and a not-so-good copy concept can be a difference of 100 percent or more in terms of advertising response rates and the profitability of your product sales. That can mean the difference between a business that doubles in size every year for three or four years and one that barely grows at all or flattens out and dies.

When you are starting your business, you may have a few ideas about how to sell your product—what features and benefits to emphasize and what words to use. But the only way you can discover the best copy platform is by testing it. Whenever I work with a client to launch a new product, we test as many different media as we can at two or three different prices and using at least two completely different copy platforms.

Finding out which media will work for you is quick and easy. Testing the price takes a little longer, but is simple to do. It is the copy platform that requires more time and subtlety, because it is impossible to know when you've come up with the best approach. You just have to keep trying different things to find out.

If you have no experience writing advertising copy, you will probably be better off hiring a professional copywriter to create your ads for you. You can locate competent copywriters by consulting with trade associations and checking out online copywriting listing services, such as the one provided by American Writers & Artists Inc. (www.awaionline.com), which trains new copywriters. Finding a good copywriter is an important component of this part of the selling process, because the right one will write much stronger copy for you. But even if you find the best copywriter in your industry, you cannot abandon your job as your company's master marketer. You have to direct the copywriter to use his or her skills to sell your particular product at a particular price to a particular market. Nobody but you can be in charge of that.

THE POWER OF COMPARISONS

If you want to create a price-driven offer but can't afford to discount the price as much as you feel the market dictates, the next best thing is to create the impression of a large discount by increasing the product's perceived value.

Back in the late 1960s, I spent a summer selling aluminum siding on Long Island. The typical package we sold retailed for about $2,600. Our primary sales pitch focused on the benefits of aluminum siding: beauty, ease, and durability.* I became pretty skilled at helping my prospects imagine how much better, easier, and fuller their lives would be once the asbestos shingles that covered their homes were hidden beneath a fine, shiny façade of bright, white aluminum.

After I had been canvassing the streets for a few weeks, Harvey, my boss, joined me for a day to see how well I was doing. Observing my routine, he complimented me on "selling the sandwich," as he said, but suggested that I would improve my closing ratio by learning how to "sell the spread."

He explained that since the neighborhood was full of competing tin men (as we called ourselves), all of the homeowners had a pretty good idea of the price. Since our price was average and therefore not a selling point, we had to do something to make it seem like a good value.

This is how Harvey did it:

After getting some young couple to imagine how much nicer their house would look clad in aluminum, how much the neighbors would

*None of which turned out to be true. But back then, aluminum was a space-age material.

THE POWER OF COMPARISONS (*Continued*)

admire them, and how generally happy they'd be, Harvey would ask them, "Now, Mr. and Mrs. Smith, tell me this. How much would you guess it would cost you to cover your house in solid oak?"

"Oak?" they would ask. "But we thought . . ."

"I'm serious," Harvey would insist. "How much would it cost?"

It was the husbands who always ventured the first guess. "I don't know—maybe five thousand dollars?"

"Five thousand dollars?" Harvey would look at the wife. "Do you think you could do it for five thousand dollars?"

"Gee, I don't know. Probably not."

The number would go up—$6,000, $7,000, $8,000. To each new estimate, Harvey would shake his head sadly and say, "You should be so lucky."

Harvey would pause for a good while, giving the frazzled customers a chance to imagine how they were going to come up with the $10,000 this was bound to cost, and then "hit them with the zinger" (as he liked to call it): "Let me give you 10 good reasons why aluminum siding is *better* than solid oak!"

It wasn't logical, but it was effective. By the time Harvey finished enumerating the 10 reasons aluminum was better than oak, they were mentally prepared to spend $10,000. When Harvey told them they'd have to fork out only $2,600, they practically jumped with joy.

"If you want to make the price of liverwurst look cheap," Harvey told me, "compare it to the price of fancy French pâté."*

*In his book *Influence: The Psychology of Persuasion*, Robert Cialdini puts a label to this technique. He calls it "the principle of contrast," and illustrates it with a story he heard from Leo Rosten about the Drubeck brothers, Sid and Harry, who owned a men's tailor shop in Rosten's neighborhood while he was growing up in the 1930s: Whenever the salesman, Sid, had a new customer trying on suits in front of the shop's three-sided mirror, he would admit to a hearing problem, and, as they talked, he would repeatedly request that the man speak more loudly to him. Once the customer had found a suit he liked and had asked for the price, Sid would call to his brother, the head tailor, at the back of the room, "Harry, how much for this suit?" Looking up from his work—and greatly exaggerating the suit's true price—Harry would call back, "For that beautiful all-wool suit, $42." Pretending not to have heard and cupping his hand to his ear, Sid would ask again. Once more, Harry would reply, "$42." At this point, Sid would turn to the customer and report, "He says $22." Many a man would hurry to buy the suit and scramble out of the shop with his "expensive=good" bargain before poor Sid discovered the "mistake."

Source: Robert Cialdini, *Influence: The Psychology of Persuasion*, rev. ed. (New York: William Morrow and Company, 1993), 10–11.

Four Ways to Make Sure You Have Killer Copy

Directing a copywriter to write good copy is not as daunting as it may sound. There are just four things to pay attention to, and you can learn all of them pretty quickly.

I will go over each key aspect of killer copy in the next chapter.

CHAPTER SIX

MASTERING THE COPY SIDE OF SELLING

As your company's chief executive, the creation of advertising copy is an essential part of your job.

But you don't have to be a copywriter to create copy. You need only know how it's done and what great copy looks like. You can learn the basics very quickly. In fact, you will know them by the time you finish reading this chapter. The next step is to create a copy platform for your product using the cheat sheet I'll give you at the end of this chapter. That will take you just a few hours to complete. The last step is to hire a competent professional copywriter—preferably someone who has experience writing for your industry—and explain what you want done.

Designing an advertising campaign is like designing a house. You have to begin with an idea of what you want—the purpose of the house (first home, second home, pied-à-terre, etc.) and how you want to enjoy it (formal dinners, reading by the fire, plenty of room for children's playthings, etc.). Then you have to translate those needs and desires into a structure (the number and size of the rooms and how they flow together). Finally, you have to tie it all together with a style, something that tells your guests (and reminds you) just what kind of a family lives in that house.

NOBODY KNOWS BETTER THAN YOU

As the person who is starting the business, nobody knows the product better than you do. And if you do what I suggested in Chapter 5 to develop your optimum selling strategy (OSS), you'll be an expert on your customers too. In working with a copywriter, you will bring these two critical understandings to the table. The copywriter will be responsible for the expression of them—but you will have the tools to evaluate the effectiveness of the copy.

Becoming your company's best marketer is critical when your business is in Stage One, because nobody but you has the same need to discover the optimum selling strategy. Your employees are dependent on your company's success, but they don't give it much thought. They are thinking more about their next paycheck. The consultants and freelance talent you hire, including the copywriters, graphic artists, and media specialists, realize that it's better for them if you succeed so they will have repeat business. But if you fail, they get paid anyway.

As the owner of a start-up business, you are making the biggest commitment: You have invested your future in it—so don't let anyone else take the ultimate responsibility for its success. You can learn what you need to know relatively quickly. Invest the time. Do it.

That's how it can work for you as creative director of your new business. After doing the research described in Chapter 5 and absorbing the information in this chapter, you will be able to tell a copywriter (or an advertising director) what you want your copy to accomplish in terms of conveying a "Big Idea" (more about this later) and stirring the emotions of your customers.

You will also be able to give the copywriter specifics about the product, the pricing, the offer, and the media you'd like to work with. From that, you'll agree on an advertising budget. And then the copywriter will start coming up with suggestions.

You will be able to respond intelligently to his suggestions and provide direction, because you will know exactly what you are trying to accomplish. You will understand what your customer wants to get from a product like yours, and you will have complete knowledge of all your product's features and their corresponding benefits. Finally, you will understand the architecture of a successful advertisement and/or sales pitch. You will know all that . . . because you are about to learn it.

There are only four concepts you need to understand in order to design and direct the advertising for your business. Each of these concepts will take you less than half an hour to learn. When you have mastered them all, you will be astonished at how easy it will be for you to come up with great advertising ideas and to direct copywriters— even the most experienced copywriters—in creating copy for your product.

FOUR KEY CONCEPTS EVERY MARKETING GENIUS MUST KNOW

To be able to create great copy and work intelligently with great copywriters, there are four marketing concepts you need to learn:

1. The difference between wants and needs.
2. The difference between features and benefits.
3. How to establish a unique selling proposition (USP) for your product.
4. How to sell the USP.

Let's start with the first concept, the difference between wants and needs.

The Difference Between Wants and Needs

In today's consumer-driven economy, it's easy to mistake a want for a need. How many times have you heard one of the following statements?

- "Sally needs a new wardrobe. The clothes she's wearing make her look silly."
- "John hates the way his hair looks. He says he needs a better barber."

- "I simply have to have that new handbag!"
- "We need a bigger house."
- "We need a nicer car."
- "We need a bigger lawn."

None of those things are needs—something you can't live without. Our needs are really few and simple: air, water, food, shelter, transportation (sometimes), clothing (usually), the tools of our trade, and so on. Just about everything else that we buy is based on our wants.

And even when it comes to needs, like food and clothing, our buying decisions are often based on wants. We want a certain type of bread, a specific brand of clothing, a house in a particular neighborhood, and so forth.

Recognizing that you are in the *want* business will help you become a better marketer and salesperson, because you will recognize that you have to create *want* in your customers' hearts. Many first-time marketers make the mistake of creating sales campaigns that are logical and rational: X number of ways their product is better than someone else's. If your product really is a necessity, like a tractor or heating oil, you could get away with that kind of pitch. But that won't work for most products, because it doesn't do what copy has to do when you are selling wants—and that is to stimulate emotions.

You have to stimulate emotions in your customers, but not just any emotions. You want emotions that will help you sell your product. To create those emotions, you need to get potential customers thinking about how your product is going to enhance their lives. The way to do that is to subject them to advertising copy that demonstrates one or several benefits of your product.

The Difference Between Features and Benefits

Advertising teachers like to teach the principle of features versus benefits by using the example of a No. 2 pencil. So let's do that here. Let's pretend that the product you are trying to sell is a No. 2 pencil.

You would start your examination of the pencil by taking out a sheet of paper and drawing a vertical line through it. At the top of the left-hand side of this worksheet, you would write "Features." At the top of the right-hand side, you would write "Benefits."

Then you would list all the features you could think of—everything the pencil is or has or does. For example, your No. 2 pencil:

- Is made of wood.
- Has a specific diameter.
- Contains a lead-composite filler.
- Has an eraser at the end.

In listing these features, you are describing the objective qualities of the pencil. And if buying were strictly a rational process, selling it would be that simple—listing all these features, these objective qualities, so your customer could evaluate them and make a logical buying decision.

Happily, buying is not entirely rational. In fact, rationality comes into play only after the irrational process—the emotional persuasion—has already taken place. This is good news for you as a marketer of No. 2 pencils, because you want to sell as many of them as you can—even to people who might have enough pencils or to people who don't use pencils.

You are hoping to arouse in your prospective customer a feeling of irrational exuberance regarding pencils, and the purpose of your advertising campaign will be to do just that. So now you shift over to the right-hand side of your worksheet. And for every feature you listed for your No. 2 pencil, you come up with as many related benefits as you can think of—what those features mean to your customer. Things like this:

Features	Benefits
Is made of wood	Easy to sharpen
Has a specific diameter	Comfortable to hold
Contains a lead-composite filler	Creates an impressive line
Has an eraser at the end	Makes correcting easy

This list will go on and on. I've conducted workshops on features and benefits using a No. 2 pencil that have resulted in the identification of more than 200 benefits.

But don't stop with ordinary benefits. Go deeper.

In our example, what might be a deeper benefit of having a pencil that sharpens easily? To figure that out, you need to ask yourself, "Who are my target customers? And why, exactly, would they want little things (like sharpening pencils) to be easy?"

Of course, there's no single answer to such questions. If your target customers are busy executives, their deeper reasons are going to be different than those of a busy housewife.

Perhaps the executives want the little things in life to be easier because they are buried in minutiae. Perhaps they sense that if they could just get a little more spare time in their day they could catch up on their work. And if they could finally get their in-boxes conquered and their e-mail cleaned up, perhaps they could write that memo or make that phone call that would boost their career.

They are not thinking these things consciously, but such thoughts occasionally cross their minds. And when these thoughts appear, it is because the executive is feeling some emotion—in this case, probably frustration. So you should list that deeper benefit—"Reduces the frustration of falling behind at work and feeling like you will never get ahead"—on your worksheet, even though it may seem like an exaggeration (or even irrational).

Deconstruct every benefit you list into deeper benefits. And don't use abstract language. If you feel that your customers are looking for success, define success in concrete terms. What, exactly, do they want? More money? More prestige? And if so, why? A bigger home? A nicer car? What? And why do they want those things? To please their families? To impress their friends? And why do they want to please their families and impress their friends?

Keep going until you have described very specific benefits or desires that feel important and true to you. They should be based on emotions that are tempting or taunting your customers—fantasies they dream about during the day or fears that keep them up at night.

If you can figure out how your product can provide benefits to your customers that satisfy their deeper and stronger emotions, your advertising copy will be powerful.

How to Establish a Unique Selling Proposition for Your Product

You can sell your product very well by talking about its many benefits, but you will find that the most successful advertisements are those that highlight a single benefit above all the rest. When this benefit can be presented as uniquely characteristic of your product, you have an advertising proposition that can last and last and last.

I am talking about establishing a unique selling proposition (USP) for your product.

The importance of establishing a unique selling proposition is widely accepted and widely proclaimed by business experts, schools, and publications. Yet more than 90 percent of all new products that come to market come without any distinguishing characteristics.

Walk through any supermarket or department store. Most of the products you'll see are fundamentally the same as others of their type. And when new business ideas are suggested to me, they are mostly copycat ideas. In the past few months, for example, I've heard the following:

- An investment advisory newsletter on exchange-traded funds (ETFs).
- A website providing natural remedies for health problems.
- A chain of retail stores selling imported accessories for women.
- A website containing inspirational and motivational messages.
- A seminar business that teaches public speaking.

None of these ideas were in any way unique. Yet that didn't faze the people who were promoting them. And some of those people were reasonably experienced entrepreneurs. When I asked them how they could distinguish their businesses from the competition, they looked at me as if I were speaking Swahili.

If you want your best chance of selling a new product into an established market, it helps if you do one of two things:

1. Make it—in some way—*better* than the competition.
2. Make it—in some way—*seem* better.

An example of the first is FedEx. An example of the second is 7-Up.

The Case of FedEx

In creating FedEx, Fred Smith came up with a unique new way to deliver packages. Instead of the conventional express shipping methods used by the U.S. Postal Service and United Parcel Service (UPS), he emulated the banking industry's method of clearing checks overnight. What individual banks did was send all their checks to a central facility that processed and returned them overnight. FedEx did the same thing with packages by creating a hub-and-spoke system in Memphis.

Twenty-four-hour delivery was a genuine improvement over what the competition was offering. But the innovation itself wasn't enough. FedEx had to sell it. In its initial campaign to launch the new service, FedEx emphasized this advantage in every single print ad and television and radio commercial it ran. It employed the slogan "When it absolutely, positively has to get there overnight" to drive the message home.

The campaign (and FedEx's performance) worked. The line was later shortened to "Absolutely, positively," but was still instantly associated by customers with FedEx's promise of overnight delivery.

The Case of 7-Up

To introduce 7-Up to the marketplace, company executives had a different challenge. The product itself offered no real benefit to the consumer. Its only distinction was its lack of color, which was a benefit to the manufacturer because it reduced production costs. The problem was solved when the executives asked themselves, "How could this be a good thing for our customers?"

What they decided to do was pitch the product as better because it was different.* It was a cola and yet not a cola. It tasted good but it was somehow more refreshing. To catch the attention of hundreds of millions of cola drinkers worldwide, they promoted 7-Up's lighter look and positioned it accordingly by calling it "the Uncola."† And

---

*The company that marketed Volkswagens in the 1970s did the same thing when executives asked themselves, "How can we turn owning a small, ugly car into a good thing?" At that time, Volkswagens were sold by appealing to younger people who, by and large, considered themselves to be nonconformists. So Volkswagen emphasized the car's quirkiness in its advertising pitch—how different it was from the conventional American sedan.

†One classic 7-Up commercial from the early 1970s featured a Caribbean planter explaining how the soft drink is made from crisp, refreshing "uncola nuts" (lemons and limes). One of the most memorable TV commercials ever created, it had an immediate effect on sales.

the concept worked. From the start of the "Uncola" campaign in 1968, net sales went from $87.7 million to $190 million a decade later.

It is easier to sell a product if it really does have a substantial benefit that the competition lacks. FedEx gained market dominance by promising overnight delivery, and Apple did a great job of selling the iPhone by emphasizing its large glass screen.

But when your product isn't clearly distinct and better than the competition, you can still make it *feel* so by emphasizing a unique secondary characteristic, which is what 7-Up did so successfully. Not only was the benefit unique, it was desirable and easy to communicate.

DOES EVERY PRODUCT HAVE TO BE UNIQUE?

Of course, not every product can—or should—be unique.

Billions of dollars are made each year by businesses that sell me-too products (their own versions of products that are currently hot in the marketplace) at discount prices. Underpricing the competition is a good and proven approach.

John D. Rockefeller dominated the oil industry by buying up production and delivery, and thus was able to offer oil and gas at prices his competitors couldn't touch. Likewise, Andrew Carnegie made a fortune by producing inexpensive steel. Marshall Field brought down the cost of retail shopping. Sam Walton is known for his discount stores, Henry Ford for making autos within the financial reach of the average person, and the Mellons for making money cheap.

When you are starting a new business, you'd be crazy not to make the concept of underpricing a core part of your growth and marketing strategy. And if your business is mature, underpricing your competition is still the single strongest way to introduce a new product or product line or to enter a new market.

But if you *can't* compete on price—and most new businesses can't— you have to compete with your product. And that means positioning it as somehow *different from* and *better than* other products of its kind.

The Unique Selling Proposition as a Method of Positioning

Coming up with the right USP can make the difference between a mediocre product launch (which could mean a complete failure for a start-up company) and a big success (like 7-Up, FedEx, the iPhone, etc.).

In their classic marketing book *Positioning*, Al Ries and Jack Trout explain why developing a USP is so essential:

> To succeed in our overcommunicated society, a company must create a position in the prospect's mind, a position that takes into account not only a company's own strengths and weaknesses, but those of its competitors as well. Advertising is entering an era where strategy is king. In the positioning era, it's not enough to invent or discover something. It may not even be necessary. You must, however, be first to get in the prospect's mind.[1]

Ries and Trout say that people spend very little time considering new information—usually just a second or two. So if you want your product to have a strong position in the marketplace, you have to come up with a unique position. Then you have to find a way to communicate that position clearly and concisely, so it will be understood in the few moments of attention you are likely to get for it. And finally, they argue, in selling the product you have to emphasize that USP all the time so that you eventually "dominate" that position in the hearts and minds of the marketplace.

"If you provide a product or service that is just like an existing product or service, you will probably not succeed," says Seth Godin in *If You're Clueless About Starting Your Own Business*. "You need to be faster, more varied, slower, cheaper, easier to work with, prettier, more highly recommended—something to distinguish it."[2]

Not sure how to distinguish your product? Godin recommends looking for a niche—some narrow segment of the general market.

"We paint houses is not a niche," Godin says. "We paint Victorian houses, on the other hand, is."[3]

But is that enough?

Is it enough to say that you have a narrowly defined specialty?

There are many ways to create a USP for your products, Jay Abraham says in *Getting Everything You Can out of All You've Got*.[4] But they all must have something to do with the customer. "Being unique is interesting," Jay told me 20 years ago when we first discussed this concept. "But if it doesn't sell, it doesn't do you any good."

What Jay meant was that the unique selling proposition has to be a benefit to the buyer. The fact that you paint only Victorian houses may be interesting to customers who own a Victorian house, but unless you can explain why that specialization benefits them, they won't be motivated to work with you.

In promoting your new product, Jay recommends that you take a good look at all the other similar products on the market and try to identify gaps by recognizing "unfilled customer needs," such as:

- Faster service
- Better prices
- Superior quality
- Convenience
- Personal service
- A better guarantee

Sometimes you can create a successful USP by marketing some characteristic of your product that is not at all unique but is generally unknown to consumers. The classic example of this was done by Schlitz beer.

In the early 1920s, Abraham says, there were about 10 brewing companies competing for the same market. And all of them—including Schlitz—emphasized the same basic benefit: Our beer is pure.

To try to separate themselves from the pack, Schlitz hired a marketing consultant who began by taking a tour of their facility and asking dozens and dozens of questions. He was impressed with what he heard: that the company had conducted 1,623 experiments over five years to identify the finest mother yeast cell that could produce the richest taste and flavor; that the water was distilled by being heated to 5,000 degrees before it was used to brew beer; that the bottles were sterilized at 1,600 degrees; and that every batch of beer was tested for quality before it was shipped out.

The painstaking brewing and bottling processes fascinated the consultant. He told Schlitz management that they should describe the steps they take to assure purity to their customers. "But all brewing companies do the same thing," the managers said.

UPDATING THE USP

The most important thing to think about after coming up with a USP for your product is how you're going to make sure it doesn't become stale in the minds of your customers. The solution to that problem is to constantly update it.

Keeping the USP "unique" can be a challenge, because eventually your competitors will imitate the most appealing features of your product. Few USPs, no matter how well put together, will last long-term without a continuous effort to keep the product distinct from others on the market.

This ties in to the phenomenon of "incremental degradation": If left alone, the quality of any product (or service) will degrade over time. The remedy is to consistently make improvements, innovations that allow the product to maintain its USP and avoid becoming ordinary and unremarkable. Just doing what you have to do to keep the status quo is not enough, because your competition is always in the background, waiting to put their own spin on your ideas, sell them as their own, and steal your customers.

"But no one in your industry has ever told their customers how they do it," the consultant persisted. "If you get the word out first, you will gain distinction and prominence in the marketplace, even if you don't really deserve it."

"Through their USP, Schlitz made the word *pure* take on a very different and much more tangible meaning to all beer drinkers around the country," Abraham explains. "Schlitz began using this preemptive marketing USP, and within six months Schlitz beer moved from number eight in market sales to number one."[5]

Three Aspects of a Solid USP

In my view, every successful unique selling proposition should have three characteristics:

1. *The appearance of uniqueness.* As the Schlitz story demonstrates, the characteristic that you decide to promote in your USP does

not have to be unique to your product, but it does have to seem like it is.

2. *Usefulness.* The appearance of uniqueness is not enough. If the distinguishing characteristic of the product is not desirable, no one will want it. In deciding on your product's USP, it is better to select some feature that isn't entirely original and make it seem unique than it is to select a feature that is unique but useless.

3. *Conceptual simplicity.* If your product's USP is trendy, it is almost certainly simple too. Very few complicated things ever become trendy. It's good to remember that you have to sell the USP—and nothing sells well that is difficult to explain.

Now let's take a step back and have another look at those copycat business ideas I mentioned earlier in this chapter. As I said, the people promoting them had no idea how to distinguish their ideas from the competition—but let's see how we can create USPs for them:

An investment advisory newsletter on exchange-traded funds (ETFs)

- The only newsletter on ETFs that takes market sentiment into its calculations.
- The only investment advisory on exchange-traded funds that is written by a former Wall Street trader.
- The only astrologically based newsletter on ETFs.

A website providing natural remedies for health problems

- The only natural health website that recommends a totally natural, "caveman" approach to fitness and eating.
- The only natural health website that is written by an ayurvedic doctor.
- The only natural health website that is created by a panel of international experts.

A chain of retail stores selling imported accessories for women

- The only store where you can buy women's accessories produced by tribal designers from the Amazon jungle.

- The only chain of retail stores for women that gives 10 percent of its proceeds to breast cancer research.
- The only chain of retail stores for women that carries the [name] product line.

A website containing inspirational and motivational messages

- The only inspirational website based on the teachings of Confucius.
- The only inspirational website created by a panoply of diverse religious leaders.
- The only motivational website published by a multimillionaire.

A seminar business that teaches public speaking

- The only public speaking program that uses the science of electroneural feedback to give you confidence.
- The only public speaking seminar created by a former speechwriter for the White House.
- The only public speaking program that gives a double-your-money-back guarantee.

These are not great USPs. I put them together quickly and without a list of actual product benefits. But you can see how much stronger they are than the original descriptions, can't you?

As an entrepreneur and as a marketer, I would much rather work with an inspirational website based on the teachings of Confucius than with something more generalized. Basing the website on the teachings of Confucius makes it not only unique but also clearly beneficial (after all, what Confucius did was help people lead good lives) and easy to explain.

How to Sell the USP

Once you have established a USP for your product, you need to sell it. All effective sales efforts have four components:

1. The Big Idea
2. The Big Promise
3. Specific claims
4. Proof of those claims

The Big Idea

Much has been written about the concept of the Big Idea. And we will talk more about it in later chapters. For the purposes of this discussion, let's say that the Big Idea is the main idea you use to sell your product. The Big Idea should come from the USP, but it is not the same thing as the USP.

The USP applies to your product. The Big Idea applies to the marketing promotion—the particular sales effort you are creating with a copywriter.

In the case of our inspirational website, the USP is that it is "the only inspirational website based on the teachings of Confucius." But you can't use that for a headline in your ads. You need something more arresting and compelling. So you look for an idea—preferably an idea that is big enough to sustain not just a single ad but an entire advertising campaign.

But where do you go for that idea? Answer: back to your product's USP. In this case, you would do some research on Confucius, looking for something he said, some bit of wisdom or advice that intrigues you. Don't worry at this point about what would appeal to your customers. Look for something that excites you. You have to start there, because if you take the other route—looking for something that you think your customers might like—you will settle for appropriate but not exciting. Big Ideas need to excite you. So start with that and trust your own feelings.

Let's say you find a quote by Confucius—something like "The man who speaks well has the power of five men." You like that idea—that speaking well (whatever that means) can increase your personal power. Based on what you've seen in life, it makes sense to you. If you could put together some ancillary material on your website, you might be able to give your customers a minicourse on gaining power through making speeches. You think that's something you'd like to do yourself—that it would be exciting.

Now it's time to stop and ask yourself if your typical customer would be as excited by this Big Idea as you are. If the answer is no, go back to your research. But in this case, based on what you know about your customers, it looks like they are very interested in gaining personal power. So the answer is yes—and you may very well have discovered your Big Idea.

The Big Promise

Now you are ready to work with a professional copywriter to create a headline and lead for your ads. You have this Big Idea—that speaking well increases a person's personal power—so you have what you need to create a strong promotion.

But a Big Idea is not enough if that's all you have. It has to come with a Big Promise. In this case, the promise was tailor-made for you by Confucius. He said that the man who speaks well has the power of five men. Quintupling one's personal power is certainly a Big Promise. So you spend some time brainstorming about what that would mean in terms of how it could improve your customer's life.

Specific Claims

This is when you put on your thinking cap and work with your copywriter to come up with possible claims that you can make in your ads—lots of claims that are based on the Big Idea.

Ask: What could a person do if he quintupled his personal power? All kinds of answers will come to you. He could conceivably quintuple his income . . . or quintuple his chances of talking his way out of a traffic ticket . . . or quintuple his success with women . . . and so on.

For the sake of productivity, it's best to just throw these claims down on paper as they come to you, regardless of whether they are realistic. Don't stop to do a lot of editing or rewriting at first. But then go back and make the claims as specific as you can. Instead of "quintuple your income," for example, make it "turn a $35,000 income into $175,000."

Proof of Those Claims

Your copywriter will enjoy helping you making up claims about your product, but won't want to spend time looking for proof of them. That's your job, the copywriter thinks. But he is wrong. You are paying the copywriter to do the hard work, so insist that he get to work and provide you with lots of real-life examples of people who gained wealth and fame and prestige as a result of their ability to speak well. The copywriter should look for historical proof as well as anecdotal proof, and should collect testimonials wherever possible.

After the copywriter's job is done, you can sort through the results, making sure all the claims have some reasonable proof backing them up, and discarding or adjusting those that don't.

At this point, you don't have a word of copy (except perhaps a headline for your ad). But you have created three or four pages of material—a "copy platform" that contains everything your copywriter (or any subsequent copywriter) will need to create a breakthrough advertising campaign for you:

- A list of product features and benefits, plus one benefit (or several, if you managed to come up with more than one) that you can market as uniquely useful.
- A Big Idea and a Big Promise expressed in a headline (or, preferably, in several headlines that you can test), along with numerous specific claims and the proof that they are valid.

**YOUR CHEAT SHEET FOR CREATING YOUR
FIRST ADVERTISING CAMPAIGN**

The Big Idea for an advertising campaign comes from your product's USP. If the USP is strong, the Big Idea will be strong too.

The Big Promise comes from the Big Idea. If the Big Idea is the right kind of Big Idea, it will have a Big Promise contained within it.

Your specific marketing scheme should be based on that Big Promise. If the Big Promise is big enough, you won't have any trouble coming up with dozens of claims that will excite your potential customers and persuade them to buy your product.

Here's a checklist to walk yourself through the process:

- ☐ Make a list of every feature of your product that you can think of.
- ☐ Brainstorming with two or three creative types, make a separate list of every possible benefit those features can provide.
- ☐ Identify a rising trend in your market—a trend that is just beginning.

(continues)

**YOUR CHEAT SHEET FOR CREATING YOUR
FIRST ADVERTISING CAMPAIGN (*Continued*)**

☐ Ask yourself: "Which of my product benefits could tie into that trend?"

☐ Identify those benefits as potential USPs.

☐ By talking to experienced industry professionals and interviewing potential customers, find out which of your potential USPs are the strongest.

☐ For each of those potentially strong USPs, create a Big Idea.

☐ For each of those Big Ideas, create one or several headlines that express a Big Promise.

☐ Working with a copywriter, make a list of claims for your product, including proof of those claims.

☐ Get at least two versions of the advertisement written—each version expressing a different copy approach—and test them.

☐ Take the version that works best, and make that the basis of all your sales and marketing efforts.

As you roll out an advertising campaign, make plans to start the process again so you can keep your selling ahead of the market.

CHAPTER SEVEN

SECONDARY–YET IMPORTANT–PRIORITIES FOR STAGE ONE BUSINESSES

During the start-up phase of your new business, selling must be your top priority. It must consume 80 percent of your and your employees' time, interest, and creativity. But what about the other 20 percent? Can that be devoted to buying office furniture and business cards?

I have a story about that. About 15 years ago, I got in touch with an old high school friend who was down on his luck. A very bright and creative guy, he had begun his career in a promising fashion, but alcoholism and other personal problems got in the way. When I reconnected with him, he was sober and looking for an opportunity to make up for lost time. So I gave it to him.

Although he had no experience in the industry, I got him a job as CEO of a Stage One merchandise marketing business I was consulting with. The revenues were about $400,000 at the time and growing quickly. We had figured out the optimum selling strategy (OSS), and made it clear that his job was to make sure we just kept doing what our four employees already knew how to do: sell our only product to people whose names and addresses were on a small number of mailing lists that we had identified as being very productive for us.

There was one thing he had to pay close attention to. He had to make sure that we rented all the new names on those lists as soon as they became available. If we didn't get to those people immediately with an offer, one of our competitors would get them. And in that business, those who rented the new names first did much, much better than those who got them later. We had already established ourselves in that primary position with the list brokers, so it wasn't a matter of negotiating. All we had to do was answer the phone and say yes when they called with a new list order.

I was careful to be there with him the first three or four times those phone calls came in. It didn't surprise me at all that he handled them perfectly and ingratiated himself to the brokers. Since I had confidence that he would not fail us in this critical task, I left him alone to handle it. About a month later, looking at the sales reports, I discovered I had been wrong.

The day the biggest new list order ever was called in, my friend was not in the office. His second in command, the woman who was effectively the marketing manager, wasn't there either. The employee who took the phone call, recognizing its importance, tried to okay the order—but because it was so big, the broker insisted on getting the okay from the boss. Attempts were frantically made to contact my friend and his marketing manager. After several hours of waiting, the broker said he had no choice but to give the new names to the next company in line.

The consequences of this were huge: $400,000 in lost sales and the demotion of the business from first to second place in the pecking order for new names. I was shocked that my friend hadn't phoned me to tell me what had happened—that I had to find out weeks later by reading the sales reports.

I called him immediately, worrying that some terrible personal tragedy had kept both of them—the only two people who could have okayed the list rental—out of the office on the very day it was due to come in. But when I asked my friend where he and his marketing manager had been, he told me they were "in town shopping for picture frames."

I was sure I had misheard him, so I asked him to repeat what he just said.

"I said, we were out shopping for picture frames," he repeated.

"I don't get it," I stammered.

"I didn't think you would," he said. "But here's what happened. I had asked Sally to decorate the office when I first arrived, but she was having a hard time selecting the right picture frames to go with the office furniture . . ."

"Sally, your marketing manager?"

"Yes. I could tell that she didn't want to disappoint me. But she was uncertain about what color I might like. She brought in a few selections, but they were really off and I told her so. Finally, I could see that this task was weakening her self-confidence."

"Are we talking metaphorically or are we really talking about office decorations?"

"Since I knew that Sally's self-confidence was critical to our business, I decided that I would go shopping with her that morning and help her make the selection . . . to show her that she could do it and restore her belief in herself."

"Are you setting me up?" I asked. "Is this a joke?"

"And I was right. She was able to select just the right frames, and she came back to the office that afternoon feeling very good about herself."

"At a cost of $400,000?"

"I think it was the right decision," he said.

"You think it was a good idea to let your people know that selecting picture frames was more important than doing $400,000 in sales?"

"It wasn't about the picture frames. It was about Sally."

"And you think it was a good idea for Sally to think that this business is about her, about upgrading her decorating skills?"

"I don't think you should trivialize it," he said. "I made my decision, and I am happy with it."

I knew then that we had made a mistake in hiring my friend for that job. He had the brains to do it. It was the judgment he lacked.

Besides being there to take that phone call, what should my friend have been spending his time doing?

Here is a short list of recommendations:

- Mentoring and being mentored.
- Teaching his team more about how the business works.
- Setting business targets.

MENTORING AND BEING MENTORED

The big problem everyone has when beginning a new business is ignorance.

New entrepreneurs don't know how the business should work—where to go for customers, how much to charge for the product, how many customers are needed for the business to become profitable, and so on.

The solution to ignorance is learning. And there are basically two ways to learn about a business: (1) by attending seminars, taking programs, and reading books—all of which provide generalized, secondhand knowledge about the industry—and (2) by speaking personally with people who are in business and getting firsthand advice from them.

When a young man I had the pleasure of mentoring several years ago started a new division in a publishing company he worked for, he was "full of energy," as he told me, but "knew almost nothing about how to start the business." His solution was simple: He would ask everybody he could how to do it.

"Talking with people, at least once a week, about what to do next kept me from wasting energy on ideas that wouldn't work," he said recently. "I absorbed 20 years' worth of publishing experience in one year by constantly reaching out to my peers and my mentors about every important marketing and product decision. Their ideas didn't drown my vision, but helped enormously to refine my efforts and make them much more successful."

He was very clever in the way he took advantage of being mentored, and I'm sure that was a big factor in his success. (In less than seven years, he grew his division from nothing to more than $20 million in annual revenue. Today, it is a $50 million, highly profitable business.)

Here is what he did:

- *He was not afraid to ask questions, even obvious questions.* At his age, I was always afraid to ask questions because I didn't want to show my ignorance. Showing my ignorance was tantamount to admitting weakness. Since I imagined myself to be in a survival-of-the-fittest career, I pretended I had no weaknesses. What I didn't understand was that there were some people in my business who wanted me to learn—who knew I was ignorant and valued me anyway. At the top of that list was my boss, the guy who hired me and had a vested interest in my success. He was not only open to questions, but also welcomed them. I was that person for this young man. I was thrilled to answer every question he asked and some he didn't ask but should have—and I always made sure I gave him a full and complete answer. His success was my success too. During his year as my protégé, we spent many hours together. At the end of our mentorship, I felt he had absorbed almost everything I knew about his type of business.
- *He had multiple mentors.* He was not talking only to me. He was asking questions of lots of other people who had different perspectives on the business, including colleagues that I introduced him to. (He would take their business cards and follow up with them later.)
- *He asked up, down, and sideways.* Although his primary mentors were experienced businesspeople who had already done what he wanted to do, he had all sorts of temporary mentors, including competitors and even his own employees. Before he began a project, he sought opinions about it from anybody and everybody who might have something helpful to say.
- *He maintained the relationships by being appreciative.* He realized that the proper and just reward for a person giving advice is getting thanks. And he was always good about thanking me and his other mentors. Most of the time, he sent a personal note, which was thanks enough. Sometimes, he sent personal gifts. (Bottles of wine and hand-rolled cigars were my good fortune.)
- *He made his own decisions and took responsibility for them.* He knew that the ultimate responsibility for the success of his business lay with him, so he always made it a point to review all the advice he

MEASURABLE BENEFITS FROM MENTORING

The positive effects of mentoring are not just anecdotal, they have been documented through serious research.

There have been several studies on the subject, including one by psychology professor Lillian Eby that involved nonacademic employees of the University of Georgia. Dr. Eby found that 89 percent of those who were mentored reported satisfaction with their jobs, and more than 90 percent considered their mentor someone they could trust and confide in. More than 70 percent of the protégés also reported that their mentors helped them advance in their careers, and taught them new skills and how to navigate the university system. The mentors benefited from the relationships as well, with 74 percent believing mentoring had a positive impact on their jobs.

Dr. Eby also found that the mentorship program, which was mostly informal, was responsible for benefits to the university itself, including increased productivity, lower stress levels, and better job performance among employees.

Source: Lillian Eby, "Summary of Research Findings." Available at www.uga.edu/ psychology/faculty/ebydebrief2005.doc.

had received and make a decision that was his own. Often, it was some combination of advice he had gotten and some unique twist that came from his own imagination. After making a decision, he took full responsibility for it. If it worked, he gave credit to everyone who had helped him make it. If it failed, he accepted the loss as his.

TEACHING YOUR TEAM

At my young protégé's age, I didn't have his skill at seeking out mentors, but I was pretty good at mentoring any team I ever worked with.

Perhaps, being a child of two teachers, it was in my blood. Or maybe it was an instinct I had about how to make my future life easier. Whatever it was, I have always had an impulse to teach new employees everything I can about what I know about their business. I have never wanted to withhold a single bit of knowledge from them. The moment I learn something new, I want to pass it along.

This impulse has served me well. It has allowed me to quickly develop a core team of people who have the skills and the motivation to get the job done, whatever that job happens to be.

This is an important benefit for a Stage One business. When you are beginning an enterprise, neither you nor anyone else in your company knows exactly what needs to be done. Because the OSS hasn't yet been figured out and because you don't yet know how many customers you will be acquiring, it's foolish to try to plan your start-up business too precisely. And that includes creating an organizational chart showing who is going to be doing what.*

When you are starting out, it is much better to acknowledge that you don't know what you don't know and tell every person on your team that their job is to do whatever you tell them to do, which will be whatever is necessary to discover your OSS and attract enough qualified, responsive customers. Assure them that once the business reaches a certain size (Stage Two), you will assign specific job functions. Promise those who like organizational charts that you will let them make one up then, so long as they recognize that an organizational chart is meant to give you a snapshot of how things are organized *so far*—not dictate how things will happen in the future.

During your business's first stage of development, your employees should know that the company's main priority is selling. Even if they aren't engaged directly in the marketing or sales process, they should be encouraged to take an active interest in it. Remember that the core team you have in the beginning may very well be the managers and then the directors and eventually the vice presidents who will run your business for you when you step into semiretirement. The more you can teach them now about what makes the business work—really work—the easier it will be for the business to grow up big and strong later.

---

*Lots of business experts and readers will disagree with me on this point. They will argue that having a clear-cut job description for every employee is essential. I have met and worked with people who have made such claims. But none of them had ever successfully started their own businesses.

Here are some tips to help you do it:

- Teach instinctively if you have the instinct. Teach formally if you don't. Every time you or anyone else does something smart or discovers a useful secret, make a lesson out of it. Call everyone together, give praise where it is due, and teach the lesson.
- Don't make these lessons one-sided. You are the leader, but you are not the only one who has insights. Ask everyone, "What can we learn from this?" and listen to their answers before you offer your own. Document the shared information afterward with a written memo that should become part of an informal bible that you can give to new employees as they come into the company.
- Don't limit your lessons to successes. When someone makes a mistake, celebrate it as a learning experience. Don't criticize the person. Thank him for giving everyone the chance to learn, and help the group analyze the mistake in a positive, productive way.
- Resist the temptation to create a culture of cliques and politics in your company by sharing all your knowledge with everybody. Don't hoard your secrets. They will become stronger and more useful to you after you share them.

To teach your core employees what you know, you need to trust them, of course. You need to have faith that they are in the business for the same reason you are: to create a better and more rewarding future. Having faith in them is easy if you follow your instincts in hiring, listening to the voice inside you that recognizes good character.

Maintaining a good relationship with people of good character is easy too. All you have to do is treat them as you would like to be treated. If you have genuinely good intentions toward them, they will almost always be loyal to you.*

---

*The goodwill that you develop will accrue interest over time. This is a subject that is so important it merits its own chapter. I don't have time for that in this book, but trust me on this.

SETTING BUSINESS TARGETS

Your core employees should be motivated by your vision. And your vision should be to build an exciting, fast-growing, quality business that will enrich their lives.

The purpose of the business should not be—and this is important—to make you or your employees rich. That may happen if you are good at choosing tipping-point products and selling them, but it should not be the main objective.*

In my earlier days, I was a big proponent of setting revenue and profit targets. I don't like to use those now, because I think they send the wrong message. I want all my clients' employees to spend their time thinking about making and/or selling great products. I don't want them focused on making their boss rich, and I don't want them focused on making themselves rich either.

Though your top priority has to be selling in Stage One, creating happy customers should always be the primary focus of your company's work. You should always be in the business of servicing the customer, and that means continuing to sell—throughout the four stages of your business's growth—good products that provide big, desired, tipping-point benefits.

I know this sounds soft and fuzzy, but I am saying it as a hard-nosed businessman who has made a lot of money. I have done it both ways: with businesses run with the main purpose of enriching their officers and shareholders, and with businesses that gave top priority to their customers. Both can be equally profitable. In the long run, I believe, a customer-oriented business will be more profitable and easier to run. That is because when customers are treated well, they stick around longer, buy more products, and recommend your business to their friends and colleagues.

---

*Again, many business experts will disagree with me here. And in this case, my critics will include very successful entrepreneurs. I know from my own experience that setting financial targets for a business does work and can be helpful. But I don't believe achieving those targets should be your company's main purpose—the purpose you talk about as a leader.

If you take my advice and establish this kind of benign but fuzzy concept as your main purpose for being in business, you will be happy later. I promise.

And if your primary purpose is customer satisfaction, then you can set other, secondary objectives that will support that main purpose and yet also be specific and quantifiable in terms of your business's growth (such as targeting the right customers for your lead product and developing a system for making back-end sales).

As a new business, making sales must be your top priority. Sales bring in cash, which can help you solve most of your other new-business problems. But sales growth in and of itself should not be your main objective.

You want to develop a growing business by providing quality products to an ever-increasing base of happy, qualified customers. By qualified customers, I mean customers who will stay with you after the first sale and buy more products.

So though your primary focus should always be on customer service, your quantifiable goal as a Stage One entrepreneur should be to acquire, as fast as possible, what we call a critical mass of qualified customers (CMQC), the number of loyal customers you need in order to make all or most of your subsequent selling transactions profitable. And if you've made your primary objective customer satisfaction, selling more products to existing customers who enjoyed their prior buying experiences with you will be relatively easy, as well as cheaper and therefore more profitable.

Once you have a good number of qualified customers—hundreds or thousands or hundreds of thousands, depending on your industry—you will be in a really good position, where almost every new product you come up with will be successful because so many of your existing customers will buy it.

Several years ago, my main client brought in a former competitor who had retired to consult with us about growing the business. He gave us lots of good advice, but the most important thing he did was remind us of something we had learned and forgotten: this concept of working toward reaching a critical mass of qualified customers.

In a recent e-mail to me, our consultant put it this way:

When I showed up, everyone was fixated on a high price for the newsletter products sold mostly by direct mail that were expected to generate a large subscriber base, the idea being that the higher the price, the more the perceived value. This is certainly true, but it does not outweigh the reality of elasticity in our industry—the fact that the number of subscribers we get almost always varies inversely with the price that we charge. The maxim is that if the price is reduced by half, the number of subscribers will double, all other things being equal. You guys continued to harp on the idea of lowering the return on investment (ROI) target on marketing campaigns (no one listened) until it became obvious that by lowering the price *and* lowering the ROI, the number of subscribers would expand exponentially.

Although your eyes glazed over when you looked at the convoluted formulas in my spreadsheet that modeled Allowable Order Cost, you immediately understood the dynamics of generating long-term profits through the development of a large-circulation, low-cost product sold at a loss on marketing by up-selling high-end products to this larger base. Extensive market testing proved the point, and even your best marketer was forced to concede (through his actions but not directly) that a lower tested price was better than the higher price pulled out of one's hat.

His "convoluted formulas" were based on one thing—the minimum number of qualified customers that we knew we needed in order to achieve profitability on our back-end sales. For that business at that time, the number was 10,000. Since then it has changed, because the Internet has changed the way we do our initial marketing. But the principle is the same: You need to identify a specific CMQC—a target number of qualified customers who will make most of your subsequent marketing efforts profitable.

What our consultant helped us discover was that we could hit that number faster by lowering both our product price and our allowable acquisition cost. (I explained how to calculate that cost in Chapter 5.)

You can apply this same line of thinking to your Stage One business by giving your core team two specific, quantifiable numbers to aim for: a certain number of qualified customers acquired at a certain cost to the company.

As long as you keep checking your math, you won't need to talk about revenues or profits to achieve those targets. When you hit your CMQC by marketing at your allowable acquisition cost, you will have reached a major financial milestone.

Best of all, by not making revenues or profits your main business objective, you can train yourself and your core team to focus on the most important thing: growing a business that provides great products to a growing base of happy customers.

CHAPTER EIGHT

A QUICK REVIEW OF THE PROBLEMS, CHALLENGES, AND OPPORTUNITIES FACED BY THE STAGE ONE ENTREPRENEUR

Getting a business (or new product) started is like moving a stopped train. It takes a lot of energy to break it free from its stationary physics, but once it is put in motion it accelerates with relative ease.

Keep this metaphor in mind when you begin your entrepreneurial venture. Imagine your challenge as an immense train, sitting dead still on a set of shiny new tracks that lead directly—and with a slight downward slope—to a Golden City. That city is waiting to welcome you as its newest citizen and shower you with its golden benefits.

You just have to get it moving.

**A LESSON FROM SCOTT MOORE:
EXPECT FAILURE IN THE BEGINNING**

For some entrepreneurs, the biggest challenge at Stage One is maintaining faith in the face of setbacks. Scott Moore, a protégé of mine who started a multimillion-dollar financial public relations company, said he had trouble "learning to balance the emotions of believing in [his] business while being objective enough to change course when things are not working."

Most of Scott's early marketing ideas didn't work, but he persisted because he could see that there was a definite market for his services. There were other successful businesses out there making money, he thought. So why couldn't he?

When one strategy failed, he tried another. It took him almost three years to find his optimum selling strategy (OSS). Nowadays, he has more business than he can handle. "If I had stuck to one selling strategy," says Scott, "I would still be floundering. Being flexible was the key. Sooner or later, your experiences will show you the way. Just keep trying different things."

I have had the good fortune to be involved with hundreds, literally hundreds, of new products and business start-ups. And every single one of them took effort—usually more effort than anticipated—to get rolling.

But once in motion, things get easier. You will run into difficulties later on, but they will seldom be as challenging as the difficulties of starting out. You should keep that in mind during the first stage—the infancy—of your business. Remind yourself that as soon as the business is moving quickly down the track, you will be able to relax a bit and allow the weight of the train to propel itself forward.

And don't worry too much if you are afraid of hard work. Being afraid of hard work is natural and intelligent. Smart people go into business precisely because they want an easier life. No entrepreneur I ever met has said, "I'm going to start a new business so I can work myself sick and keep away from my family."

A LESSON FROM TOM LAWRENCE:
BE READY TO MAKE CHANGES

"Starting a business from scratch is both the most challenging and the most rewarding phase," says Tom Lawrence, a protégé of mine. "It is also the most frustrating time. Because no matter how long you have been in business and how successful you've been before, your expectations for success always turn out to have been too optimistic."

Tom points out, "The market is a creature of immense inertia, which makes it very difficult to get a new business growing. When you have troubles, you won't know what's to blame. Is it your technical support that's at fault? Or your creative efforts? Is it the product? The marketing? The market?"

His advice: "To find out what's going on, you have to know the key numbers. You need to analyze your sales and conversion figures carefully so that you can recognize problems and shortcomings. And when you do spot problems, you must be ready to revise your ideas. At the end of the process, your business plan may look quite different from the one you started with. That's the way it should be. What matters is success."

The nature of an entrepreneur is to want it quick and easy. That's why how-to books and programs sold to entrepreneurs use those very words. We get ideas about how life could be so much easier . . . if. And then we get to work on our new business. But we never believe for one moment that we will have to work as hard as we do.

I can't tell you how many times a successful businessperson has confided in me, "If I'd had any idea it would be this hard, I would never have done it."

And I used to say the same thing. But I don't say that anymore, because I can't pretend to myself or my clients that launching a new business will be quick and easy. I know it will be hard work. In spite of that, we go forward, because we know that although the work we will have to do will be more than we expect, there will be pleasure in doing it—more than enough pleasure to keep us motivated.

Plus, I have learned a lot about starting new businesses and launching new products over the years. And all that knowledge has, in fact, made the process faster and easier. In the early chapters of this book, I told you some of what I've learned. The most important lesson—by far—is how critical it is to devote most of your time and effort in the beginning to selling the product.

When you ignore that lesson and spend too much time fooling around with fun things like fixing up the office or refining the product, the business doesn't go anywhere. It's like that train, sitting stock-still on the tracks. If you want to get it going, you shouldn't spend time polishing it. You should put coal in the furnace and get the boiler hot. Steam runs the pistons; polish doesn't.

Steam is revenue; sales are fuel. To get your train running, focus on the fuel and let the steam drive the engine.

That said, here are some of the most important ideas that I want you to take away from this book to help you become a product-selling genius and a master at starting new businesses:

- *Don't waste your time on corporate marketing.* Don't be lured into the fun of creating fancy brochures, cards, websites, or any other corporate marketing materials. You can think about selling your business later, if you want to. (My main client's business is almost $300 million big and we haven't yet decided to spend any time or effort on selling it.) Stage One is the time to sell your product, not your company.
- *Don't waste money on invisible (to your customers) business extras like office space, furnishings, equipment, and the like.* Acquire as much of this as you can by borrowing, by begging, and by using castoffs. You can upgrade your business lifestyle later, after the company is profitable. Enjoy the fun of starting in your basement or kitchen. It will make a good rags-to-riches story that you can repeat endlessly to new employees in the future.
- *Don't be misled by phony business experts.* Most people who are out there peddling ideas have never started a single business except for the business they started when they started giving advice. Listen to people who have done what you want to do—and have done it not just once but repeatedly.
- *Be proud of your business acumen, but don't be arrogant about your particular business ideas.* If you want to become successful at start-ing businesses, you must learn the process—which is pretty well

explained in this book. If you can master the process, you will be able to start many successful businesses. But being good at the process doesn't mean every one of your business ideas will be successful. Know beforehand that some of your ideas will work and some will not. Don't attach your ego to any particular business or product idea. Attach your confidence to the process.

- *Ask for advice from smart people.* Smart people include formal mentors (people who have more experience than you and have agreed to help you) and temporary mentors (peers and subordinates who are happy to answer your questions). In the first stage of your business, everything is new, including the business relationships. You may feel uneasy about asking too many questions, because you may feel that doing so puts you in a subordinate position psychologically. Don't let that stop you. There is a way to ask questions that is empowering. Learn it. However successful you become, never be ashamed to ask for advice. When you get an idea that excites you, make a list of half a dozen people who have experience doing what you want to do. Send them a personal note or make a phone call. Ask for their advice. And treat that advice like gold—because it is gold. Even if you don't use it, let all of your advisers know how much you value their generosity.

- *Don't ever believe you know more than the market.* If you have had some business success in the past, you may have strong feelings about what sort of product or sales campaign will work for your new business. Use your instincts to shape your plans, but never commit the bulk of your capital to a project until you have tested your idea. Remember that your customers, not you, are the ultimate arbiters of what is good and valuable and exciting. The sooner you can find out what they think—whether it supports or contradicts your judgment—the better.

- *Make sales your company's top priority.* Spend 80 percent of your time overseeing marketing and sales. Don't delegate this role to someone else. Do consult with and hire good marketers and copywriters, but never let them run your business for you. In the first stage, the driving force of your business is sales. As CEO, you need to be in the driver's seat.

- *Learn everything you can about sales and marketing.* In your spare time, read books, take courses, speak to experts. The education you give yourself in sales and marketing will be the most valuable investment you will ever make. Not only will it help you successfully start your business, it will also give you the knowledge and confidence to start a second and then a third business when it succeeds (or restart it if it founders).

- *Discover the optimum selling strategy (OSS) for your business—the particular combination of media, pricing, and positioning that will bring you the most qualified customers.* Your OSS will probably be similar to the OSS of your major competitors, but there should be at least one element of it that is distinct—an advertising medium that you dominate, a clever pricing structure that no one else has, or a unique selling proposition (USP) that is better than your competitors'. Once you know your OSS, run with it. This is your fast-track pass to growth and profitability.

- *In determining your OSS, understand how pricing and other aspects of your offer affect sales.* Recognize that your initial marketing goal is to achieve a certain critical mass of qualified customers (CMQC). To accomplish that goal, you need to determine an allowable acquisition cost (AAC)—how much you are able to "pay" to bring in a new customer. Generally speaking, the less you charge for your lead (front-end) product, the more customers you will acquire. The trick is to bring in as many customers as you can without degrading their quality (i.e., the amount of money they will spend with you in the future on your back-end products) or running out of cash.

- *Give your marketing team one main goal: to bring in a certain number of qualified customers.* Hitting that target should achieve two purposes—profitability and cash flow, enough cash flow to fund further business growth.

- *If possible, use direct mail or direct e-mail to discover your optimum selling strategy.* Direct marketing is the best way to test new ideas, because it is fast and cheap. Most important, direct marketing is more reliable than other methods, because with direct marketing you can do more than ask people what they *might* do (which is what you do with customer surveys and focus groups). You can give them a chance to actually do it—by selling them your product. Whatever media you choose for marketing your product—television, space ads, retail, whatever—there is almost always a way to test new ideas by direct marketing. If you possibly can, figure out how to do that.

- *In testing price to determine your OSS, favor the downside.* Ultimately, your long-term profits will probably come from selling higher-priced products to your best, most loyal, and most well-heeled customers. But in the beginning, you want volume to achieve your targeted critical mass of qualified customers as soon as possible.

- *Don't invest in a lot of inventory before you have figured out your OSS.* Instead, find some way of pretesting your idea before you create the product. There are many ways to pretest new product ideas. You can sell them in advance of producing them as a special marketing test. You can purchase other, similar products but sell them with your unique selling proposition attached to them. You can dry-test a marketing strategy by selling without the product and then refunding all the money the test brings in. The bottom line: Get the selling part right before you build or perfect the product.

PART THREE

STAGE TWO:

CHILDHOOD

CHAPTER NINE

FROM $1 MILLION TO $10 MILLION AND BEYOND

How to Break through the One-Product-Company Syndrome

"Innovation distinguishes between a leader and a follower."

—Steve Jobs

You have gotten your business started and have recorded your first million-dollar year. If you followed the program outlined in the preceding chapters for Stage One (start-up) businesses, you are ready for Stage Two: getting your business from $1 million to $10 million in revenues. You have learned a lot of important things—actually, the most important things—about doing business in your industry. You have:

- Located your core market—where your best customers are.
- Figured out the best media to reach them.
- Determined the best price for your lead product.

> **STAGE TWO: CHILDHOOD—$1 MILLION TO $10 MILLION**
> **IN REVENUE**
>
> Main Problem: You are only breaking even or may even be losing money.
> Main Challenge: Creating additional, profitable products quickly.
> Main Opportunity: Becoming a business of innovation, increasing cash
>   flow, and becoming profitable.
> **Additional Skill Needed: Coming up with a constant stream of new**
> **and potentially tipping-point ideas.**

- Identified a unique selling proposition (USP) for your product.
- Tied that USP into a Big Idea.
- Used that Big Idea to create compelling marketing copy.
- Tested all of the above—media, offer, and copy—repeatedly.

In short, you have figured out the optimal selling strategy (OSS) for the lead product of your business. Having an OSS means you understand how to bring in new customers cost-effectively. And that—the efficient acquisition of new customers—is the most important thing you can do as a Stage One entrepreneur.

It feels good to be in the market selling your lead product. You feel proud to have broken through all the entry barriers that once kept you out. Now, as sales come in and revenue grows, you can tend to other matters—tweak the product, hire a few employees. But you don't have to worry if sales slow down a bit. You can get them going again, because you understand how to sell your lead product from the inside out.*

You are not yet a marketing genius, but you know how to sell one product, and that's enough to take your business through its infancy.

That is the *good* news.

The *bad* news is that this brilliant thing you have been doing so far—this unique selling strategy that has caused your business to

---

*And if, for any reason, you had to start your business from scratch again, you could do it—in less time and with fewer mistakes.

grow—is not going to keep working indefinitely. Sooner or later, it will stop. Yes, you have developed a good product, and yes, you have discovered its OSS. But even the best products and selling strategies don't last forever.

ARE YOU FLEXIBLE ENOUGH TO GO ALL THE WAY?

When your business is ready for change, you must change it. If you don't, things will get bad. Sales will slow or refunds will soar or your best employees will walk out on you. If you stubbornly insist on sticking with the old ways, the damage could become irreversible.

As I've explained, an entrepreneurial business has four stages of growth. Each stage has its unique problems, challenges, and opportunities. The business strategy that allows you to successfully grow through one stage will not be entirely suitable for the following stage. Adjustments and additions need to be made.

If you can teach yourself to welcome change, you can lead your business through each of the four stages of business growth. That is a very satisfactory accomplishment—being at the helm of a business not only at its inception but also later when its revenues are $50 million, $100 million, or even $500 million.

Most entrepreneurs never get to enjoy those Stage Four revenues because—for whatever reason—they can't make the personal changes necessary to create the corporate changes. If you want to bring your start-up to the highest level, you will have to:

- Recognize when the dynamics of your business and/or industry have shifted and change is needed. (This you will learn by reading this book.)
- Welcome those changes emotionally (because you see them as opportunities to increase your market share by being faster and smarter than the competition).
- Encourage your employees to embrace the necessary changes.
- Retain the knowledge and skills you have acquired (because they will become useful later on).

GETTING CAUGHT IN STAGE ONE LIMBO

Stage One growth slows down when you have exhausted the market for your lead product.

You will recognize this when it happens to you. At first, sales will be sporadic as you struggle to discover your OSS. Once that is ascertained, growth will be steep. Then sales will dip for a little while as you make adjustments to the OSS: finding new media, raising or lowering the price, coming up with a new Big Idea for an advertising campaign.

This second leg of first-stage growth will continue, in dips and peaks, for a good deal of time—usually longer than the fast-growth first leg. But eventually, all the tweaking you are doing will prove futile. Sales will slow and, no matter what you try, they won't improve.

The problem is usually pretty simple: Your lead product, which got you where you are, has finally exhausted itself. Most potential customers in your market have either bought it or considered it and decided against buying.

There is still a reasonable amount of buying as new customers come into the market. But the days of increasing sales are gone. What to do?

At this point, many entrepreneurs will exchange their multimillion-dollar business dreams for something more "sensible" and "realistic." They cut back on operating expenses, discontinue their less profitable advertising, and eke out a meager salary for themselves and a small profit of $50,000 or $100,000 or $150,000.

If the market doesn't decline, they go on that way indefinitely, running a modest business that provides a modest income with a few perks thrown in on the side. It is the most common choice that entrepreneurs make at this juncture. In fact, according to research firm BizStats, 95 percent of businesses in the United States didn't exceed the million-dollar revenue threshold in 2006 (based on 2006 tax returns).[1]

SELF-EMPLOYMENT COMPANIES VERSUS EQUITY BUSINESSES

I think of such businesses as *self-employment companies*—businesses that provide the owners with guaranteed jobs and compensation that is about what they would make if they were working for someone else.*

In my view, having a self-employment business is better than being a salaried employee because, for me, independence is more important than security.† But when you start a business, you should get more out of it than a CEO's salary and the feeling of being in charge of your future. You should get the wealth-building power of equity, and the excitement that comes with watching your company grow.

You can get that only from a business with revenues—and, eventually, profits—that are growing. So if you feel the way I do, you shouldn't allow your business to stall at Stage One, even if you are grossing $1 million and netting $250,000. To transform your business into an equity-building machine, you have to get it past what it is: a one-product Stage One business.

You can do that. But it requires making changes—because the problems, challenges, and opportunities you will face at this stage will be significantly different from the problems, challenges, and opportunities you faced when you started out.

Each of these differences will demand a different way of running the business and a different set of skills.

> **Entrepreneurial Axiom:** *Every time your business changes, so must its leader—you.*

THE NATURE OF STAGE TWO GROWTH

Let's talk about the differences.

If the major problem you faced when starting out in Stage One was ignorance—specifically, not knowing how to sell your lead product—what is your major problem now? If your major challenge was discovering your OSS so you could make your first profitable sales,

---

*Or, to put it differently, what they would have to pay someone else, someone of their own caliber, to come in and run their business for them.

†And let's face it, the days of lifetime employment are gone. Nowadays, a good employee can feel just as secure as a good professional athlete. That is to say, he shouldn't feel secure at all.

what is your major challenge now? If your main opportunity was to get the business to the point where you had a sizable number of loyal customers, what is your biggest opportunity now?

To answer those questions, let's look back at the observation I made at the beginning of this book. I said that when we first charted the growth of a number of companies I consulted with in recent years, I noticed that once they hit the $1 million mark, their pace of growth *accelerated very quickly*. Without exception, they grew from $1 million to $10 million within five years.

Why would that be? Why would half a dozen entirely different companies with Stage One growth that varied from one to five years all subsequently grow to $10 million so quickly?

I looked at my records. I talked to the people who had been there during those growth spurts. Gradually, a theme began to emerge. And the theme was this: In every case, they had made a fundamental change from being a company that was marketing one product to a business that was marketing many products.

Although each of these businesses had different leaders, product lines, management styles, and so on, the one thing they all had in common was *an aggressive proliferation of new products*.

HOW TO DOUBLE YOUR REVENUES . . . AGAIN AND AGAIN AND AGAIN

Let's take a short step back and look at the situation logically.

Getting your business started is a matter of breaking into an existing market by selling some new product effectively. Once you have figured out how to do that (figured out your OSS), what you do is keep on keeping on, making adjustments as you go, until the market gets tired of your product.

At this point, sales are slowing and you know that you must do something different. But what could that something be?

Can you stimulate further growth by changing your accounting? Or your database management? Or your customer service or other aspects of your operations?

Maybe a tiny bit, but not significantly.

Can you create sales by finding a new market for your product? In theory, yes. But in practice, probably not. There is always a theoretical possibility that there are new media in which you can advertise—but in reality, if you have hit the $1 million mark it is because you have sold your product very hard, using every marketing trick in the book and buying market entry wherever you could find it.

The one big opportunity you have for growth—to double your million dollars in sales and then to double that again and again and again (which will bring you to $16 million)—*is to start selling more new products*.

That is a fundamental fact of entrepreneurial growth at this second stage. It is so important that I will repeat it in different words:

> **Entrepreneurial Axiom:** *The primary factor in Stage Two growth is the development and marketing of new products. The faster you can develop and sell those new products, the faster your business will grow.*

Does this seem obvious to you?

It does to me now. But it wasn't so obvious to me when I first started working with fledgling businesses. Back then, I spent a lot of my time looking for bigger markets—a bigger flea market where we could sell costume jewelry, a magazine with a wider circulation where we could place ads for our inexpensive watches, or a larger mailing list for our direct-mail business book promotions. It was only gradually, after years of stumbling around, that I was able to look back at my business career and see the thread of success, the pattern of happy accidents that created growth.

SOME PERSONAL EXPERIENCE WITH STAGE TWO GROWTH

I learned about the importance of aggressive product development in the early 1980s when I became editorial director for a publishing business that was based in South Florida.

When I joined the business, it was publishing about half a dozen business-to-business newsletters. Revenues were hovering at the million-dollar mark. After I had been there for about a week, my boss called me into his office and told me that he wanted me to help him launch a new line of newsletters. Instead of targeting the business market, he said he wanted to sell newsletters aimed at consumers.

Since he had been in the investment business in a prior life, his idea was to publish investment newsletters (an industry that was in its infancy back then). He told me that he felt the business-to-business newsletter marketplace was overcrowded and in decline. He said that the best way for us to grow the business quickly was to "go where the growth is."

I told him that I didn't know anything about direct-to-consumer publishing. All my experience to that point had been business-to-business and academic publishing. He told me that he wasn't worried about our lack of experience, that we could "learn as we go." The main thing, he said, was for us to get involved soon, while the market was still growing. "A rising tide," he said, "lifts all boats."

AN EASY, IF FLAWED, WAY TO CREATE NEW PRODUCTS

His strategy for growth was as simple as it was uninventive: Look at the marketplace for consumer newsletters, find out what is hot, and "knock it off."

At that time, I had so little experience in business that I didn't feel I had the right to disagree with him. But the idea of knocking off a competitor seemed wrong to me. We discussed it, and he challenged me: If I would help him create knock-off products, he would help me create an original one. We could "let the market decide"* which one of us was right. I happily agreed, flattered that he would give me the chance to prove my theory.

The first of the knock-off consumer products we developed was a digest of a dozen personal finance newsletters that were successful in the market. My boss believed that the fastest and easiest way for us to get into the investment newsletter market was by selling a digest. A digest, after all, was the best ideas of the best people, rolled into one easy-to-read format. Not only could our customers get our competitors' best

---

*That was the first time I heard that very valuable phrase—"let the market decide"—and because of the experiences that followed, I never forgot it.

investing ideas in a single place, they could get them all for less than *half the price* that they were currently paying for a single newsletter!

What a deal that would be, my boss thought. And, as it turned out, he was right.

The publishers we "covered" didn't like us very much. They correctly surmised that we were capitalizing on their assets. But because we were careful to follow the "fair use" rules related to copyright protection, they couldn't do much about it. Some of them refused to rent us their lists of subscriber names for our direct-mail marketing efforts, but most of them were happy to take our money and grumble.

I was secretly hoping my boss's first knock-off product would fail—to prove him wrong. But it didn't. In fact, it became an almost instant best seller in our industry. The subscription base went from zero to 30,000 in less than a year. At $39 per subscription, cash up front, that put us at the million-dollar-plus sales level.

HITTING THE STAGE ONE PLATEAU

During that first amazing year of selling the digest, we felt like sales would never slow down. Every month that passed brought in a record-breaking number of new subscriptions. Contrary to what I feared, it appeared that the digest was the financial newsletter breakthrough of all time—the product that was going to prove that "we" (I never shared my doubts with the outside world) were brilliant marketers—and that it would provide us with growth forever and ever.

But just as we hit the million-dollar mark in revenues, our direct-marketing promotions began to fail. At first, we blamed it on the post office. We had heard rumors that they sometimes dumped third-class mail, and since our newsletters were being delivered third class, we figured that must be the problem.

When we switched to first-class mail, results picked up—but just a little bit, not enough to reverse our losses. We tested new prices, offers, and copy, but nothing worked for more than a few weeks. After several months of beating our heads against the wall, we sat down and talked it out. "Maybe digests aren't like magazines," we concluded. "Maybe they are more like movies or books that come and go."

Our conclusion wasn't entirely right. I have learned since that it is perfectly possible to keep a newsletter alive and profitable for more than 20 years if it is good. But when the product is trendy and/or insubstantial, it is likely that its curve of success with the public may be steep (both upward and downward), just like most best-selling books or popular movies.

To combat crashing sales, we invented a second product—another financial newsletter. It wasn't a digest this time, but it focused on the same investment sector. I didn't understand why my boss wanted to make our second newsletter so similar to the first one. It seemed to me that we ought to cover more ground by branching out. But he assured me that we would grow more quickly if we stuck "close to what works," so that's what we did. Within six months, this second publication had more subscribers than the digest.

Now we were excited. We brought in a copywriter we knew and spent two days brainstorming new ideas. The first two products we came up with were low-cap stock advisories. Both of them worked well with our target market. By the end of that second year, we were publishing four newsletters with a combined circulation of more than 100,000 subscribers.

This meant that we had taken the business from being stalled at $1 million to booming at $4 million in about 12 months. That sold me on the power of launching new products.

Three years later, we were publishing more than 40 newsletters and had revenues of about $35 million. The company was very profitable.

IF IT WORKS WELL THE FIRST TIME, DO IT AGAIN

Soon thereafter, we switched from the direct-to-consumer newsletter business to product marketing—as partners, this time. In that new business, we used the same growth strategy: focusing on selling a single product the first year and then pushing out as many new products as we could once we had the cash flow and creative resources to do so.

Our first product in this business was a collection of cheap perfumes made to look like designer brands—the kind of perfumes you see in flea markets. Back then, they were a rarity. It took a while to find a market that would buy our perfumes, but gradually we found a group of mailing lists that worked for us. At about the million-dollar sales level, we began selling other inexpensive knock-off consumer goods, such as watches, sunglasses, and jewelry.

At one point, we were selling thousands of these items every month. The business was growing by leaps and bounds. In fact, we blew right through Stage Two and had sales in excess of $30 million in less than three years. Needless to say, those were frantic years. We were constantly running into problems with vendors that could not keep up with our ever-increasing sales, and so we were having trouble fulfilling our orders. As a result, refund requests started climbing.

After trying to solve our operational problems internally, we brought in a consultant who told us to hire a professional manager. We were reluctant to pay the salary that the best candidate was asking, but we capitulated—and I, for one, was glad we did.

By reorganizing the company, we were able to resolve the operational problems that had been upsetting our customers. Our profit margins went down with the implementation of all the new management systems, but that was temporary. Gradually, as refunds started receding, we climbed back to the margins we had enjoyed earlier.

When things were running smoothly again, we opened up another line of products—informational products that might appeal to the same group of customers who were buying our knock-off merchandise: a magazine and a series of books about gambling, sweepstakes, contests, and the like. These were not subjects I had any interest in, but our customers did—and that's what mattered.

Next, we started selling inexpensive electronic goods (again, to the same market), including radios, portable tape recorders, and television sets. At one point, we were selling more than 10,000 black-and-white TVs per month.

When my partner had a heart attack several years later, we broke up the business and sold it off to employees and colleagues. At that time, sales were an astounding $135 million.

After taking some time off—18 months that I refer to as my first retirement,* I was lured back into the newsletter publishing business by one of our prior competitors.

---

*During this time, I wrote poetry and short stories ... and made a total of $900 in 18 months for my efforts.

I welcomed the opportunity to work with this new company, because I liked its owner, admired its products, and believed I had something useful that I could contribute. Under the leadership of its owner, the company had been successfully launched and had reached $8 million in sales by increasing its product line from a single monthly newsletter on travel to include newsletters on investing and personal finance.

My job as a consultant was to help grow the company. After what I had learned about product development and marketing, I felt confident I could do it. Getting this $8 million company to break through the $10 million barrier would be easy, I knew, simply by increasing the number of newsletters we published.

I was right. Getting beyond the $10 million hurdle took less than 12 months. This occurred because of a combination of one very strong advertising campaign and about half a dozen new product launches (some large, some small), which was more than twice the rate at which the company had been launching products before.

GETTING TO $80 MILLION

For a period of about six years thereafter, we were able to increase the company's revenues from $8 million to $80 million. This strong growth was especially impressive because it occurred during a period of time when the marketplace for newsletters was static.

In retrospect, it is clear that our growth was the result of two calculated marketing strategies:

1. Capturing a larger share of the static market by producing and selling a flurry of new newsletters.
2. Increasing our yearly revenue per customer by selling higher-priced back-end products.

The second strategy involved selling products to existing customers—products that were similar to what they had bought before, but cut and polished in a more elegant way so as to fetch higher prices. If a group of customers had recently bought a newsletter on international investing for $99, for example, we would then offer them a special report on Swiss banking for $299.

UNDERSTANDING THE DIFFERENCE BETWEEN FRONT-END AND BACK-END MARKETING

For entrepreneurs, there are few marketing distinctions more important than the difference between front-end and back-end marketing. Understanding how each works is critical to accelerating growth and maximizing profitability.

Front-end sales are those that come from prospects—people who have never bought anything from you before.

Back-end sales are those that come from your existing customers.

The purpose of the front-end sale is to acquire a new customer. The purpose of the back-end sale is to produce a profit. If you understand this concept, you are ahead of the pack. Many businesspeople never discover this important business-growing secret.

When you start a business, your top priority is to collect as many qualified customers as you can as quickly as you can. You do that by discovering the optimum selling strategy for your lead product. But bringing in hundreds or thousands or even hundreds of thousands of new customers isn't how you should expect to generate your profits. Selling those customers other (i.e., back-end) products is.

Most businesses can make profitable front-end sales by keeping expenses within given margins. But if you can increase the number of qualified customers you bring in by increasing your marketing budget, you should do so, because all those extra customers will buy more products from you later on.

To bring in as many qualified customers as possible, you must be willing to just break even on your front-end marketing, or even take a loss. But that doesn't matter so long as you can go back to them and sell them your back-end products.

Back-end marketing is extremely easy. All you have to do is tell your customers about your new products and give them some incentive—almost any incentive—to buy. If someone has bought from you once and found it to be a pleasant experience, that customer will be happy to buy from you again. Just be consistent with your products and your pitch, and you'll have that customer buying back-end products from you right and left.

The company had done very little back-end product development and marketing before I got there. But they were extremely good at selling at the front end—marketing new products to noncustomers. Because of that strength, they had paid little attention to renewals and had produced no specialized products for their existing customers.

Because their customers had never been sold back-end products before, they were extremely receptive to our back-end offers. Half of our growth from $10 million to $80 million came from the back-end marketing.

As a result of this experience, I became a big advocate of product development as a strategy for growth. I don't believe it is a good idea to create a lot of products when you are just beginning. It's much better to sell one good product extremely well. But once that product is producing cash and you have the personnel and other resources to produce new products, you should do so.

HOW TO CHANGE YOUR COMPANY (AND YOURSELF) AT STAGE TWO

Developing and selling lots of new products is a growth formula that works, but it's not something you can do simply by saying, "Let's do it!"

To push your company past the $10 million mark, you will probably have to make some big changes. You will certainly have to learn and then teach your key people two new entrepreneurial skills in addition to the one you already mastered: selling a single product.*

> **Entrepreneurial Axiom:** *Every stage of business growth has its own set of problems, challenges, and opportunities. To succeed at every stage, the business owner must change the fundamental orientation of the business and develop the skills necessary to effect that change.*

---

*Selling a single product was your primary job as a Stage One entrepreneur. Selling a million dollars' worth of that product to get your business to Stage Two qualifies you—at least in my book—to call yourself a *master of marketing*.

I will tell you what those skills are and how to develop them in Chapter 10 and Chapter 11. The main idea that you should take from this chapter is simple: To get your business from $1 million to $10 million, you need to get more products to the marketplace.

First, you must replace your stale lead (front-end) product with one or several new ones to continue to attract new customers.

And then you must create a line of back-end products and sell them to your existing customers.

Generally speaking, the more products you produce during the second stage of your company's development, the faster you will grow.*

As a successful Stage One entrepreneur, you built a business that is great at marketing a single front-end product. As a Stage Two business leader, you have to transform your company so it can both produce and market many more.

---

*Many business experts will disagree with me on this. They will argue that it is much better to introduce a limited number of really good products than a raft of mediocre ones. That makes good theoretical sense, but I have found through experience that it is nearly impossible to tell which products are really good when they are in the conception stage. The only way you know for sure is to launch them. Since you can reasonably expect to wind up with only one good product out of two or three, and one excellent product out of five or 10, the pragmatic approach is to get good at launching many products—and then to fold the weak ones and nurture the strong ones. I'll discuss this approach in more detail in the following chapters.

CHAPTER TEN

INNOVATION—
THE KEY TO
SECOND-STAGE
GROWTH

In his business best seller *The Tipping Point*, Malcolm Gladwell looked at the way new products sometimes "take over" the consumer marketplace. His particular interest was in what he called "tipping-point" innovations. Why is it, he wanted to know, that some products—such as Hush Puppies or Slinkys or iPods—suddenly become enormous trends?

The traditional view is that these are breakthroughs—completely new and different products that, for whatever reason, capture the imagination of a given market. Gladwell's research led him to a different conclusion: that trendsetting products are not revolutionary at all; rather, they are variations on a growing theme.

WHY INNOVATIONS AREN'T
USUALLY REVOLUTIONARY

Most of the biggest social trends of modern times, Gladwell contends, were not stark departures from the past but minor variations on ideas that were already in the collective consciousness:

Merely by manipulating the size of a group, we can dramatically improve its receptivity to new ideas. By tinkering with the presentation of information, we can significantly improve its stickiness. Simply by finding and reaching those few special people who hold so much social power, we can shape the course of social epidemics. In the end, Tipping Points are a reaffirmation of the potential for change and the power of intelligent action. Look at the world around you. It may seem like an immovable, implacable place. It is not. With the slightest push—in just the right place—it can be tipped.[1]

The tipping point is a metaphor that describes this phenomenon. It refers to a common high school experiment wherein a glass of water is filled to the brim with water, and then the teacher begins to add, one by one, additional droplets of water. What the students discover is that, contrary to their expectations, the additional droplets remain for a while on top, forming a mound of water that is actually higher than the rim of the glass. Drop by drop, the mound gets higher. And then, suddenly, one single extra drop causes the mound of water to collapse and run down the sides of the glass.

That is how trends work, Gladwell argues. In any given social context, many people share the same basic idea about some innovation that is needed. Spurred by that common notion of what should come next, individual innovators make changes, but most of these changes are absorbed into the culture without producing any significant reaction. They are, metaphorically, the additional droplets that form the mound.

These minor variations do not change the culture, but they are noticed by other innovators who can see the trend (see, in effect, the mound forming) and recognize that, sooner or later, the weight of all these little innovations will have the necessary effect and there will be a sudden overflow of movement in the new direction.

Consumers aren't looking for brand-new products. They are looking for clever new adaptations of products they already know and love. When it comes to new, the human brain can take only a little bit of it. Eighty percent of the old and 20 percent of the new is a good ratio.

What does all this mean to the Stage Two entrepreneur?

For one thing, it means that your goal is *not* to develop brand-new ideas, but to notice trends that are beginning and develop products that anticipate that trend by a little—just enough to catch your customers' attention.

It also means that you must be humble. Innovation isn't usually about genius. It is more often about trial and error. If you are always trying to come up with product ideas that are completely new and different, you will likely have a very poor success record.

My former partner's strategy of knocking off competitors' products was half right in this regard. He was correct in paying attention to trends and creating products that resembled ones that were already working. But he was wrong in duplicating them.

WHAT'S WRONG WITH KNOCK-OFFS?

When you create me-too products, you are imitating something that is already being sold. As such, you are *following* the market. To be consistently successful, you have to *anticipate* the market, not follow it. And the way to do that is by creating products that are not entirely new, just a little bit better than the hottest thing out there.

Remember, it's the tipping-point effect you are going for, that one extra droplet of water that is added to many more that have been dropped before.

When my former partner and I got out of the knock-off business and into the innovation business, our sales and profits skyrocketed. Eventually, we became market leaders. Then we got our payback when other people began knocking *us* off.

When that became the norm, we devised a strategy to contend with it. Rather than wait for a competitor to knock off a good product, we would knock it off ourselves—but creatively—by inventing a new and better version almost as soon as we knew the first product was selling well.

Imitation doesn't work, because it is always too little and too late. But noticing what products are working and then creating new products with features that are somehow more advanced—that's how you get the breakthroughs.

The secret, as we used to say in the 1960s, is evolution, not revolution.

And your job as your company's innovation leader is to be sensitive to industry trends and to develop all sorts of new and better versions of products that are already trending upward.

THE PRINCIPLE OF "ONE STEP REMOVED"

When developing new products, you don't want to make the mistake of investing in something that is two or more steps away from what you know how to do.

That's because your chances of success decrease geometrically with each step. Take one step, and you are fine. Two steps, and you are on thin ice. Three steps, and you are up to your neck in very cold water.

Let's say, for example, that you own a successful neighborhood restaurant called The Steak House. Your basic business is selling a certain kind of eating experience to the local community.

Over a few drinks with friends, you come up with two new business ideas:

1. The first is to open a local restaurant called The Fish House.
2. The second is to go into the wholesale steak-selling business.

Both of these businesses have several elements that relate to what you are already doing. The Fish House is almost identical, except for one difference: You will be selling fish, not steak. All other key aspects—how you attract new customers, how you create a profit margin, and how you control your costs to deliver a bottom line—remain the same.

Starting a wholesale steak-selling business is about selling steaks. And that's what you do. But in this case, there are many differences. For one thing, the market is different. You are not selling to local diners but to regional businesses. This means the selling strategy is different, the profit margin is different, and so on.

THE PRINCIPLE OF "ONE STEP REMOVED" (*Continued*)

Opening up The Fish House is an example of starting a new business that is only one step removed from what you know. Opening up a wholesale steak-selling business is three or four steps removed.

The first business has a good chance of succeeding. The only unknown: Will there be a big enough local market for a fish restaurant? The second business has a poor chance of succeeding. There are simply too many things you don't know about it . . . too many inside secrets that are blocked from your view.

It is possible, of course, to succeed with a product that is wildly different from one you're selling now. It's just highly unlikely. Successful entrepreneurs take calculated risks (i.e., they act only when their calculations suggest they have a good chance of winning).

IN PRAISE OF MALCOLM GLADWELL

I have to stop here and qualify Malcolm Gladwell's tipping-point idea. Of all the marketing ideas I have heard in recent years, this one has been the most useful to me. It has helped me understand, in a very clear way, why some of my seemingly great ideas worked so well and why some of them were shocking failures.

It makes such complete sense, because it corresponds to what every good marketer learns sooner or later: You can't dictate to the market; you must let the market tell you what to do. All of the very successful product launches I've been associated with were—I realize now—evolutionary, not revolutionary processes. And all of the big failures—the product launches that lost more than half a million dollars—were brand-new ideas that the market had, until that point, shown no interest in.

I will be eternally grateful to Malcolm Gladwell for giving me the idea of the tipping point. It was, evidently, a tipping-point idea in itself, because it changed him from being a well-liked but relatively little-known writer for *The New Yorker* to being a national best-selling author.

Now, having established my gratitude and respect for the tipping-point concept, I want to say that I don't believe it's *only* tipping-point products that make money. Plenty of very ordinary me-too products are profitably sold each year. In fact, I believe that most of the business revenues and profits that occur are spurred by these ordinary products.

That has certainly been true for the businesses I've been involved in. Whether it was newsletters, television sets, inexpensive jewelry, or Latin American real estate, the lion's share of the revenues these businesses earned came from mundane products.

But that doesn't mean you shouldn't worry about coming up with tipping-point innovations. On the contrary, doing so is and should be your main job during the second stage of your company's growth.

Let me explain.

Tipping-point innovations are much, much stronger than ordinary me-too products. They will bring you new customers at double or triple or quadruple the rate you could get by marketing ordinary things. You need tipping-point innovations to break into new markets or to revive your business when it is flagging. Tipping-point products are hard to come by, but they can grow your business by leaps and bounds.

Ordinary products won't start or save your business, but they can create millions and millions of dollars of profits for you.

BACK TO OUR FRONT-END/BACK-END DISCUSSION . . .

To understand this, we have to go back to the difference between front-end and back-end marketing.

To bring in new customers in a competitive market, ordinary products won't do. Tipping-point innovations are what you need. One single tipping-point product is normally enough to launch a successful business. If you can produce another one every year or two, you'll be sitting pretty all the way to the top of the ride.

Your tipping-point (front-end) products will bring in your new customers. And those customers, as I have already pointed out, will be highly disposed to buy lots more products from you—so long as you treat them well and continue to present them with appropriate buying opportunities. That's your back end.

And here's the amazingly wonderful thing about the back end. It is a much easier and much more profitable sale than the front end.

Front-end products need to be tipping-point to create significant growth. But back-end products can be very ordinary, and they will still bring in lots and lots of money. Because you already have a relationship with your customers, they are much more likely to buy from you. They know you. They trust you. And, most important, they trust you to sell them more of what they have already bought from you—which is exactly what you want to do!

If they bought one pair of shoes from you because they were just "so cool," they will buy other pairs from you even if they don't seem quite as great. This willingness to buy non-tipping-point products is what we call *goodwill*. If you've ever wondered if goodwill has any value in business, you can stop wondering.

Because of goodwill, the likelihood that an existing customer will buy again is very, very high. That makes the back-end sale much more profitable, because your back-end marketing costs are proportionately smaller. Not only will existing customers buy at a much higher rate than first-time customers, they will also spend more money.

If your tipping-point product was priced at $50, chances are your typical back-end product can sell very successfully at $60 or $70 or even $100.* The combination of a higher response rate and a higher average price point results in a much more profitable sale.

Before I go on, let's stop for a moment to review the three fundamental marketing facts I've been talking about here:

1. The secret to breaking into new markets or reviving a flagging business is to create tipping-point products.
2. The secret to creating tipping-point products is to find hot products in rising markets and come up with some way to make them new and different.

---

*You have probably had that experience yourself as a consumer. You buy a new cologne because it is being talked about and because it is being sold at a discount. Then, because you like the product, you fall into a pattern of buying several other products in the same line—scented lotion, soap, dusting powder, and the like—even though they are pricey.

3. You need tipping-point products for your front end, but you can make lots of money on the back end with ordinary products, so long as you make the effort to sell them to your existing customers.

WHY YOU HAVE TO SET HIGH STANDARDS FOR INNOVATION

So that's your winning Stage Two formula: Create a small number of tipping-point products for your front end—to enter new markets and to replace any front-end products that are flagging. And create lots of ordinary products for your back end.

Of course, it's not easy to create tipping-point products. In fact, it is very difficult, even if you are aware of rising trends and try to anticipate them by making small but significant improvements to products that are already out there. To create a tipping-point product, you have to work hard. You have to surround yourself with smart, plugged-in people. And you have to find a productive way to engage them so that you become, as a group, a tipping-point machine.

If you do that (and I'll talk about how to do it in a few moments), you will produce tipping-point products—but probably only one time out of every 10 times you try. And that's the reason you have to always try to come up with new tipping-point products, even though you know you can make lots of money with ordinary products on the back end. By always trying to be innovative, you wind up with exactly what you need: nine ordinary products for your back end and one tipping-point product for your front end.

If you allow your creative team (and your creative team at this stage—before your business has taken its first leap forward in employee growth—should be all your executives) to produce ordinary products, your chances of producing a tipping-point product will be next to nil. Raise the standard of creativity in your company as high as you can. Make it clear that when you get together to brainstorm new-product ideas, you are looking for amazing results.

This brings us to another fundamental fact:

If your new-product idea feels like a breakthrough, it might be (but probably won't be). But if it feels ordinary, it will be ordinary. So always keep working on it until it feels really good.

FIRST ISN'T ALWAYS BETTER

The first product to market isn't always the winner. Best sellers usually come later, in the second wave. Often these second-wave winners are knock-offs marketed by Fortune 500 companies. Sometimes, though, a smaller company's timing and product mesh together perfectly and it enjoys the lead position.

Taking first place, though, should never be your objective. It is wasteful and foolish to always aim to be number one. The smart businessperson understands that long-term growth is built on multiple front-runners, none of which need to be number one.

Smart companies aim to catch trends when they are rising. Companies that can do that two out of three times will grow very quickly.

Look behind any of today's most popular products, from Apple's iPods to Hublot's Big Bang watches, and you will find that the innovations they represent (in Apple's case, portable, personalized record collections; in Hublot's, sports watches made of high-tech metals) were already being developed in slightly different ways by other, competing companies at about the same time. The reason one innovation becomes a trend and a similar innovation becomes a footnote in marketing history is a matter of timing.

Malcolm Gladwell demonstrated that most first-to-market innovations are absorbed into the culture without creating a splash. Being second (or third or fourth) is often the best place to be. The point is to be out there competing with your innovation during the height of the trend so that it has the best chance of being the droplet that causes the flood.

NEW-PRODUCT IDEAS: HOW TO PRODUCE LOTS AND LOTS OF THEM

You need a tipping-point product to replace the one that launched your business. And you need lots of ordinary products to sell on the back end. How do you come up with ideas?

One of the most effective ways I know of is to work as a member of a creative team, not to fly solo. This is a lesson that I learned the hard way.

After the first tipping-point product I came up with (an investment newsletter that operated like a private club) exploded onto its market, I quickly developed a reputation as a marketing force to be reckoned with. My boss gave me a sign that read "Marketing Genius." I loved that sign, and fell in love with the idea that I really was a marketing genius.

If I had created one breakthrough product, I reasoned, I could create another one. All I had to do was tap into the genius that was located somewhere between my ears.

But my record after that first success was piebald. I did have some hits, but they were not at the same level. And I had some failures too. What was going on?

It took me several years to realize that the success of my first tipping-point product was not due entirely to my marketing genius. It was due to a combination of timing (the market was ready for something different in the way that this was different) and collaboration. My boss didn't invent the product or write any of the advertising copy. But he did critique everything I did over and over again. And the changes I made based on his recommendations, I now realize, made the product what it was.

Nowadays, I don't even try to be a solo creator. I know that I will get much better results much faster by working with a creative team. I do, sometimes, get ideas by myself while showering or sitting on an airplane. But I don't act on those ideas. I write them down and bring them up when I'm brainstorming with the group.

My Formula for Creative Brainstorming

I've developed a formula for creative brainstorming. I can't say that I have ever seen it proved out in research, but it works for me.

1. *A quorum of three.* You need a minimum of three people to brainstorm. Two works better than one, but three works much better than two. The problem with two is that you often find the discussion getting into a rut. You say one thing. Your brainstorming partner says something else. You repeat your position. She repeats hers. Eventually, the conversation stalls. With three people, this seldom happens. I'm not sure why exactly. It may be that

the third person represents an audience. Even if only two people are talking, having someone there to listen forces you to be at your best, to work hard to present your ideas in their strongest form. Whatever the reason, I'm so convinced that three is better than two that I insist on three even if the third person is not normally involved in brainstorming.

2. *A maximum of eight.* In his book *The Tipping Point*, Malcolm Gladwell showed that there is a limit to the number of people you can efficiently group together at a time. That limit is six or seven. My preference is six, but I will tolerate eight if necessary. Keeping your brainstorming sessions small speeds up the process. And speed—as we'll discuss in the next chapter—is an essential part of the innovative process. Better to brainstorm twice for an hour with two groups of six people than once for two hours with 12.

3. *A limit of time.* Brainstorming is like professional basketball. Nothing really important happens until the last five minutes. I have attended countless full-day and even two- or three-day creative sessions, and have always felt that most of the time was spent fooling around. Yes, we did come up with good ideas in the end. But those good ideas, I always believed, could have been generated much more quickly if we'd had less time to do it. Parkinson's Law says that "work expands so as to fill the time available for its completion." Masterson's Law is very similar: *The length of time it takes to generate a good idea is equal to the length of time allowed minus 30 minutes.* For me, a creative session should be one to three hours, never more.

4. *Established goals.* Don't be vague about what you want. Be specific. This is a good rule for any sort of goal setting, and it is very useful in brainstorming sessions. Determine beforehand the specific objective of the meeting. The specificity should involve the number of ideas you want to generate. (If, for example, you want to come up with a new-product idea for your line of Nicaraguan cigars, let everyone know that you want to develop five good ideas at the meeting so that one of them will work, since your historic success ratio is one out of five.) It should also involve the type of ideas you are looking for. (Since maduro cigars are hot now, let your brainstorming

team know that you want to focus only on that segment of the market.)

5. *High standards.* Your objective is to develop ideas that have a pretty good chance of working. To accomplish that goal, they must at least feel like marketing breakthroughs. When ordinary ideas are put forward, keep pushing to make them better. Keep asking "How can we improve on that?" until you get good answers.

6. *A code of equality.* Creative sessions work best when everyone contributes. But that will never happen if your creative team is divided into the smart people and the rest. The usual situation is that preference is given to the marketers and product people because it's their job, normally, to come up with ideas. But if that were true, you wouldn't need brainstorming sessions at all. You are all there for a reason—to generate fresh ideas—and they will come faster and be judged more fairly if everyone on the team feels like he has an equal right to be there.

7. *Strict rules.* It may seem counterintuitive, but the best way to encourage a free flow of ideas is to establish and maintain strict rules. Those rules should indicate how ideas should be suggested and evaluated, and also limit the time any one person is allowed to speak. In addition, I usually impose the following:

   a. Specific suggestions only. Nobody is allowed to speak in generalities or make general comments. They waste time, confuse people, and give rise to long-winded discussions.

   b. No specific criticism. When an idea is suggested, I will take a poll to see how many people in the group like it—but I don't allow any specific criticism of the idea, because that is distracting and counterproductive. Just tell me whether you like it or not and move on. We don't have time to hear why.

   c. Be positive. I try to say something positive about every idea that is contributed, even the weak ones. If an idea gets a mediocre reception, I ask, "How could we make that better?" rather than "Here's what's wrong with that."

   d. Encourage the meek and cut the windbags short. To keep up a steady generation of ideas, you have to be willing to control

the conversation. The moment someone begins to pontif-
icate—and you will know the second that happens—derail
his speech by asking a question. Encourage the wallflowers
to speak by prodding them with questions and compliment-
ing their answers. Get the group working toward the goal of
coming up with new ideas by reminding them of it over and
over.

8. *A culture of creativity.* Ultimately, you need an entire workforce
of creative people to be an innovative company. I will talk more
about how to achieve that later in this chapter.

Coming Up with New Ideas by Using the Magic Product Cube

Getting through the second stage of entrepreneurial growth requires
you to come up with a lot of new-product ideas. Here is the easiest
way to do that.

Think of product development as a cube that has, as cubes have,
three dimensions. One dimension is going to be price. A second will
be product type. And the third will be the unique selling proposition
(USP), which I have already discussed at length.

Let's say you are in the business of selling golf equipment. The three
dimensions of your new-product cube could be:

Price: You have three levels of pricing—inexpensive, moderate,
and expensive.
Product type: You sell golf clubs, golf paraphernalia, and golf
balls.
USP: You have three golf pros under contract who will endorse
products for you—Tiger Woods, Bubba Watson, and Joe Bailey.

Thus, you have a cube of three times three times three, or 27
possible products.

Your Tiger Woods collection would include three different price
levels of clubs, three different price levels of paraphernalia, and three
different price levels of balls. The same goes for your Bubba Watson
and Joe Bailey collections. Each collection has nine options to offer.
That gives your customers 27 different choices.

Customers might start with your cheapest offer—the Joe Bailey Budget Collection, say—and gradually upgrade twice, eventually purchasing everything you sell in that collection (which might be a hundred possible items in all). Or, at some point, they could switch to the Bubba Watson series, if they decide that's more appropriate for them, and continue upgrading their arsenals of golf equipment with that line.

If you get another pro to sign on, that gives you an additional nine categories of products. Your customers benefit by seeing their range of choices increase from 27 to 36. Add a fourth price level (super-expensive) and a fourth type of product (golf memorabilia)—which is certainly possible in the golf industry—and your product selection increases geometrically. Now you are at four times four times four, or 64 product lines!

I like using the product cube at the beginning of a Stage Two business because it reminds me—and our creative team—about how many possibilities there are. Coming up with half a dozen or a dozen or even 64 product ideas doesn't seem so crazy when you break it down this way. You can see very quickly how many of those ideas are simply variations on a geometric theme.

The product cube is very useful as a planning tool, but it shouldn't be used to dictate new-product development. It shows you very quickly all the products you could possibly create. Determining which ones you actually develop requires a less formal way of doing things. That requires observation and intuition—paying attention to the market you are in and getting a feeling for what is working and what is not.

CHANGING THE CULTURE OF YOUR BUSINESS

Businesses are often compared to machines, with structures and frameworks and cogs and wheels and other moving parts. In fact, they are more like living organisms that respond to their natural environment according to certain evolutionary rules.

Like living beings, businesses are in a constant state of growth. Sometimes that growth is enormous and sometimes it is barely perceptible, but a business is never actually static—even if it looks static—unless it is dead.* Just like living beings, businesses grow by renovation—continuous change at a cellular level. For a business to stay healthy, this change needs to be positive. When change becomes negative, its growth becomes negative too. Like cancer, negative changes in business, though not detectable from the outside, can be deadly.

Viewed from an organic perspective, therefore, it makes sense to say that the primary purpose of a business is to grow—not always to grow by leaps and bounds, but to constantly change in small ways that are positive and stimulate overall growth.

The best way to spur growth is through innovation. You were the innovator during your company's first stage of growth—but to get it through the next stage, you are going to need to get everyone involved.

In a healthy, growing Stage Two company, every employee is an innovator.

BECOMING AN ADVOCATE OF INNOVATION

Getting your business through Stage One to the beginning of Stage Two—from zero to $1 million in revenue—took a lot of mental pushing. You had to push your key employees to spend most of their time thinking about selling. ("How can we sell more? Where can we find more customers?")

To take your business to the next level, you have to get everyone involved in innovation. You must persuade them that their work lives will improve in every way if the company continues to grow, and that the best way to cause that growth is to become really good at putting out new products.

Explain to them that it is natural for the product that spurred the company's first growth to be replaced, when it tires, by another. Teach them the difference between front-end and back-end marketing, and show them how each is necessary to your future growth.

---

*When we say that a business has been flat, what we are usually describing is the accumulated financial activities of that business. But if you look below the surface, you will see all sorts of ups and downs, including the individual sales and refunds of all the products, the fluctuating costs, the additional (sometimes marginal) cash flows, and so on.

NOT ALL CHANGE-RELATED STRESS IS BAD

As Timothy Ferriss points out in *The 4-Hour Workweek*, there is a difference between good stress, which he calls *eustress*, and bad stress, which he calls *distress*.

"Distress refers to harmful stimuli that make you weaker, less confident, and less able," he says. "Destructive criticism, abusive bosses, and smashing your face in the curb are examples of this. These are things we want to avoid." Eustress, in contrast, is something that the entrepreneur should seek out. Role models who push us to exceed our limits, physical training that removes our spare tires, and risks that expand our sphere of comfortable action are all examples of eustress—stress that is healthful and the stimulus for growth.

Source: Timothy Ferriss, *The 4-Hour Workweek* (New York: Crown Publishing Group, 2007).

Make them understand that, from now on, change will be their constant companion. Every day, there will be new problems; every week, new challenges. Every month, they will have to come up with new systems and solutions. And every six months to a year, you will all have to get together and change the way the business works in some fundamental way.

Be sure they understand that all of that change will bring stress—and that if they want to grow along with the business, they have to learn to tolerate stress and embrace change.

CREATING A CULTURE OF INNOVATION

It's not enough to make speeches about embracing change. You have to demonstrate it for your employees.

As problems mount, you must keep your cool. Criticize the mistake, but praise the mistake maker. "Thank you for bringing this mistake to my attention," you should say. "Now come back with a plan to prevent it from happening in the future."

Teach your employees to share what they have learned with each other. Let them know that errors and failures are inevitable for a growing company. Challenge them to be open about problems and challenges and to communicate with one another. Let them know that you want to accelerate and publicize mistakes, not to retard and hide them. As long as everyone learns from them, mistakes are good.

Being a leader of innovation means showing your employees that change is fun, but also being sensitive to those employees whose job it is to implement and coordinate the change. Never allow your business to become divided between *innovators* and *implementers*. If you do, you will discover that too many good ideas are subverted by accidents, unexpected obstacles, and competing obligations. Make every employee a part of the company's commitment to innovation. Praise the action people (implementers) as much as you praise the idea makers (innovators).

The process starts with you. To make your company good at innovation, you have to become an instigator of new ideas. Some of those ideas will be big ones—ideas for new products. But most of those ideas will be smaller—ideas about improving product delivery or taking orders or buying advertising.

Accelerating your company's growth through product development requires all sorts of new ideas. So be sure that all your employees—not just your research and development (R&D) people or your marketers—think of themselves as innovators. Let your employees know how much you appreciate good new ideas, including ideas for order taking, customer service, accounting, database management, marketing, sales, and product development.

A FINAL TIP ON BEING INNOVATIVE

If you have been in business for any length of time, you have had the following experience: You are at a meeting. Somebody comes up with a great idea for a new product. Everybody is excited about how it will boost sales and increase profits. Somebody at the meeting is put in charge of moving the new idea forward, of roughing out a model of what it will look like and creating a preliminary marketing plan.

The meeting is adjourned with high expectations. And then, at a meeting two months later, someone asks, "What's going on with that great idea?" The person responsible for implementing the idea provides a list of obstacles that have delayed the project. He assures everyone that these problems are being resolved and the idea will be put into action in the near future.

Three months later, at another meeting, the question is asked again. More problems were encountered, the implementer explains, but the idea is now ready to be put into action. "By this time next Monday, we will have it in place," he says. On Tuesday, you ask for a report, excited to hear the results. The report is disappointing. The idea was a complete failure. You wonder how that could be.

You ask to see the product model and the marketing plan. What you are given is only vaguely related to the original idea. You don't remember the details, but you do remember that the original idea was brilliant and had you excited. This three-month-old iteration is very ordinary—even insipid.

You wonder if you might have been mistaken at the first meeting. Perhaps you were temporarily delusional—falling in love with an idea that was dull as dishwater. But then you remember that everybody else loved the original idea too. When you ask for opinions on the product model and marketing plan, everyone expresses the same reaction you are having: disappointment.

So what happened?

What happened was that the truly brilliant aspects of the idea—the twists or turns that made it a tipping-point idea when you first discussed it—have been lost because the idea withered on the vine.

Fresh product ideas, like fresh dairy products, go bad over time. Good ideas are usually developed through animated discussions where one idea adds on to a previous one. With each new comment or suggestion, the idea takes shape and becomes better and more exciting. Finally, someone says something that seems to perfectly incorporate the culmination of all this brainstorming.

The great idea is captured in a phrase, but that phrase itself is only a handful of words in a sentence. Unless that sentence is soon turned into something more—at least several pages of advertising copy, for example—there is a good chance that everything that made the idea brilliant in the first place will be forgotten.

You can't just write that sentence down and expect to use it to re-create the great new idea months later. There are too many unwritten feelings and associations that need to be captured. To deliver the idea in all its tipping-point brilliance, you need to create both a model that resembles the product idea and the headline and lead for a promotion that might sell it. If you can do that, then you can proceed.

THE 24-HOUR RULE FOR PRESERVING THE INSPIRATION OF GENIUS

In addition to the brainstorming rules listed earlier, I have two extra rules I have begun to impose at product development meetings to prevent good ideas from going bad.

1. The entire brainstorming session must be tape-recorded.
2. When a tipping-point idea is suggested, a short advertising piece that encapsulates it must be written within 24 hours.

Take, for example, a brilliant idea for a new marketing campaign. After four hours of brainstorming, somebody utters a phrase that seems to perfectly capture it. Everybody in attendance is excited about it. And one person, usually a copywriter, is charged with creating the advertisement that will embody it.

Normally, the completion of any sort of advertising promotion takes weeks or even months. But I always insist that the copywriter come back with something by the end of the following day.

I do that to ensure that the idea we came up with—the brilliant, tipping-point idea that we all agreed would be our next big break-through—is accurately reflected in the advertisement. I have learned over the years that unless I see that great idea articulated in a short period of time, I will never see it produced at its full strength.

I don't need to see the entire advertisement. I only need to see the headline and lead. But since the headline and lead are responsible for 80 percent of the impact of any sales effort, I am very happy to get them back quickly so I can compare them to my memory of the concept while that memory is still fresh in my mind.

And because I insist that brainstorming sessions are tape-recorded, I have an audio record to refer to, if I need to, of the conversation that led up to our "Aha!" moment.

When it comes to getting brilliant innovations actualized, time is your enemy. Time fogs the memory, erases important details, and eventually dissolves all great ideas.* The faster you can get a great idea out of the realm of the conceptual and into action, the better your chances of preserving its original brilliance.

This brings us to our next topic: the virtue of speed.

---

*There is a reason for this. Great ideas are, as Malcolm Gladwell points out in *The Tipping Point*, minor variations on commonly held ideas. What separates ideas that cause floods from those that are merely absorbed into the marketplace are those minor variations. Details matter.

CHAPTER ELEVEN

SPEED

Putting *Ready, Fire, Aim* into Your Business

In the preceding chapter, I talked about innovation. I said that to create significant second-stage growth, an entrepreneur must transform his business from a single-product company into an organization that is able to create and market many products.

In this chapter, I am going to talk about speed.

When innovation and speed are combined, the results can be astonishing.

A SIMPLE FORMULA FOR SECOND-STAGE GROWTH

To change your company from a mom-and-pop, one-dimensional business into a product-producing machine, you will have to become good not just at innovation but also at speed. It probably took several years to produce and market your first product. To take your company to the next level, you will have to move faster—at least twice as fast as you are comfortable moving right now.

I am talking about increasing the *velocity of innovation*. This includes the time it takes to brainstorm, develop, test, and produce new products. In Chapter 10, I talked about how you can get better at coming up with good ideas. But I also pointed out that if you don't execute good ideas quickly, they will degenerate over time.

Innovation matters. And so does speed. Combined, they give your business extraordinary growing power. Incorporate them into your company's culture, and you will have no problem breaking through the one-product, million-dollar barrier.

Let's put this in mathematical terms:

$$80\% \text{ of } G = IV^2$$

Where G equals second-stage growth, I equals innovation and V equals velocity.

If you prefer verbal axioms, remember it this way:

The amount of growth a company can expect at the second stage of its development is directly related to its ability to generate and test new-product ideas quickly.

As your company's leader, you are responsible for its growth. Therefore, most of the time you spend during this stage of development should be given to generating and executing new-product ideas. You don't need to spend tons of time brainstorming. If you run your creative sessions as suggested in Chapter 10, you will be able to come up with plenty of good new-product ideas by spending just a day or two every two or three months drumming them up. But you will need to spend a good deal of time pushing those new ideas along to fruition—conducting follow-up meetings, sending out follow-up memos, making phone calls, and reading reports.

There are, of course, plenty of other things you feel pressured to do during your typical workday, but you should do as few of them as you can. By now, you should have at least half a dozen people to whom you can delegate important responsibilities. Let them be in charge of operational tasks. Let them worry about customer service issues. Let them market your existing product(s). They should know how to handle all those things. If they don't, you have not been teaching them properly.

There is a time for everything, and now is the time to develop new products. Imagining and effecting improvements is now your most important role.

THREE THINGS THAT YOU SHOULD FEEL PASSIONATE ABOUT

To succeed as a product innovator, you should have or develop passionate feelings about three things.

First, you should love good ideas. And it shouldn't matter a whit to you whether the idea is yours or someone else's. If it sounds like it can effect a big change, love it.

Second, you should hate sluggishness. When working with new ideas, you should feel anxious about time passing. The moment a new idea surfaces, you should have a strong impulse to begin working on it right away. You should feel anxious if weeks go by and you hear nothing about it. You should get angry when you discover that someone has been letting it sit.

Third, you should enjoy the process. Taking a new idea from concept to execution is often a long and laborious procedure. If you find it tedious, you may pull away from the action and leave too much to chance. Allow your executives to do most of the work, but identify key decisions that you can participate in making. Set deadlines for making those decisions and keep them.

Teach your key people that when ideas are left in limbo, details are forgotten. Obstacles arise. Enthusiasm wanes. And, finally, the idea is forgotten or—worse—executed so weakly that it fails. The space of time that stands between the conception of an idea and its execution is filled with the potential for failure.

"MONEY LOVES SPEED"

Joe Vitale, author of *Buying Trances: A New Psychology of Sales and Marketing*, is a big proponent of speed.

At an EarlytoRise.com seminar, he told an amusing story that illustrated a principle he espouses: Money loves speed. To boost traffic to a new website, Vitale came up with the whacky idea of selling Elvis Mermaid Dolls on eBay. What was an Elvis Mermaid Doll? He wasn't quite sure. But he knew that every month, millions of people go online and do a search for the word "Elvis." What would happen if they saw something that said Elvis Mermaid Doll? How would they react?

It felt like a very good idea—maybe even a tipping-point idea—so Joe didn't waste any time. Within 24 hours, he had created an image of an Elvis mermaid (by using Photoshop) and posted it on his website.

Within seconds, he said, he had hundreds of people visiting his site.

"If I had stopped to think about this for very long," he admitted, "I probably would have realized that there were problems with using Elvis's name. There are legal issues involved in using any celebrity name for commercial purposes. If I had the habit of moving slowly and carefully, I'm sure I would have found them out. But, luckily for me, I moved quickly. I didn't fool around with anything. I just moved. The idea turned out to be a huge traffic builder for me."

When it comes to implementing new product and marketing ideas, Vitale told the seminar audience, "keep one thing in mind: Money loves speed."

That's the right instinct for a business builder: to implement good ideas as fast as possible.

FASTER TESTING MEANS MORE PRODUCTS, WHICH MEANS MORE PROFITS

At a business retreat that I recently attended, the CEO of a publishing company explained how her newsletter division led her company's growth over the past five years.

"Historically, we've been very good at recognizing good ideas," she said. "Because we have a license to emulate successful publications of a sister company in the United States, coming up with breakthrough ideas has never been a big problem. The process, in fact, is pretty easy: See what's hot there, adapt it to local conditions, and test it. More often than not, if it works in the States, it works here.

"So we have that advantage in terms of innovation," she continued. "But for many years, our growth was hampered because of how long it took us to get new products going. Even with the advantage that our idea-borrowing program gave us, it took us, on average, over two years to test and launch a new product.

"We were hamstrung by all the regular things," she explained, "a limited budget, a limited staff, and lots of accounting and legal regulations. But after so many years of putting up with how long it took, we came up with a new idea."

Her idea was very simple:

"If we could decrease by half the time it took us to bring a new product to market, we could double the number of new products we could test. Doubling the new products didn't guarantee a doubling of sales or profits, but—based on our track record of successful efforts—it seemed like a very good move."

When she introduced the policy, a few people quit because they didn't want to do the extra work. "But almost everybody else was excited by the challenge," she said. "And it turned out that once we got the system figured out, we were able to have more fun producing more products in less time."

Borrowing from something she had seen another division in the company do, she replaced the old, laborious, two-year launching program with a new, streamlined approach that takes only a year from start to finish.

When her team gets an idea for a newsletter, they create a short business plan that requires them to answer some very basic questions —such as how the publication is unique, how it fits into the existing product line, and to whom it will be marketed.

"This doesn't tell us if the new product will succeed," she said, "but it does indicate if we've made any major errors in thinking, such as planning a product for which there isn't a sufficiently large market or projecting sales without a realistic marketing plan based on past performance—selling similar products to the same market."*

Next, they create a rough sketch of what the newsletter will do, how it will look, who will write it, and so forth, and they write a short sales piece for it, based on that rough sketch.

Then they hire the person who will write the newsletter and give him a three-month contract to produce prototype issues. At the same time, they get a good copywriter to produce a relatively short (four- to eight-page) sales letter announcing and selling the new product. They run this ad on their website, offering 100 readers the chance to get the

---

*These are, in my experience, two of the most common mistakes experienced marketers make.

newsletter for free for 90 days in return for their willingness to provide feedback.

Several hundred people usually volunteer right away, she said. They select 100 of them and begin delivering the new product to those sample subscribers through the Internet (even if it is intended to be produced in print later on).

"During this time, we ask them a lot of questions about what they like and don't like about the newsletter," she told us. "And at the end of the 90-day trial period, we bring everybody together for a full-day focus group.

"By the end of the trial period, we end up with a much better and more focused product than we had at the beginning, because of all the specific feedback we get from our test group," she said. "And we also have better ideas about how to sell it."

When asked what she felt was the biggest obstacle she overcame in growing her division, she had an immediate answer: "It was the idea that going fast is risky," she said. "We have a reputation for liking exactness. So getting everybody used to moving so quickly was a big challenge."

But by cutting in half the time it took to test and launch new products, she was able to reduce costs (the average cost of testing decreased by approximately a hundred thousand dollars) and radically increase her division's sales. The result: In five years, sales went from $5 million to $22 million, while their profit margin actually increased.

HOW TESTING CAN LEAD TO SPEED, SAFETY, AND PROFITS

Not every business has the option of launching new products by testing them first with existing customers—but if you can do it, you should. It is fast, safe, and profitable. Here's why:

- Your existing customer base should always be your best market. If the new product launch doesn't sell quickly (for free) to those customers, it almost certainly won't work if you advertise it elsewhere.

- Because the new product is advertised as a test and given away for free, it doesn't have to be polished. That saves a lot of money.
- Test-launching the product this way gives you customer feedback before it is officially launched. All that feedback has got to improve the product.
- It gives the marketing team compelling personal testimonials about the value of the product—some of which might be expressed with dramatic stories that can be used in your advertising.
- And, finally, the announcement to your existing customers that a new product is being tested creates anticipation that can result in higher responsiveness when you market the product to them later on.

HOW TO INCREASE SPEED: A CASE STUDY

For my main client, a Baltimore-based international publishing company, business grew dramatically when employees were encouraged to come up with their own new ideas and to implement them as quickly as possible. In five years' time the business boomed, with revenues skyrocketing from $100 million to $300 million. "Most of this growth," CEO and founder BB says, "came from ideas that our employees thought of."

The company encourages innovation and speed by preaching two sermons repeatedly. The first one is *accelerated failure*. The second one is *Ready, Fire, Aim*.

The Principle of Accelerated Failure

BB explains accelerated failure this way:

> We must remain humble enough to realize that many, if not most, of our good ideas will be rejected by our customers. It certainly helps to have good gut instincts and some market data handy when it comes time to launch a new product, but in the end it's our customers that make the final decisions.
>
> Because we are fallible, we must accept failure as part of our process. By accelerating our failures, we can also accelerate our successes.

It's not enough simply to accelerate failure. If that's all the company did, accelerated failure would be a principle for failure, not success. The idea is to become more efficient over time by learning from mistakes and thus gradually increase your ratio of successes over failures.

To ensure that employees learn from their mistakes, the company publicizes them. Executives are encouraged to talk freely at meetings and at seminars about failed attempts, and marketing failures are documented in company files that are available for study, along with details of successful promotions, on various corporate websites. Before a new product or promotion is launched, the originator can compare the idea to everything similar that's been done before. Keeping that knowledge fresh in everyone's mind makes it less likely that foolish mistakes will be made in the future.

Another component of making this principle work is an attitude that says it's *okay* to fail. So long as the company's innovators take advantage of the knowledge that has been so expensively acquired, they are never criticized for failure. BB doesn't do it. And neither do any of his top executives. That message—that it's okay to fail*—is understood companywide.

By the way, the newsletter publisher I referred to a little earlier takes this pro-failure attitude one step further by actually giving rewards to product managers who quickly kill products or promotions that aren't working.

The Strategy of *Ready, Fire, Aim*

The second sermon preached constantly by this client is *Ready, Fire, Aim*.

Ready, Fire, Aim means what it says. When you have an idea that has the potential to grow your business, test it as soon as it is ready. Don't fiddle with it, trying to get it perfect. You can make adjustments later, after you know the idea is working.

The *Ready, Fire, Aim* strategy is fundamental to the amazing growth the company has experienced in the past seven years. Around 2000,

---

*It's okay to fail, as long as you have been intelligent in the effort by researching what has been tested before and doing certain get-ready tasks that I will spell out in Chapter 12.

there was a lot of discussion about the Internet and how important it would be to their future. Most thought it was significant, but many believed it would never be more than a secondary source of additional revenue.

Another topic of debate was about what road to take. Some wanted to build big websites and bring in new customers through search engine optimization, viral marketing, and other "pull" marketing methods. Others wanted to stick to what the company knew best—"push" marketing—by going out to the Internet market with paid advertisements for low-priced products in order to create a list of buyers and then sell those buyers higher-priced, back-end products via e-mail.

They could have spent years and millions of dollars investigating, planning, and preparing for this change. In fact, many of the company's competitors did just that. But because BB believed in *Ready, Fire, Aim* and *accelerated failure*, he encouraged each division head to take whatever path he wanted—push or pull—and to individualize the effort in some unique way so that, by the end of a year or two of such experimentation, the company would be able to have failed a good deal and, hopefully, succeeded as well.

"Do whatever you think makes the most sense," BB told his senior executives. "But do it quickly."

Not every division head listened to his advice. One decided to "wait and see" the results. "We'll see how the others do before we spend our time and money on this," he said. "We'll learn from their mistakes."

For two years, the company's marketers and product managers were extremely busy trying to keep the old direct-mail-based business going while building a new business based on different ideas about how the Internet should work for them. So many people were doing different things at such speed that it became impossible for operations and accounting to keep up with it all.

Problems cropped up, and those problems were discussed openly at company meetings and through e-mail. Senior management tried to interpret marketing data when it seemed contradictory and to communicate lessons learned when they seemed definitive. By about the end of 2002, one of the company's Internet publications was working well—growing quickly and showing very good profits. Some of the other divisions' Internet efforts were working, too, but none was showing as much growth as this one.

Almost immediately, three of the other division heads changed their programs to reflect its success.

Inside of 30 months, my client had gone from knowing nothing about Internet marketing to having a working model that was growing at the rate of 30 percent to 50 percent per year.

Meanwhile, the one division that didn't want to risk failure with a *Ready, Fire, Aim* plunge into the Internet market was experiencing a significant downtrend in sales. Partly due to the growth of Internet publishing, the response they were getting to their direct-mail promotions was dwindling and their profits—battered by escalating printing and postage costs—were quickly diminishing. By the time the wait-and-see division head finally decided it was time to get into the Internet, his business was losing money and the competition was already miles ahead of him.

The Methodology of *Ready, Fire, Aim*

Spend the greatest part of your time, money, and corporate resources getting the idea ready for testing. All other things that you might want to do to perfect the concept (which tend to be costly and disruptive, because they will involve changes and affect many aspects of your operation) should be done, to the greatest extent possible, later on—if and when the idea has proven itself to be viable.

The goal is twofold: to increase the speed at which new ideas are tested, and to decrease the total corporate cost of each one.

Ready, Fire, Aim is a way of testing more innovations, good or bad, in order to increase the number of good ones that get implemented.

In theory, *Ready, Fire, Aim* comes with a cost: the additional expenses involved in fixing later what could have been fixed at the beginning. The expression "A stitch in time saves nine" comes to mind. But, in fact, *Ready, Fire, Aim* saves money—and for a very good reason. Let me explain.

The Economic Efficiency of *Ready, Fire, Aim*

Let's say you're in the soft-drink business, and you have an idea about producing a new version of an existing product—a colorless version of your best-selling cola. In discussing the idea at a brainstorming session, you realize that making the product work involves two separate uncertainties:

1. Will the market like the taste of the new product?
2. Will the market be willing to drink a colorless cola?

To answer both questions with certainty, you would have to develop a great-tasting, colorless cola before you do anything else. That would probably take you several years and cost you hundreds of thousands (or millions) of dollars. But if you break the innovation down into its two separate components and test each one separately, you can speed up the testing process.

The obvious strategy would be to test the colorless idea first by trying to sell it to a sample marketing group as soon as you possibly could. As long as the test was conducted scientifically, you would find out whether the core idea—the colorless concept—could work. If it didn't work, you could avoid the time and expense of developing the right flavor. If it worked, then you would probably do the next quickest thing, which would be to track customer reaction to a colorless cola that tasted exactly the same as your best-selling product.

I don't know whether this was the strategy implemented by 7-Up when Charles Griggs' Howdy Corporation introduced it in 1929. But if I had been Howdy's marketing director at that time, it is the kind of *Ready, Fire, Aim* approach I would have taken.

Ready, Fire, Aim as a Management Tool

Although it is primarily a method of accelerating good product ideas, *Ready, Fire, Aim* can also be applied to operational innovations.

Let's say you have an idea about improving customer service. You have read somewhere that when customers are given something for free, they feel a moral obligation to reciprocate.[1] If your customers feel that way, you reason, they will buy more products from you in the future. So your idea is to send your new customers little gifts in the mail to thank them for their patronage.

You could begin by hiring consultants and doing market research. You could spend months and lots of money on a feasibility study that would tell you what the theoreticians have said about this idea in the past. Or . . . you could select a group of 200 new customers, send them the gifts, and track their buying habits over a six-month period (being sure to sell them reasonably aggressively during that time). At the end of the six months, the effectiveness of your idea would have been pretty accurately tested. You would have accomplished your management goal (seeing if the gifts affected your customers' buying habits) in a fraction of the time it would have taken you otherwise, and also at a fraction of the cost.*

Creating a *Ready, Fire, Aim* culture in your business will shorten the time it takes you to do just about everything. It will reduce the cost of failure, increase the likelihood of success, and diminish the damaging impact that time has on all good ideas.

Here are eight guidelines to help you speed up the implementation of good ideas in your business:

1. *Explain the key concepts.* If you try to introduce a *Ready, Fire, Aim* culture by announcing it to your people, you will create a good deal of resistance. And some of that will come from your best people. Sit down with your core team and tell them what you want to do. Explain to them the relationship between innovation, speed, and growth. Make them understand why velocity is necessary. Then explain to each one, individually, how growth will benefit him personally. Get everyone emotionally involved in your vision.

2. *Support management.* Some parts of your business will take longer to accelerate than others. Data management is probably one of the most problematic. Assure your key employees that you mean to maintain the highest possible level of efficiency in all operational areas, and that you will support everyone on the management side of growth by giving them what they need to accommodate change.

---

*There is no better test than a test that replicates exactly the thing you want to achieve. In the case of new-product sales, the test should involve selling some *Ready, Fire, Aim* version of the product to a sample group of customers. In the case of testing this particular idea of sending customers gifts, you would need to see their actual buying patterns before you could be sure of what that test would be.

3. *Walk the walk.* In implementing all major changes, your key employees will follow your actions, not your words. Preaching the principles of *accelerated failure* and *Ready, Fire, Aim* will do you no good if you are yelling at people for making mistakes. Lead them by obeying Dale Carnegie's three commandments: Don't criticize. Don't condemn. And don't complain.

4. *Establish parameters.* Your employees need to know how fast you want them to go. Saying "faster" doesn't help. Break the idea-to-production cycle down into its component parts and establish for each of those parts timelines that, taken together, will give you the speed you are looking for.

5. *Get agreement.* Timelines will work as long as your key executives support them. Make sure they do by getting them to tell you they do, in person, in a group meeting.

6. *Accelerate gradually.* At Stage One, your business is a Celica, not a Ferrari. You can't go to Stage Two—from cruising at 55 to a speed of 155—in just a few weeks. If your ultimate goal is to produce 50 new products per year and you have so far produced only one in three years, make 50 a three-to-five-year target.

7. *Provide support as you go.* As your business grows, the problems will mount. It is extremely important that you keep up with those problems by honoring the promise you made to management. Be liberal about hiring new employees but strict about firing weak ones. When your information technology (IT) people want to lease new equipment, be open to the idea, but remind them that the company's growth is only beginning.

8. *Follow the program.* The methodology is *Ready, Fire, Aim.* That means readying the gun before you shoot it. In the next chapter, I will talk about how to get your new product ideas ready quickly. In the chapter after that, I will talk about refining—aiming—those ideas.

CHAPTER TWELVE

GETTING READY

The *Ready, Fire, Aim* concept is about velocity, about the profound benefits of moving from an idea into action at the fastest possible speed. But *Ready, Fire, Aim* doesn't mean reckless abandon. It doesn't mean bolting into action before you are ready. It's *Ready, Fire, Aim*, not *Fire at Will*.

It's bringing the gun to your shoulder and pointing, not shooting from the hip.

Ready, Fire, Aim is a wonderful strategy for increasing your company's production capacity. After you have exhausted your first product's potential, it's the best way to encourage growth.

Ready, Fire, Aim can and should be applied to almost every aspect of your business, including the generation of both front-end and back-end products.

Speeding up production will definitely allow you to sell more products, and selling more products will definitely boost revenues. The challenge is making sure those revenues are profitable. You can do that by taking just a little bit of time during the *Ready* phase to ask and answer the following seven essential questions:

1. Do I have a good idea?
2. Does it feel like it will work?
3. Are my sales targets realistic?
4. Can I afford to test the idea?
5. Do I know the basic tasks that need to be done?

6. Do I have the people who can do them?
7. Do I have a Plan B, an exit plan, in case my good idea turns out to be a bad one?

Let's look at each of these questions individually.

DO YOU HAVE A *GOOD* IDEA?

It's unlikely that you would launch a product you didn't believe in. But beliefs are sometimes mistaken. Product development is a costly endeavor. There are capital requirements and time commitments (usually from your best people). You will never know how good your product idea is until you test it in the market, but in the beginning—when you are brainstorming the idea—it pays to take a moment to ask this question.

Start by defining what *good* means to you. How is the product good? Good in the sense that it is better than some other product? Good in the sense that you believe the market needs it? These are common motivations for new-product development, but they are not sufficient for your business purpose. Your objective is to grow your business by selling lots of products. But each and every product must be sold in certain minimum quantities. Unless your product can sell that minimum amount, it can't be said to be good.

I can't tell you how many times, in the beginning of my career, I was involved in the launch of products that had no chance whatsoever of being profitable. My standard of goodness then was imprecise and personal, as in "Wouldn't it be cool if . . . ?" If I had a thousand dollars now for every $10,000 we stupidly invested in products that had no chance of being profitable, I could buy you a Bentley. Maybe two.

Because entrepreneurs are driven by emotion, they often don't have the patience to question—even for a minute—their business impulses. To make matters worse, they are usually strong-minded and persuasive, which means that the people around them (even if they are very good and smart) will sometimes go along with an idea even when they don't like it.

If you are strong-minded, driven, and persuasive, be happy—because these qualities will make you an effective leader. But they

---

YOU HAVE A GOOD IDEA: WHAT'S THAT WORTH?

Best-selling author and *Early to Rise* columnist Robert Ringer is an expert at *Ready, Fire, Aim*. In his book, *Action! Nothing Happens Until Something Moves* (which I strongly recommend), he says:

> An idea, of and by itself, has no intrinsic value. It must be accompanied by action. It is action that cuts the umbilical cord and brings an idea out of the womb. I can assure you that Fred Smith, the founder of Federal Express, wasn't the only person to come up with the idea of starting an overnight delivery service to compete with the woefully incompetent U.S. Postal Service. . . .
>
> Further, I do not for a second think that I was the only other person to ponder the idea of an overnight mail-delivery service. In fact, I would be surprised if literally thousands of other entrepreneurs weren't simultaneously mulling over the same idea. What made Fred Smith different from the rest of us was that he didn't just think about the idea; he took action. Action converts an idea into an experience. Action creates reality.

Source: Robert Ringer, *Action! Nothing Happens Until Something Moves* (New York: M. Evans and Company, 2004), 14–15.

---

will get you into trouble if you don't temper them with a bit of humility and the habit of asking questions. That's what the *Ready* phase is all about: taking a moment to question whether your product idea is good.

How to Quantify *Good*

So before you launch a product, talk to your core marketing team (the six or eight people who will be most involved in the launch) about a sales target. Explain your thoughts. Ask for their input. Based on that conversation, set the target. Then make it clear to everyone who is working for you, directly or indirectly, who could possibly affect the outcome of the launch, and get them committed.

Frame the discussion in terms of *good*, as in "I want to make this a really good product." *You* know that "really good" means that it will sell really well, but you don't want to overemphasize the target sales number. Make that number a visible target by posting it where everyone can see it. But when you talk about it, use the word *good*.

If someone, for example, doubts the target you establish, say, "Okay, John, if you don't think the product as we imagine it is good enough to sell 10,000 copies, how can we improve it? How can we make it good enough to reach our target?"

Speaking in terms of quality is more productive, because it focuses everyone's thinking on the customer. And that's where the thinking should always be. If this product is as good as you think it is, the marketplace should love it. It should be easy to sell, because it is so damned good. And once people start buying it and using it, word-of-mouth sales will surge.

That's the attitude you should have about any product you're about to bring to market. And if you can maintain that attitude, you will be able to keep your employees happy, motivated, and super-productive through your company's growing pains.

One of my former protégés, Katie Yeakle, embodies this attitude in everything she does. When I asked her what she learned about product development while growing her business—American Writers & Artists Inc. (AWAI)—from zero to more than $10 million in 10 years, she didn't hesitate:

> The most important thing, by far, is starting with a good product, a product that provides a big benefit to the customer. The benefit has to be so big, in fact, that it's easy to communicate. The moment your customer hears about it, he has to be able to see himself benefiting from it. That's a good product, one that offers that kind of huge, instant appeal.

That's how Katie talks to her employees—always phrasing everything in terms of what's good for the customer. By taking that position, she makes it feel *good* to work for her business. Her employees get it, and so do her customers.

If you walk into the AWAI offices, you will see that the walls are lined with framed letters from customers. There are hundreds of frames on the wall, and hundreds more in boxes, waiting for more wall space to become available. These are testimonials to the effect of Katie's expressing her business objectives in terms of what is good for the customer.

> ## GOOD AND GREAT: BACK-END VERSUS FRONT-END PRODUCTS
>
> Front-end products must have very high sales targets. Their purpose, after all, is to bring in as many new customers as possible. To achieve very high sales targets, front-end products must be tipping-point good. In addition to providing a big and easily communicated benefit to the customer, they must also be on the cutting edge of an industry trend.
>
> Back-end products usually have lower sales targets because the cost of selling to your existing customer base is generally much lower than selling to prospects. In addition to lower marketing costs, back-end sales often enjoy the benefits of high response rates and higher prices. This is a wonderful combination that produces profits even when the quantities sold are relatively small.
>
> When I am involved in creating a front-end product, I keep asking, "Could this be a tipping-point product?" When I am involved in back-end marketing, I simply ask, "Is it good?" Because I know that its chances of success are so very high. It's not a matter of will it work, but how well.

Katie has been thinking and speaking this way since the beginning. So today, when you sit in on a creative session with her, there is no distinction between goodness and success. A good product is one that provides a big and clearly communicable benefit. If a product does that, of course it will sell!

DOES IT FEEL LIKE IT WILL WORK?

Given a choice between (a) methodically analyzing whether a business idea is good enough to be successful in the marketplace and (b) relying on the intuition of an experienced person, I'd opt for intuition.

Intuition is more reliable at anticipating future events than formal analysis is, because it incorporates years and years of information collected through careful observation, much of which can no longer be consciously remembered but still informs the decision-making process.

Let me illustrate that with a true story about a vitamin company that wanted to spur growth by breaking into a new segment of the market. They brainstormed and brainstormed and finally came up with a "great" idea.

"Let's produce and sell vitamins tailored to people in different professions," they said, "such as vitamins for firefighters, vitamins for secretaries, and so on.

"After all," they reasoned, "jobs differ in terms of physical demands and stress. So wouldn't it make sense to design different lines of vitamins that could be tailored to those different jobs?"

The marketing idea was logical, and the marketing plan—targeting large groups of professionals, such as teachers and nurses—would be easy to execute.

There was one problem: The businessman who had been mentoring them since the beginning had a bad feeling about it. When they brought the idea to him, he said, "I know how excited you are about this project, so I hate to say this. But I've tried this type of thing before—creating product lines for customer groupings—and it has never worked. My gut tells me this won't either."

"But we have numbers to show you," they said. And they did—all sorts of charts and graphs and reports from professional consultants who believed, as they did, that the idea was a good one.

It was about 40 against one—overwhelming odds by any standard—except that the mentor's intuition was based on experience, and all the research and calculations of the consultants were not.

So they agreed on a compromise: They would test the idea but limit the losses (if it didn't work) to a quarter of a million dollars.

They closed the project when it hit that number, and the final losses were about $350,000.

Experience-based intuition is fractal, not linear—and fractal thinking can interpret many more factors than you can possibly calculate on a spreadsheet. A checklist for evaluating the feasibility of a new-product idea might include 10, 20, or even 100 questions. But the gut instinct of a veteran businessperson is based on thousands or even tens of thousands of experiences.

You probably already have more of a feel for what a "good" product is than you realize. Don't ignore it. But pay more attention to the advice of those who have much more experience bringing new products to market.

THE STUDY OF HUMAN INTUITION

Nobel laureate Herbert A. Simon, a professor of psychology and computer science at Carnegie Mellon University who has studied decision making for decades, believes that experience enables people to "chunk" information so that they can store and retrieve it easily. He believes that even the most sophisticated gut judgments can be broken into patterns and rules. In chess, for example, he found that grand masters are able to recognize and recall perhaps 50,000 significant patterns of the astronomical number of ways in which the various pieces can be arranged on a board.

Advanced intuition is developed by what Simon and other experts call "cross-indexing"—finding patterns in one area that correspond to patterns in another. Thus, a marketing executive might see something in a health-oriented advertising campaign that reminds him of something he should do in a financial promotion.

So gut instincts are really subconscious suggestions that arise from all the patterns we have observed. They tell us more than we can logically know, because they represent much more information than our brains can logically process.

To develop a great gut instinct for business, pay attention to every business deal you do. Assess its outcome objectively. Ask others for their opinions. What worked? What didn't? Resist the temptation to revise the facts later. Resist the impulse to make yourself right in retrospect.

The conclusions you draw from your actual primary business experiences are the most valuable resources you have. Make sure they are valid. If you do that, your instinct for what to do in any situation will inevitably get better.

ARE YOUR SALES TARGETS REALISTIC?

Your product idea is good. It provides a big and easily expressed benefit to your customer. It feels right, too. And when you compare this product to other products of its kind, you get excited. You have stopped to think about how well it will sell, and you've set specific sales targets. Now you have to ask, "Are these targets realistic?"

If you have done everything I've advised you to do so far, the answer will almost certainly be yes. But because results in business seldom are quite as good as expectations, you should spend a little time doing some quick "What if I'm wrong?" calculations:

1. Ask yourself how much it will cost to make the idea come to life. Take that number and double it.
2. Figure out how many units it will sell (or how much extra cash it will bring in), and cut that number in half.

If the net result of doubling your anticipated costs and halving your expected returns still looks like you've got a profitable venture, go ahead with it. If it looks marginal or negative, drop it and move on to the next new idea.

This simple bit arithmetic is not definitive, but it will probably be very close to accurate—and you can do it in five or 10 minutes and feel comfortable with the results.

CAN YOU TEST THE IDEA?

Like scientific hypotheses, business ideas can be tested in controlled environments before they are put into action. When ideas are important or costly to implement, it makes sense to do that if you can.

Testing ideas is standard operating procedure for direct marketers, which is one of the reasons I believe that almost every business should have a direct-marketing component. With direct marketing, you can test your idea relatively cheaply by selling it to a sample group and then, if it works, roll out with it to the general market.

Not every new product idea can be tested to sample groups by direct marketing, but many can.

Let's say you are in the pet food business, and your new-product idea is kosher dog food. The market, presumably, would be the millions of pet owners out there who eat kosher food themselves. Instead of spending a huge amount of money launching your kosher vittles to the market en masse, you identify a hundred or a thousand of your existing customers who eat kosher food, and you mail a targeted sales promotion to them.

Your eventual plan might be to sell your kosher pet food with space ads in large-circulation magazines. Nevertheless, the targeted mailing you do to this small test group will give you a very good indication of how successful your product will be with the general market. That's because target marketing usually gets a much higher response rate than general advertising. So if it doesn't work on a targeted basis—to a group of customers who are already predisposed to buy kosher food—you can safely assume it won't work on a larger scale.

If your idea does work in a targeted arena, that doesn't prove it can work elsewhere. But if the response is strong, you can be encouraged.

DO YOU KNOW THE TASKS THAT NEED TO BE DONE?

Before you put your ideas into action, it pays to create a short list of the primary tasks that need to be completed.

Such a list needn't be elaborately detailed, and it shouldn't take more than a few hours to create. But it could prove very useful in identifying obstacles, estimating costs, and—most important—determining the team you will eventually put in charge of the product.

A sample task list for a test mailing to promote your kosher pet food might look like Table 12.1.

TABLE 12.1 Sample Task List for a Test Mailing

Task	Doer	Comment
Identify customers who eat/buy kosher food	Marketing department	Done to collect data necessary for test mailing
Design and write promotion	Copywriters	Copy must appeal to this group
Mail test promotions to these customers	Circulation department	To test the salability of kosher pet food
Analyze results	Marketing department	To determine if test was successful enough to launch to general market

> **LOCATING CHAMPIONS, WORKHORSES, AND SUPERSTARS**
>
> Finding the right people to execute your plan is perhaps the most important "get ready" activity.
>
> You have to nail down who can help you start and run the business, and who can provide valuable advice (leading experts in the field). You should create a network of all of these individuals that you can draw on when you need to. A big network is a steady source of opportunity.

DO YOU HAVE THE PEOPLE WHO CAN DO THE TASKS?

Every great idea needs great people to make it succeed. Before you move into action on any significant business idea, stop to ask yourself, "Who can help me get this done?"

Start by choosing a primary champion for the main idea—a person you think has the personality to get the idea actualized. A champion must (1) believe in the idea, (2) have the authority to execute it, and (3) have the experience to make wise decisions along the way. If you have no champion and no time to champion the idea yourself, it may be better to postpone implementing it.

In addition to a primary champion, a good idea may need other talented people to play key roles. Who can produce the product? Who can test it in the marketplace? Who can be in charge of fulfillment and operations?

At this early point in time, it's not necessary to have a full roster of support people. But you should at least know who your champion will be and have some idea about who will be your supplier/producer, marketer/seller, and fulfillment/operations person.

DO YOU HAVE A PLAN B?

Sometimes (not often, but sometimes) everything is there—the idea is good, it feels right, it tests well, and it has good people behind it—yet the product falls on its face when you roll it out. Rather than being blindsided by such an unlikely event, why not plan for it in advance? That way, if it happens, you and everyone else involved in the project won't be demoralized.

By having a Plan B—a "What if it fails?" plan—you will be much better prepared to act if that time comes.

For much of my career, I was a pedal-to-the-metal product developer who never thought in terms of failure. I thought that was a good thing. I'd get an idea, talk it over with someone smart, and then, if it still seemed like a good idea, have it put into action as soon as humanly possible. From go-ahead day to the day the test results were in, my approach was full speed ahead.

Often this fire-without-getting-ready approach worked. But often it didn't. Sometimes, those failures resulted in significant fulfillment obligations without a business to support them—and it was stressful to have to solve such problems on the spot.

Eventually, I learned to come up with Plan B before an idea was put into action.

Like other aspects of "getting ready," developing a good Plan B doesn't need to take a lot of time. Details can be easily worked out later if you know what your get-out strategy is before you start.

The key to making a Plan B is to set stop-loss points at the outset—measurable points that determine, ahead of time, whether you will continue to invest money in the project or drop it.

Don't make the mistake of thinking that failure won't ever happen to you.

I can tell you stories about great projects that failed: a seemingly brilliant idea for a new record club that cost one of my clients $125,000 . . . a "can't-miss" celebrity health newsletter that lost $780,000 before we gave up on it . . . and a magazine that was going to make millions that cost us millions instead.

I remember reading that when Ted Turner was planning CNN, he found that he had done such a good job promoting the idea that his partners and top executives weren't willing to even entertain the idea that it might not work. Since he knew full well the value of being prepared, he kept asking the question "What if it fails?" until his associates gave in and put together a fallback plan.

CNN started off terrifically, and when the company hit financial problems seven years later, they already had a solution. In this case, it was to sell a portion of the business to cable operators. Turner's early insistence on a Plan B allowed the crisis to be overcome without anyone breaking a sweat.[1]

How to Create a Plan B

Business schools teach formal systems for creating backup plans. My favorite method is much simpler.

Imagine a conversation between two of your main competitors. They are talking about your business. They have heard some very bad news about your company (bad for you, not so bad for them). What is it?

Did you lose your biggest account? Did you blow your product launch? Did your three top executives leave you? Did your bank close your line of credit?

Once you have a better idea of exactly what might go wrong, it's relatively easy to create your Plan B. For each scenario, come up with a survival plan that makes sense. What would you do, for example, if:

- Your cost of goods suddenly increased by 15 percent?
- Your main customer dropped you?
- Your most important employee suddenly quit?
- Your building burned down?

That last scenario actually happened to one of my clients—a book publisher in France—several years ago. The building burned to the ground one night. Everything was lost. Fortunately, the owner had a Plan B in place: a very substantial insurance policy and a copy of every manuscript locked in a fireproof vault.

Think about your business. Ask yourself the above question and spend an hour or so coming up with answers. If you have someone who can help you, take advantage. Jot down some preliminary thoughts. Mull over those thoughts for a few days, and then write up your "What if it fails?" plan. Put the written document somewhere safe, and keep a copy with a trusted colleague.

Do it. It may seem like extra work right now, but you'll feel much better when it's done.

> **THE IMPORTANCE OF BEING COMPREHENSIVE**
>
> By forcing yourself to do a business plan, including a budget, and by revising it when needed, you will develop a much better and more realistic understanding of what will make your business succeed, why customers will buy your product, how your industry works, and what numbers (and activities) are critical when it comes to long-term profits. You must take into account everything that can go wrong, but on the positive side ask "How big can this get?"

THE *READY, FIRE, AIM* BUSINESS PROPOSAL

When someone comes to me for advice about a business idea that will require a considerable expenditure of time and money, I often ask for a *Ready, Fire, Aim* business proposal.

The purpose is not to slow down the start-up process but to outline goals, identify costs (obvious and overlooked), and analyze expectations to make sure they're realistic. To keep the momentum going, I tell them that the proposal has to be finished and delivered to me within 24 hours.

The ideal *Ready, Fire, Aim* business proposal looks like this:

- It is more than one page but no longer than four.
- It includes ballpark financial projections, including costs.
- It identifies critical tasks.
- It identifies a project champion and key support people.
- It has a timeline for major tasks to be completed.
- It describes Plan B.

BREVITY IS THE SOUL OF VELOCITY

If you routinely spend months or even weeks planning every new business venture, you are probably wasting time.

That's mostly because you don't know the most important secrets about the new (to you) market.

What's most critical to know about any business is invisible to newcomers. No amount of planning or preparation is going to change that. The key to being successful with start-ups is having a good general idea of what you want to do but being flexible enough to change plans quickly as you discover the invisible secrets of the market you've jumped into.

If you can develop the habit of (1) asking yourself the seven essential questions I presented in this chapter and (2) coming up with a *Ready, Fire, Aim* business proposal for every new product or project you attempt, your chances for success in business will skyrocket—even if the ideas you have aren't always brilliant.

CHAPTER THIRTEEN

WHAT ARE YOU WAITING FOR? START FIRING ALREADY!

What is there to say about *firing*?

You have an idea for a new product. You have asked the seven "get ready" questions. The idea is good. You and your team are excited about it. You have established realistic sales targets and have halved, and halved again, your anticipated returns. Everything looks encouraging. Everyone knows his responsibilities. You've even written a short business plan that you can refer to, if you need to, later on. Now it's time to launch the thing. So what's there to talk about?

Nothing. Except if . . .

Except if . . . after you are ready, something unexpected happens—a family problem, a business issue, some little chores that you have to take care of before you start.

TWO REASONS WHY MOST GOOD IDEAS NEVER GET IMPLEMENTED

There are two reasons why most good business ideas and good product ideas never get off the ground. They are:

1. A desire for perfection
2. Little chores

The first one, I've talked about: the need to get everything right before getting started. I can't tell you how many times I've seen exciting ideas for new business and product ideas linger and eventually die on the development vine while the people who championed them tried to fix every potential problem they—or anyone else they talked to—could think of.

The nothing-less-than-perfect attitude has been the theme of many success stories, but it is exactly the wrong notion to have in your head when it's time to launch a new product or business. When the time is right to fire, you must fire. If you spend another moment aiming, the opportunity to hit your target may pass you by.

In an article in the *Early to Rise* e-zine, Robert Ringer put it this way:

> I believe all successful people share this trait [the willingness to move ahead with a good but imperfect product]. You cannot be action-oriented unless you are willing to make mistakes—even willing to look foolish or stupid. Remember the Michael Jordan ads where Jordan said that he's missed something like 22 game-winning shots? He then finished by adding, "I succeed because I fail."
>
> People who are obsessed with playing the "what if" game are destined never to get out of the starting gate. In doing a brain scan on Bill Gates, the one thing I zeroed in on, above all else, was his strategy for getting Microsoft's software out to the public as quickly as possible—bugs be damned!
>
> Clearly, Gates' philosophy has been that Microsoft can always deal with the predictable bugs and customer backlash down the road. And the biggest Microsoft haters in the world would have to admit that it's a strategy that hasn't worked out all that badly for Bill & Friends.

Microsoft is a perfect example of *Ready, Fire, Aim* in action. And if you think that Apple always gets everything right before launching a product, how do you account for their constant upgrades? Yes, Apple's new products are always good. Good is what you are looking for. But they are almost never perfect at the outset. You can't upgrade something that's perfect.

Apple is a good company to keep in mind if you are having trouble accepting this idea of launching imperfect products. Apple's products

---

READY, FIRE, AIM **IN A NUTSHELL**

The *Ready, Fire, Aim* formula has three simple rules:

1. Begin when you are ready—excited by the idea because your gut tells you that it will work.
2. Don't waste time perfecting your product or planning for every contingency, since you can't know what will work until your idea is in action.
3. Only after the idea has proven itself in some way (when you know for sure that it will work) should you make adjustments to improve it.

---

are generally better-designed than Microsoft's—or so Apple customers would have you believe. But they are always subject to improvement. Imperfections are really just profit opportunities waiting to be seized. You certainly should never launch a product that is seriously flawed. Such a product isn't good. The objective is to fire when you are ready. And you are ready only after you've answered the seven questions I presented in Chapter 12, the first of which is: Do I have a good idea?

My argument, in a single sentence, is this: *Getting things going quickly is more important than planning them perfectly.*

So get your products ready. Then launch them. There will be plenty of time to perfect them later, if they sell well now. (Think about the history of laptops, for example.) In the next chapter, I will talk about why and how you should seek to perfect good products. The purpose of this chapter is to get you emotionally ready to fire when the time comes.

Keep this thought in mind: For every product or business idea that has failed because it wasn't properly perfected before it was launched, a hundred never got launched because their champions (entrepreneurs or executives) got caught up in the make-it-perfect-first game.

THOSE LITTLE CHORES THAT NEVER GET DONE

In the world of entrepreneurship, product stillbirths are born from a two-headed monster. One head is the God of Perfectionism. The other is the God of Procrastination.

"I will get to it as soon as I finish up with such and such."

That is the most common thing I hear when, after someone tells me excitedly about a new business idea they have, I ask them when they are going to get started.

When I hear that excuse, I think: "This person is a loser."

That's not a nice thing to think. And I feel bad about having the thought each time I have it. But experience has taught me that the thought is right even if the emotion is wrong. These people may be successful in many ways, but if they are telling me that they will start something later, chances are they won't start it at all.

At least not without some sort of intervention.

I have been the one who did the intervening several times. After listening to a friend or colleague blather on about something he was going to do "just as soon as . . ." I challenged him to put up or shut up.

The challenge itself probably wouldn't have been enough. To give the person an incentive, I usually offered to be his partner. "Okay," I'd say. "Here's what we can do. I'll give you some general advice. You learn the business and you do all the work. I'll take the money risk. You take the time risk. In the end, we'll be partners."

In most cases, they agreed without hesitation. But there were a few people who actually told me that they would take me up on my offer . . . but only after they finished a couple of little chores. I was offering to help them realize their long-held dream. They weren't taking any financial risk. All they had to do was get going. How these people could have put off such a chance in order to take care of chores baffled me. I knew they would never come back to me, and they didn't.

Those who took me up on my offer, without a single exception, all succeeded. Two built $10+ million nutritional-supplement businesses. Three became multimillion-dollar publishers. One developed a million-dollar income providing public relations services to public companies. Still another created the largest and most successful training program for copywriters in the world.

After talking about their dreams for so long, these people were all emotionally ready. Some of them hadn't bothered to ask the seven questions (I hadn't yet formulated them) or write a short business plan, but they were all ready to get going the moment I made the offer.

In all, I have about a dozen such success stories. It is not a large sample, but it is large enough for me. It made me realize how much a part of success taking action is. What separated these 12 entrepreneurs from the three or four who turned me down was not skill or knowledge or experience. It was just their willingness to fire when the time was right for firing.

The Psychology of Procrastination

I never thought for a moment that the people who turned me down seriously intended to take me up on my offer after they had finished doing whatever it was they said they had to do. Taking care of those little chores was just their way of putting off action.

When I think about business, I find it hard to understand why anybody would procrastinate. When I get or hear about a good product idea, all my emotions lock into forward gear. I can't wait to get going and make the idea a reality.

But just because I am naturally inclined toward action in business doesn't mean I don't understand procrastination. As longtime readers of my articles in *Early to Rise* know very well, I have been struggling to be a novelist for most of my adult life. I can write books about wealth and business as easily as I can brush my teeth, but when I sit down to write fiction, I am attacked by the two-headed monster. "I'll start my novel as soon as I've finished this business book," I tell myself. And then when I do start writing it, I have trouble getting past the third chapter, because I keep revising the first two—trying to make them perfect.

Where is my Michael Masterson to get me over these stupid obstacles I keep putting in my own way?

Don't Make Me Say No to You ... Please

Whenever I mention, in print, the success I've had mentoring people, I get dozens of letters from people who would like to give me the opportunity to do it again with them. When I turned 50, I promised myself that I would take on no more business projects. When I turned 55—last year—I promised my wife the same thing.

I don't intend to disappoint my wife. So please don't write me one of those letters. If you are having a problem with procrastination or perfectionism, you'll find a solution in this chapter. If you don't find it the first time you read it, read it again.

Procrastination is a problem—a troublesome emotional barrier. You can overcome it even without someone stepping in and helping you, but it will take effort.

A PROFILE IN COURAGE

Several years ago, I gave a speech at a wealth-building seminar about what it takes to be a successful entrepreneur. I held nothing back. I revealed all my secrets. I felt good about my presentation when I was done.

That evening, at a seminar cocktail party, one of the attendees—Susan Thomas—buttonholed me. She was very disappointed in my speech, she told me. I didn't need to ask her to tell me her complaints. She spent the next 15 minutes listing them. She had technical criticisms about the way I articulated my ideas and about my posture, but she also had some very substantial condemnations. She said that what I said about action—the importance of being emotionally ready to fire when it was time to fire—was a "total waste of time" and an "insult to anyone of intelligence."

What Susan wanted me to tell her, she said, were "specific things" about business, like how to form a corporation or how to check for references when hiring.

I told her that she could get that kind of information from anyone. Business schools have courses that are taught by people who are experts in those subjects, and retail bookstores have entire sections devoted to answering those sorts of questions. "I could probably do a pretty good job of explaining all that stuff to you," I told her. "But that isn't what interests me. And I don't think it should be what interests you."

"What do you mean by that?" she asked. She seemed defensive.

I said I meant that she had paid good money to listen to me speak, and for that money she had a right to expect me to tell her what I think is important. If I am an expert at anything, it is the process of helping people successfully start businesses, I told her. That is pretty much all I've been doing for 25 years, I explained. And it has occupied a big part of my thinking.

"If I tell you that taking action is critical to entrepreneurial success, it's because I have seen so many would-be entrepreneurs fail from lack of action. I promise you, I am not trying to waste your time. I'm telling you the good stuff."

Susan wasn't happy with that assurance, so I reached over, took her hand, and said, "I'm genuinely sorry you are disappointed. Tell me about yourself. Tell me about your dreams. Tell me how I can help you."

She started talking, slowly at first, but picking up speed and confidence. After an hour of this one-way conversation, she was finished. I had heard the story of a woman who was at one time at the top of a professional career, but had been hit by a set of scary health problems and then by an unexpected dissolution of her marriage. She was healthy now, and on her way back to having a stable social life. But her financial situation was in shambles. She had paid for the seminar with the last of her savings. If she didn't find the answers she was looking for, she would be lost.

Susan's objective was to start a business that she could grow into something substantial. The business would be based on a skill she had, which turned out to be graphic arts. It didn't take me long to figure out that she was a genuine expert at this prodigious skill. I told her that there was a big and vibrant market for information on that subject. Although I couldn't help her by being her partner (I was honoring my 55th-birthday commitment), I told her that I could give her some ideas. And if and when she launched her business, I would help her promote it.

The important thing to know, I told her, was that she was already *ready* to start that business. She had the knowledge. She had a good idea for her first product (how-to workshops). I had told her that the market was viable, and had even offered to help her get started. All she had to do was write some articles about graphic arts to get her name out to people who might be interested in improving their skills at her workshops. "You can do that tomorrow," I told her. "It won't make you rich right away, but at least you'll be started."

Susan thanked me for my help, but she didn't get started the next day. In fact, she got busy taking care of some chores that came up.

I almost gave up on her, but didn't. And after three years of stalling, she somehow drummed up the courage to take action and did what she had to do to begin her business.

This isn't a story that *already* has a happy ending. I am certain it will, though, because I am certain that she will eventually succeed.

The important thing to me is that she is no longer a wannabe. She found a way to put herself into action. I didn't do it for her. She did it herself. I recently asked Susan to tell the readers of this book how she did it. This is what she wrote:

Susan's Story

One of my goals for 2005 was to learn how to make it much bigger in business. I knew I had been playing life too small, yet I also knew I had been successful by anybody's standards—except in the area of being financially independent.

Because I want people to do well—especially if I'm paying to listen and learn from them—I gave Michael the feedback on his seminar presentation that I believed he needed to hear.

What I had not counted on was his turning the tables on me and making me fess up to my business shortcomings. Like so many people who go into business for themselves (in my case, as a self-employed graphic artist), I was excellent at what I did, but really inadequate in the area of business building.

Uncertainty about how to proceed, and perfectionism combined with the idea that I never knew enough, made a perfect recipe for procrastination. Trying to overcome my lack of direction, I read volumes on what one needed to do to build a business. Unfortunately, I only became more confused.

One thing I did know was that I needed to develop products to grow my business. I had the idea of holding workshops to help people improve their graphic arts skills—but, once again, being uncertain of what I really wanted to do, I did nothing.

During my conversation with Michael, he said I could turn my business around in eight months. One of his suggestions, since I have a master's degree in journalism, was to start submitting articles to various publications. That was the first step.

After starting to write my articles, it quickly became obvious that I needed a web site that I could use to promote my products. Though it took far longer than I thought it would to develop my site, eventually it was good enough that I was willing to be associated with it. That was step two.

The next step was to develop products. I set up my first graphic arts workshop—a big step. (Before this, I had only conducted workshops sponsored by corporations, so all I had to do was show up and conduct the training.) The workshop was recently held, and was recorded and videotaped.

Within a month's time, I will have an audio product, followed by an Internet course and then a how-to video. The way I am keeping perfectionism at bay is by thinking how exciting it will be to start working on my next project.

What has been most helpful to me in this moving-into-action process?

- *First, making a decision to move in a profitable direction—no matter how long it takes.*
- *Being fortunate enough to have a mentor (Michael Masterson), someone with expertise, someone who can look at a business situation dispassionately to see what needs to be done, someone who I know is on my side.*
- *Attending that wealth-building seminar. What that did for me was put me in touch with like-minded people and show me that other levels of achievement and success are possible for me.*

A decision I made, an emotional shove in the right direction, and the support of someone I respect. That's what got me moving.

What would I say to someone else to get them to get moving from a standstill?

1. *Decide on your goal, the direction you want to take—even if it's the wrong direction.*
2. *Find guidance and encouragement. Hire a coach, meet with a business friend, or join a mastermind group, but don't go it totally alone.*
3. *Make it matter. Make it important. Make it now.*
4. *Balance the time you spend learning and doing.*
5. *Discover what motivates you. Usually it is not money itself, but what comes as a result of money.*

CHAPTER FOURTEEN

AIMING THE PRODUCT

Ready, Fire, Aim doesn't mean you are willing to produce mediocre products. On the contrary, it is the best and most efficient way to achieve product quality. And product quality matters. It's how you maintain a good and productive and long-lasting relationship with your customers. Nothing else matters as much. Not even customer service.

So let's get that straight, in case you have any doubts. I am totally and completely devoted to getting the product right. The difference between the traditional do-it-right-the-first-time approach to product development and my *Ready, Fire, Aim* approach is that *Ready, Fire, Aim* is more realistic. It is a method that was developed from lots of experience—the experience of trying to do things right the first time and discovering that it doesn't usually work. *Ready, Fire, Aim* is a more practical way of developing good products. Being more practical, it is more likely to work.

Ready, Fire, Aim acknowledges that it is impossible to get a product right before the customer has had a chance to use it. *Ready, Fire, Aim* recognizes the fact that a big part of *getting it right* is making it emotionally appealing to the customer. *Ready, Fire, Aim* is a pragmatic method based on the observation that more than 90 percent of new-product ideas never materialize as actual products because they get lost in the development process.

Ready, Fire, Aim ultimately results in higher-quality products, because there is less money and time wasted on features, mechanisms, and details that customers simply don't care about. Fewer resources wasted at the *Ready* stage means more resources available at the *Aim* stage. And that's what you need in order to create good products.*

A TALE OF INCREMENTAL DEGRADATION

There is a well-known business theory that deals with the question of product quality. It's called "incremental degradation." The theory is based on the idea that product quality is the sum total of many factors, some of which, if measured individually, are not even noticeable.

The story that is usually told to illustrate this theory goes something like this: Once upon a time, there was a candy company. The company's main product, a chocolate-covered candy, was the number one candy in the country, selling at the rate of 10 million bags a year. When the founder of the company suddenly died, he was replaced by a young man who had a reputation for cutting costs and increasing profits.

The new CEO called in the company's top engineer and asked him for an analysis of all the ingredients that went into the best-selling candy and the cost of each ingredient. The following day, report in hand, the CEO brought the production team together and said to them, "Did you know that we are using 38 different ingredients to make this candy?"

They told him they did know—that, in fact, one of their jobs was to ensure that the exact amount of each of those 38 ingredients went into each and every piece.

"Well, let me ask you this," he said. "Do you think our customers can actually taste all 38 of those ingredients?"

---

*Just in case you are opening the book at this chapter: *Ready, Fire, Aim* is not a method that works for every product. Elevators, suspension bridges, and space shuttles need lots and lots of planning. But *Ready, Fire, Aim* works well for most consumer products and many business-to-business products. Remember, it's *Ready, Fire, Aim,* not Fire at Will!

No, the production team admitted, the customers certainly could not.

"Then what would happen if we eliminated one of those ingredients?" the new CEO asked.

The production team said nothing in response to this question, but the CEO could see by the way they fidgeted that they were uncomfortable even thinking about it.

"I'll tell you what would happen," he said. "Our customers wouldn't notice a damn thing, and we would save money."

They looked at him, still uneasy.

"And do you know how much money we would save if we eliminated ingredient number 16, for example?"

They did not know.

"We would save $3.6 million a year."

The production team looked impressed but still doubtful.

"And do you know what I'd do with 10 percent of that $3.6 million if we could save it?" the CEO asked.

They had no idea.

"I'd allocate it as a bonus for all of you," he said, "because you would be implementing this cost-saving change and so you would deserve a little reward!"

Now the production team perked up. Smiles appeared. Heads were nodding.

"But I want to make one thing very clear," the CEO added. "Our customers are our first priority. Their satisfaction is paramount. To make sure we aren't making a mistake by eliminating ingredient number 16, we are going to taste-test the new product before putting it into production. If our customers can notice the difference—even a little bit—we will not move forward. Is that clear?"

This last assurance seemed to sway even the most stalwart doubters. A spontaneous burst of applause erupted, and the meeting ended with everyone talking animatedly and giving many thanks to the new CEO for his "vision" and "concern for the customer."

The production team lost no time in implementing the idea. Within a month, a test version of the new product was available and a taste test was conducted with a sample of typical customers. The CEO and the production team waited anxiously to hear the results—and when it was announced that the test group could detect no difference between the two samples, everyone stood up and cheered.

A month later, all the members of the production team got their bonuses, and the CEO was written up in *The Wall Street Journal*.

A month after that, another production meeting was called, and everyone came into the room feeling happy and proud of what they had done. The CEO thanked them for their efforts, and announced that he had two questions for them to answer.

"First," he said, "do you know that ingredient number seven costs us $8.6 million a year?"

They were impressed.

"And second, do you know what 10 percent of $8.6 million is?"

The applause was immediate. The production team went to work, and a month later another taste test was successfully conducted. Ingredient number seven was dropped, and, again, no decrease in sales was detected. Congratulations and bonus checks were passed around.

With such a happy pattern established, it took only one more meeting to initiate a series of cost-cutting measures that resulted in, over a 12-month period, 19 of the 38 ingredients in the candy being eliminated. Before they eliminated each one of those ingredients, a taste test was conducted. And each time, the testers could not detect any difference.

At the end of the year, costs were down so much that the company's stock price soared. Investors were happy, the company was named "business of the year" by *Business Week*, and the CEO became $26 million richer through stock options.

And for several months thereafter, it seemed like everything was lovely. The CEO had proven what he had proven so many times before: that you can make a lot more money if you simply spend less on the product, and that since customers don't notice small reductions in quality, there is no point in not making them.

Then, suddenly, something happened. Sales started tumbling. Without explanation and without warning, the number one candy in the country suddenly dropped to number two and then to number three and, by the end of the year, to number 11.

The CEO called in his marketing team and accused them of doing something wrong—but they all insisted that everything was being done exactly as it always had been.

HOW IMPORTANT ARE THOSE INGREDIENTS, ANYWAY?

The story about the candy manufacturer has been told so many times that it must be considered apocryphal. But there are many documented cases of the damaging effect of incremental degradation.

One is about a formerly popular beer.

In 1974, the Schlitz brewery decided to increase profits by lowering production costs. The cost-cutting initiative, which was presented to customers as a technological advancement in brewing, involved the fermentation process and included, among other things, replacing several of the beer's ingredients with cheaper alternatives. Instead of barley malt, Schlitz began using corn syrup. Hop pellets were used in place of actual hops. A powerful preservative, known as "Chill-garde," was added to extend shelf life.

The changes were noticed by Schlitz drinkers. The new preservative caused small white flakes to float around in the beer. To make matters worse, the lack of barley malt meant there was no head on the beer. Longtime customers rejected the inferior product and Schlitz sales went from 24 million barrels a year down to 15 million by 1980.

Schlitz had gone from a serious competitor of industry giant Anheuser-Busch to a minor player with small market share.

Source: Adam Horowitz and the editors of *Business 2.0*, *The Dumbest Moments in Business History*, compiled by Mark Athitakis and Mark Lasswell (New York: Portfolio, a member of the Penguin Group, 2004).

"Maybe it's all the cost-cutting you did," one of them suggested.

"That's impossible!" the CEO shouted. "We tested those reductions every step of the way!"

The CEO was completely confounded by the problem, and insisted that his marketing people must find a way to solve it. Then one day, sitting in his office stewing, he began munching on a bag of the candies. "Damn, these are good!" he thought. "The reductions definitely were not the problem."

But then he looked at the package and noticed it was an old one, produced before the first change had been made. He asked for a new package—just to see—and tasted a piece of candy from that one. He was shocked to find that it tasted completely different.

"How is that possible?" He wondered. "We tested each change every step of the way." And then his mistake occurred to him: He had been testing each change against the previous change. He should have been testing each new version of the product against the original.

He called his production team in and explained his thinking. "I am afraid we made a great mistake," he said. "Our customers could not tell the difference when our candy was reduced by a single ingredient. But those incremental degradations added up, until now the candy is no longer appealing to them."

So he ordered them to start producing the original product, and he brought his marketing team in and told them to begin promoting the original candy to their old customers. They were reluctant to try it, but it worked. After five years and almost a billion dollars in lost revenues, sales of the candy were back where they started—at number one.

YOU CAN'T MEASURE INCREMENTS OVER THE LONG RUN

That story is told to warn entrepreneurs and executives about the danger inherent in increasing profits by decreasing costs. Although a minor reduction in the quality of a product might be imperceptible to the average customer, the process of incremental degradation is likely to have a damaging effect over time. And that effect might be catastrophic.

But does that mean you should never try to reduce the cost of your products?

Of course not. You can, and should, attempt to lower production costs whenever the reduction does not diminish the quality of the product. A creative person can always find clever ways to reduce costs without lowering standards. Oftentimes, you can actually improve products by cutting costs prudently. Thanks to the Internet, all sorts of information products—from movies to books to audiotapes—can now be delivered faster and more reliably, and also much more cheaply, by converting them to digital products that can simply be downloaded by the customer.

Sometimes you are not sure whether the cost-reducing change will decrease or improve quality, because quality is based on perception. For example, you might be able to reduce the cost of producing a line of painted toys by using a different sort of paint that is a slightly different color. Would children find the new color more—or less—appealing?

The easy answer is: Test it. If you could put the newly colored toys in half of the toy stores in a segment of your market and test sales for a month or so, you could determine, with a high degree of confidence, the effect on quality.

For testing to work, it has to be done scientifically. And when done correctly, it helps you refine your products. But it is unlikely that you will be able to test every idea you have. And even if you could, testing alone isn't a reliable indicator for refining products, because testing tells you what is going on now but not what will happen in the future.

Building a successful business is about building long-term relationships with your customers. You can't measure the long-term effect on them of lowering the quality of a product in some way unless you create a long-term test and produce both "before" and "after" versions of the product for that long term.

So where does that leave you?

DECONSTRUCTING BUSINESS BEHAVIOR: THE GOLDEN RULE OR THE RULE OF GOLD?

Ultimately, what you do about refining (aiming) your products will depend on how you think the world of business works.

I have found that businesspeople—actually, all people—fall into one of two groups: (1) those who feel, mostly on an instinctual level, that the universe is fixed and disconnected (i.e., it has a definite size and all of its component parts are independent of each other), and (2) those who feel it is interconnected and infinitely expanding.

Those who feel that the universe is limited and disconnected think of wealth as something that is limited and, thus, must be hoarded. Those who feel the opposite—that the universe is unlimited and interconnected—think of wealth as something that can be expanded indefinitely and thus shared.

In our personal lives, these subconscious feelings determine how we treat family members, friends, strangers, and even enemies. In our business lives, they dictate how we treat employees, colleagues, competitors . . . and our customers.

Seeing the universe as limited, hoarders develop notions that are based on scarcity. Since there is a limited amount of wealth, hoarders believe that the right way to act is the way that gives the individual the greatest amount of personal wealth. That means competing with others to acquire wealth, and then hoarding it.

Hoarders are willing to share their wealth, but generally in proportion to the likelihood that they can get something of equal value in return. A hoarder's idea about how to treat people is built on concentric circles around him: He believes in treating those closest to him better than those further away. Thus his immediate family and close friends are treated better than distant relatives and strangers.

In business, hoarders believe in treating key employees very well (because key employees give so much back) and other employees less well. Some hoarders not only consider their customers to be very far away from them, but also see their customers as competing with them for their profits. Thus, they are inclined to make their products as cheaply as possible. The bigger the profit margin, the better they like it.

Sharers have a completely different way of looking at the universe. They feel that the universe is infinitely expanding. Thus, they feel that wealth, too, can be expanded infinitely. Sharers believe the right way to act is to give as much as they can—as generously to a stranger as they would to a close friend or family member.*

Sharers follow a principle that is so universal (both to secular ethical codes and to religious doctrine) that it has come to be known as the Golden Rule: Do unto others as you would have others do unto you.

---

*You have probably noticed that the Christian idea of "giving to the least of your brethren" is based on this same morality. Many professed Christians, of course, don't follow all of Christ's teachings. Being hoarders, they do not practice the ethic of giving to the least of their brethren. To justify their own self-centered behavior, they have created another saying: "God helps those who help themselves."

In business, a sharer's code of conduct is very similar:

Treat your customers as you like to be treated when you are a customer.

But hoarders believe that in every business transaction there is a winner and a loser. The winner is the person who gets more than his fair share of the deal. The loser is a sucker.

Therefore, hoarders have a different code of conduct when it comes to customers, the Rule of Gold:

The less I give to customers, the more I will have left for myself.

Again, they see wealth as limited, so they cannot conceive of getting more by giving their customers more. They look at it the opposite way: "If I can cut my costs by a nickel, that's a nickel more that ends up on my bottom line."

Hoarders, in my opinion, are wrong about the world in general—and not just wrong, but stupid.

During the 30 years that I have been in business, I have worked with people on both sides of the divide. It saddens me to say it, but I have encountered more businesspeople who follow the Rule of Gold than the Golden Rule. Worse, I have followed it myself. It was a foolish, self-destructive, and degrading experience. And it cost me a lot of money. I know that now.

I know I can make more money more easily by following the Golden Rule—by treating colleagues, employees, vendors, and customers as I like being treated as a colleague, employee, vendor, and customer. I know that if I give more I will get more, and that if I share more, more will be shared with me.

Hoarders think they don't need to give or to share, because they are geniuses at getting. They know how to transfer wealth from others to themselves by persuading others to do business with them. They think they don't have to worry about giving or sharing, because they think there are other suckers out there to take from. When it comes to product quality, hoarders provide as little as they possibly can. Their idea of good business is to promise customers everything but give them as little as possible.

CAN YOU RECOGNIZE A HOARDER?

It is easy to spot businesspeople who follow the Rule of Gold. They are often very good at selling but very weak in customer service. Their products are made as cheaply as they possibly can be. They don't honor their refunds—or they just barely honor them—and they pride themselves on creating profits by cutting costs.

If you could hear these entrepreneurs talking privately about their customers, you would think: "Gee, I'm glad I'm not buying from them." They see customers as either suckers or enemies. When they make speeches—even public speeches—they speak about business as if it were a battlefield.

Business should not be like war. It should be like love, like loving your neighbor.

Remember, most of your profits will come from back-end sales, which means that the easiest way to grow your company is to develop good, long-term relationships with your customers and produce really good products for them.

Hoarders don't realize that they are building their business on a base of quicksand. Although they may be able to turn a deaf ear to their customers' complaints, customers are talking among themselves (increasingly so nowadays, thanks to the Internet), and what they are saying about the hoarders' cheesy products and service isn't flattering.

HOW TO SHARE THE WEALTH: INCREMENTAL IMPROVEMENT

If you want your business to grow quickly and easily, commit yourself to giving your customers as much as you possibly can. *Ready, Fire, Aim* is a business-building strategy that works best for people who want to give, because it is about improving the product (and thus the relationship with the customer) after the sales transaction has already taken place. *Ready, Fire, Aim* results in better-quality products, because it gives you more resources for aiming your product (and thus improving it) after you start selling it.

If you want to develop a business that keeps growing, don't spend all your time trying to reduce your product costs. Spend a good deal of time asking, "How can we make this better?"

Because you readied yourself before firing, you jumped into the marketplace with a product that you already knew was good. And your customers seem to be happy with it. But because you believe in the Golden Rule, *good* is not good enough for you. You want your customers to be more than happy with everything they buy from you.

If they are happy with their purchases, they will reward you by making more purchases. If they are more than happy—impressed or astonished by the quality of the product—they will recommend you to friends and colleagues. In the long run, it will be easier to grow your business if your products continue to improve.

To ensure that, you must engage in a program of incremental improvement—regularly upgrading your products by small degrees, even when there is no evidence that your customers are in any way unhappy.

Incremental improvement is an ongoing process. Once or twice a year, you get together with your product development team and figure out how to make the product (and the experience of buying the product) more useful and/or enjoyable.

Profits count. You know that. Keeping your business profitable is the best and only way to ensure that it can continue to pursue its mission, which is to provide your customers with increasingly better products over time. In making improvements, therefore, you have to make sure that the improvements are paid for out of your profit margin. When it comes to improving the product, keep in mind that you are competing for quality dominance in a narrow market.

The idea is not to produce the world's best watch for only $39, but to produce the world's best $39 watch.

Incremental Improvement Works

I dumped my Rule of Gold partners because what they wanted to do didn't correspond to how I felt about myself and my world. Yes, we made lots of money by putting ourselves first. But there was no natural momentum to the business. It worked because we pushed hard and were good at selling. But I always had the feeling that sooner or later things would fall apart, because we weren't creating extra wealth by producing great products; we were just hoarding some of that wealth for ourselves.

Since I got out of those hoarding businesses and began working exclusively with sharers, I have been doubly blessed. First, and most important, I discovered that I really like to work when I feel that I am doing something valuable. Second—and this is much less important to me at this point in my life but gratifying nonetheless—I am doing better than ever financially.

Adopt the Golden Rule as a business principle. Don't pay attention to people who believe that cutting product quality is okay so long as customers don't really notice. And don't partner up, or do business in any way, with people who speak badly of their customers. Take the high path. Improve your products. Be smart about it, but improve them. You'll be glad you did.

HOW TO CREATE GREAT PRODUCTS THAT KEEP GETTING BETTER

My approach to product quality is very simple:

If it ain't broke ... fix it!

For our purposes, "broke" means not selling well, as in your customers are not buying it. If your customers are not buying it, you should *not* fix it. This advice runs contrary to what most business experts will say. But I have found, over and over again through the years, that it is almost impossible to make a bad (weak-selling) product good (strong-selling) by improving it incrementally. It is much smarter to drop it, go back to the drawing board, and come up with something significantly different.

Let me say that again to emphasize my point: If the product fails to sell well, trash it. If it *does* sell, improve it.

There are no proven rules about how to improve products. Everything I recommend to my clients is based on instinct and intuition (which, of course, is based on experience). My policy is to improve best-selling products as much and as often as we possibly can, and to let our customers know that they are always getting better.

Products that sell moderately well should be improved too, but only after the top-selling ones have been taken care of.

To avoid putting your employees through incremental-improvement hell, you should come to an agreement about how to deal with ideas for product improvement—how to determine if they are actually better, how to calculate their potential costs and benefits, and how to schedule them into production so you don't overburden the system.

I have become such a compulsive product improver that most of the CEOs I deal with have developed ways to manage my constant suggestions. I recognize that not all of my ideas will actually improve things, so I never insist on any particular improvement. I make suggestions and have faith that over the long run things will get better.

How Often Should You Make Improvements?

Several of the businesses I work with hold yearly meetings to brainstorm and plan product improvements. Several others do this once every two years, and one works on a once-every-five-years schedule. In contrast, my clients who are in the business of selling digital information products via the Internet are able to improve their products almost instantaneously.

How often you improve the product depends on how much hardware the product has. As a general rule, the more fixed parts the product has, the less frequently you can improve it.

But the main rule is: Improve your products as often as you can.

How Big Should the Improvements Be?

Again, there is no science to this, but my preference is to make small changes incrementally. Since I have made many mistakes about whether certain changes would be seen as favorable, I shy away from radical moves. My preference, when working with a product that is selling well (and is, therefore, good) is to change one thing at a time, and then to see how customers respond to it.

Incremental changes can easily be rescinded. Fundamental transformations cannot. I want the curve of my clients' product quality to be always angling upward. We don't need sharp upward movements. I'd rather have a gradual incline.

I think our customers like that approach. It allows them to see constant improvements and feel that they are in a relationship with a business that is always one step ahead of them. Constant, incremental improvements allow for more frequent communication with your customers too. And experience proves that the more contact you have with them, the more sales you will enjoy.

Car manufacturers have long understood the perceived value of incremental improvements. With every new improvement in the steering function or the dashboard, they enjoy an additional opportunity to distinguish their product from the competition and get past customers to exchange old models for new ones.

How Should You Communicate Those Changes?

If you make it a policy to continually improve your products incrementally, you will have many wonderful, ongoing opportunities to speak to your customers about the great new changes you are working on. Making product improvements transparent to customers (and even competitors) might seem foolish to the businessperson who sees the value of any improvements as limited. But as a businessperson who believes that wealth can be infinitely improved, you will be happy to share next year's improvements with the rest of the world, because you know that as soon as you get them into the pipeline you will be working on some others.

The product goal is constant, never-ending improvement, because the business goal is constant, never-ending sales.

CHAPTER FIFTEEN

AIMING THE MARKETING, PART 1

A Quick Crash Course

To get your business through its first stage (from zero to $1 million in revenues), you had to become an expert at selling one product to one audience of prospective customers. To get your business through the next stage (from $1 million to $10 million), you are going to have to expand your product line—and that means expanding your marketing skills.

Don't worry. You don't have to go back to school and earn an MBA. You already know what is most important about marketing. You know where prospects can be found, how to create products that appeal to them, and how to give them offers they find very hard to refuse.

Everything you will learn in this chapter is, in some way, just a refinement of what you have already learned. But let's start by talking about you—how you can improve your skills as a marketer.

HOW SALES-ORIENTED ARE YOU?

If you're a natural salesperson, that's great. If you're not, you have to recognize that as a potential drawback and compensate for it by hiring or partnering with a strong salesperson to carry the selling weight. Your chief salesperson will need adequate compensation (it could be as much as you make) and all of your support and encouragement. You are the jockey, but he is the horse that will bring you across the finish line.

Even if you aren't going to be making sales yourself, you have to be in charge of them. You have to take responsibility for sales moving up. This isn't *The Apprentice*, where you can be a team leader and blame your marketing manager or salesperson for failing. As CEO, revenues and profits are your job, even if you don't handle them directly. You don't have to be your company's main salesperson, but if you are not you have to be the full-time pusher of your salespeople.

HOW TO BE A SALES AND MARKETING GENIUS

As I said, you don't have to worry if you aren't a natural salesperson. (Nobody could have been less gifted at selling than I was when I began.) You already know the most important stuff. And you are about to learn a lot of new ideas that will astound everyone around you with your marketing savvy.

One day, you may hear yourself described as your company's resident marketing genius. You won't feel like you deserve that honor, but you probably will.

But let's begin at the beginning—from where you are right now.

STEP ONE: EXORCISING THE RIGHTEOUS DEMONS

Despite your success at creating a million dollars' worth of revenues so far, you may be harboring bad feelings about the selling process. You may still harbor negative ideas about the ethical validity of business. You may also be afraid of selling.

Don't worry. These are the thoughts and feelings that anyone who has been educated in the United States is likely to have. Having them simply means you are smart and sensitive.

But to become the marketing genius your company needs you to become, you must change those thoughts and feelings. Again, don't worry. Your transition from sales inhibitor (which you are if you don't like sales, even if you don't know it) to selling superstar will be much faster and easier if you know what you are doing.

To overcome your antipathy toward sales, rid yourself of the following three very common myths:

Myth #1: It is good to sell things that people need, like grain and milk, but it is bad to sell things that people don't need, like TiVos and gambling vacations.

Reality: More than 90 percent of what people buy is based on wants, not needs. Guess what? You don't really need a nice house, a late-model car, grade-A beef, or a new outfit for your daughter's wedding. You think you need it, but you don't. If you want to market needs, move to a third world country and sell flour. Otherwise, get over the silly notion that selling a $350,000 home is somehow nobler than selling junk jewelry or waterskis.

WANTS VERSUS NEEDS

The logical mind presumes that we buy things because we need them. And that is certainly true of some purchases. We buy gasoline when the gas tank is low and milk when the carton is almost empty. But most other purchases are made for products and services we don't need. We may think we need them, but we really don't.

Think about the last five things you bought:

1. That latte at Starbucks.
2. That 50 Cent CD at Virgin Records.
3. That Michael Masterson book at Barnes & Noble.
4. That new keyboard for your computer.
5. Those tickets to the baseball game.

(continues)

WANTS VERSUS NEEDS (*Continued*)

As much as you wanted them, none of these were needed purchases. You could have made your own coffee at home or done without coffee. You could have contented yourself with listening to the radio or one of your other CDs or given up music in favor of listening to the world around you. You certainly could have done without the Michael Masterson book and the new keyboard and the tickets. But you didn't want to do without them. And though you may have found them entertaining and even useful, you didn't need them.

It may seem that any purchase made for business (a new suit, a new laptop, etc.) is a necessary one, but that's not true. Much, if not most, of our discretionary business buying decisions are made not because we need something but because we believe it will enhance our business lives. In other words, they are made out of want.

The things we buy because we need them are called commodities. And commodities, such as rice and heating fuel, all share a common problem. Consumers don't want to pay a lot of money for them. In fact, they want to spend as little as possible.

Commodity selling is selling to needs, which is boring because the needs are obvious, and limited because once they are filled the customer won't buy any more of the commodity. Discretionary selling, on the other hand, is selling to desire, which is exciting because it involves the breadth of human psychology, and unlimited in terms of profits because you can sell into a buying binge. (More about this in Chapter 16.)

The problem with being in the commodity-selling business is that there is always enormous pressure on you to lower your prices because, thanks to modern technology, every consumer is linked up to thousands of suppliers from all over the world, and, thanks to the Internet and efficient air transport, consumers can go virtually anywhere to get the best price. All of that worldwide downward pressure on pricing can have no other effect than a reduction of profits.

This is not, of course, true for anyone who is selling a discretionary (noncommodity) product—a product that is purchased because the customer wants it. If you are selling a discretionary product, the price you charge isn't dictated by what your competition is charging but by how you position the product in the marketplace. And that is because the value of your product is not objective but perceived.

Myth #2: It is good to sell things, as long as you don't charge much more than they are worth.

Reality: What does value really mean? We say that there is a difference between intrinsic and perceived value—"intrinsic" meaning something's true value as a basic commodity, and "perceived" meaning what it is worth in psychological terms. There is some truth in that. But keep in mind that 95 percent of modern commerce is based not on selling basic commodities but on selling things that have been manufactured. Even most of the food we eat is manufactured. And when something is manufactured, there is room for quality differentiation. And when there is room for quality differentiation, there is room for perceived value. How much that little extra difference in quality is worth is entirely subjective.

Myth #3: It is good to make good things better, but it is bad to sell them.

Reality: Give me a break. If you understand that more than 90 percent of what people buy (except for the purchases of the very poorest members of our society) is based on wants, not needs, and that some significant part (sometimes more than 90 percent) of what we pay for any given item is based on perceived, not intrinsic, value (think organic vegetables, Rolex watches, luxury hotels), then you have to conclude that the world of business is more than 90 percent about vibrating molecules, not meeting basic human needs.

This brings us to the Golden Rule of Marketing Genius, which is:

> *Don't be ashamed of doing to thy neighbor that which you secretly want done to you.*

Or, to put it in more traditional terms: Treat your customers the way you want to be treated.

And how do you want to be treated?

Let me guess:

- You want to be able to buy what you want to buy.
- You want the product you buy to perform as advertised.
- You want to feel like you are paying a good-to-fair price for it.
- By a good-to-fair price, you mean relative to what other people are paying for the same quality.

- You want your product delivered quickly and in perfect condition.
- You want to be treated like a valued customer.
- You want to be able to get a prompt, courteous refund if you are unhappy with your purchase for any reason.

Have I missed anything? If so, fill it in. Make your own list. Then start running your company that way.

I establish a higher standard than "perform as advertised" for my clients' products. I want them to be the best they can possibly be for the price we're charging for them. In their segment of the market, I want them to be the best quality available.

Now let me ask you: If you could provide all of the benefits listed above to your customers, why wouldn't you want them to buy as many of your products as they possibly could?

You are, after all, providing them with everything you would want for yourself.

Deep down, it's not about the features or even the superficial benefits of your products. It's about what the buying and ownership experience does for your customers. Ultimately, your customers want you to continue shaking their molecules the way you shook them the first time when you sold them your first product. You designed your first marketing promotion. You discovered the optimum selling strategy (OSS). You know how to shake those molecules, and only you know how to do it. If they could do it themselves, they would. But they can't. They want you to shake 'em. So do it. And be proud of it.

STEP TWO: SHOOTING REVENUES THROUGH THE ROOF WITH THREE BASIC APPROACHES

Marketing genius Jay Abraham frequently points out to his business clients that there are only three ways to increase the revenues of a business:

1. You can sell your product to more people.
2. You can get your customers to buy more products from you.
3. You can charge more for the products you sell.

That's pretty simple, don't you think?

It's surprising, though, how many businesspeople don't understand it. During my 30-year career in business, I have helped turn around dozens of foundering (not just floundering, foundering!) companies—and I have never encountered one that wasn't suffering from a lack of one of those three basic selling approaches.

At Stage Two of your company's growth, you have to implement all three of them if you want to (and you do) get your revenues to grow from $1 million a year to $10 million.

Let's talk about how you are going to do that.

1. *Sell your product to more people.* To get to where you are now, you have probably sold about as many of your first lead product as you possibly can. To increase the number of new customers you are bringing in, you will have to develop other lead products. I've already talked about how to do that. It's a matter of creating an environment where innovation is everybody's top priority, and where every aspect of product development and marketing is done efficiently so you can create and test more products to more people.

2. *Sell more products to your customers.* This is what I have been referring to as the back end of your business—creating and selling many new products to your existing customer base. Because back-end sales are easier to make (for reasons I've already described), you will have a lot of success with this. A good strategy to market more back-end products to your customers is to design a series of specific sales efforts that presents all of your back-end promotions to every customer in a particular sequence soon after the first purchase is complete.

3. *Charge more for the products you sell.* It may be possible to charge more for your front-end products, but there is a danger in doing that because it will change the nature of your business in a very fundamental way. (If you want to take this path, it's usually better to launch a separate line of products under a separate brand.) But back-end products can, and should, be more pricey than front-end products. Your best customers will want to spend more money with you. Let them.

There is a problem with getting all three of these approaches running simultaneously: Your employees will feel overwhelmed and begin to focus on one kind of marketing at the expense of the other two. To avoid that, I usually recommend dividing up the responsibility at this stage—creating one marketing group that focuses on the front end and another that is devoted to the back end.

The back-end products will give you your profits, but don't make the mistake that many entrepreneurs make at this stage and devote most of your talent and time to the back end. It's natural to want to do that because that is, after all, where the profits are. But if you give in to this impulse your business will suffer and you will regret it.

The key to running a successful Stage Two marketing program is to put your best people to work on the front end. The front end is where you need tipping-point ideas, and you are not going to get tipping-point ideas with your inexperienced and/or B marketers.

Challenge your best people with the task of increasing the number of qualified new customers you bring in every year.* It is a very simple objective. But it will take everything they have to achieve it.

Put together your B team to market your back-end products. They should be direct-marketing experts, since a significant portion of your back-end sales should come from direct-marketing efforts. It doesn't matter how your front-end customers come in; there is a way to back-end them directly. You do it by gathering their addresses (postal and e-mail) and beginning a campaign of communicating with them. Talk to them about what you know they are interested in—the products and services your industry provides. Make your back-end team good at this kind of communication. Teach them to provide value so your customers become appreciative of the relationship you're building with them. The more you give your customers, the more they will reciprocate by buying products from you.

How to Super-Size the Lifetime Value of Your Customers

Increasing your base of profitable customers will always be your biggest business challenge. It will require the most experimentation (in terms of testing media and offers), and will also demand the greatest investment of capital and creative resources. Even if you are happy with the number

---

*Qualified is the key word here. You don't want them bringing in any old customer whose lifetime value may be next to nothing.

of customers you have, you will still have to replace those who leave you. And replacing them with equally profitable customers will require as much creativity and hard work as it took to get them in the first place.

Increasing the average lifetime value of your customer base is relatively easy—if you understand what good customer service is.

Customer Service Made Easy . . . and Profitable

When businesses are set up properly, the optimum selling strategy (OSS) is one that acquires as many customers as the allowable acquisition cost will allow. What that means for most businesses is that new customers are brought in at breakeven or a loss. Thus, a healthy optimum selling strategy for the front end is never going to be profitable. All the profits, when you see the business from this perspective, come from the back end.

So how do you increase back-end sales? How do you get your customers to buy more frequently from you and pay more per purchase?

The answer is customer service. Doubling, tripling, quadrupling, or quintupling your back-end sales is a matter of good customer service, and good customer service involves only three things:

1. Knowing what your customers really want.
2. Finding out how you can do that for them.
3. Talking to them about what you are happy to do.

Let me show you what I mean.

Yesterday, I was walking down a fashionable street in Bucktown in Chicago when I saw a large poster in a shop window that shouted, "Children's Yoga—Sign Up Here!"

I looked up above the poster at the store's marquee, expecting to it to be a yoga studio. Instead, it was a children's clothing store. "That's smart," I thought, "very smart."

Indeed, if the woman who owns this store knows what I think she knows, she will have a very successful, growing business. What I think she has figured out is the answer to the first requirement of good customer service: knowing what your customers really want. In this case, she knows that her customers—young women with children, for the most part—want to give their children a rich and productive growing-up experience.

She hasn't settled for the most obvious and superficial conclusion: "The people who come into my children's clothing store want clothes for their children." She knows that if clothing their offspring were their main goal, there are other stores—discount outlets and department stores—where these young women could get a wider selection at better prices.

What Your Customers Really Want

She has recognized, in renting space on a fashionable street and stocking her store with expensive, hard-to-come-by clothing, that she is going to be selling to a certain type of young mother—an affluent, educated, and upwardly mobile woman who sees the success of her children as a direct reflection of her. Perhaps because this store owner is such a mother herself, she understands that her customers are interested in much more than clothing.

What her customers really want is to do everything possible to give their children the best of everything. And for these mothers—being young and affluent and upwardly mobile—that means indulging them in all the latest trends in quality living. One of these trends is surely yoga. Yoga is practically *de rigueur* among wealthy 20- and 30-something mommies these days. If it is good for the mommies, why wouldn't it be good for the children too?

I don't know how this clothing store merchant has managed to offer kiddie yoga classes, but it's likely that she made a deal with a local yoga teacher who agreed to provide free or low-cost weekly lessons in hopes of securing other, more lucrative business from the store's customers later on.

For the merchant, the strategy has at least two obvious, commercial benefits:

1. It could bring new customers into the store who find the yoga idea fascinating.
2. It could stimulate a spurt of new buying: yoga outfits for children.

But the most profound benefit is likely be the effect it is having on her existing customers—the sense they get that this merchant is looking out for their children's well-being and that she understands the kind of experience they are trying to give their children.

Recognizing what your customers really want is the first and most important step in providing good customer service. It allows you to service not just the superficial wants that can be satisfied with a single purchase but the deeper emotional needs that can never be completely satisfied. Understanding what your customers really want allows you to take care of these desires with products and services that demonstrate your understanding. In doing so, you deepen the relationship.

The shop owner who is smart enough to offer yoga classes to her customers understands that, in doing so, she is sending them an important signal: that she understands who they are and what they really want. She is also demonstrating that she can generate new ideas—tipping-point ideas—that can help her customers achieve their deeper goals.

I can imagine the positive response her yoga promotion must have created: new customers walking into the store, asking about the classes . . . goodwill generated by her existing customer base . . . and both new and old customers feeling that the she really gets it . . . not to mention thousands of extra dollars from the sale of little yoga outfits.

Finding Out What You Can Do for Them

If the owner of this children's clothing store really does get it, the yoga classes are just a single step of a lifelong journey she is embarking upon. Understanding what her customers really want (a life of privilege and advantage for their children), what other things could she offer them?

How about carrying a line of expensive educational toys and inviting someone to lecture on early childhood education—so all of her customers can make sure their children become the geniuses they are meant to be?

Or maybe she could do something with a local music conservatory —arrange for free introductory piano lessons, perhaps, and then back end the lessons with a line of clothing appropriate for giving recitals. (Every promotion doesn't have to result in a direct sale, though. Goodwill is enough of a return on investment now and then.)

As the children of her current customers grow up, so could her product offerings. If her customer base is sufficiently large, in fact, a children's clothing store could give birth to a teenage clothing store.

Likewise, she could create new product lines that are connected to her customers' lifestyles—traveling outfits and luggage for summer, skiing outfits for the winter holidays, and so on.

With each promotion, she could give something to her customers—lectures, demonstrations, tastings, and the like. By making strategic alliances with other local businesspeople who could profit on the back end, she could provide most of these benefits to her customers without cost.

The key thing she will have to remember in developing all these back-end products and services is that everything she does has to be consistent with the understanding she has of her customers' deeper desires. She should never offer them anything, whether she charges for it or not, that is not in keeping with the reputation she is building for herself—in this case, as a woman who really understands how good it is to provide advantages to her customers' children. If she introduced anything similar to a discount business, she would lose credibility immediately.*

Talking to Them about What You Are Happy to Do

If you recognize your customers' deeper desires and provide them with more and better products more frequently, you will double or triple your back-end sales and, thus, double or triple your company's profitability.

And if you do one more thing—talk to your customers about what you are happy to do for them—your profits can skyrocket.

This is an aspect of customer service that too many entrepreneurs, even good entrepreneurs, neglect. You shouldn't do that. Talking to your customers is one of the most powerfully profitable things you can do.

If this shop owner is as good as I hope she is, she is already collecting the names and addresses (or, better yet, e-mail addresses) of all her customers and is sending them information on a regular basis. She is surely sending them announcements about special events (such as the yoga classes) and sales, but she should also be sending them advice that helps them achieve their deeper objectives.

---

*Discounts will work to affluent, high-quality markets, but they have to be presented as very special, very rare, and by invitation only.

She should be sending them a monthly newsletter that talks about all the great new parenting books and information products that are specifically geared toward affluent parents. She should be talking about what events are taking place in the store and what new ones are being planned, and including testimonials (which she should be collecting) from customers who have experienced her special events in the past.

The wonderful thing about the Internet is that it makes this sort of communication easy and affordable. Instead of printing up a four-color monthly newsletter, she can e-mail her customers informally any time she has something to say. If she reads something interesting in the *New York Times*, she can pass that along to them. If she is thinking about bringing in a piano teacher to give introductory lessons, she can ask her customers if that's something that would interest them.

With the software packages available these days, it would be easy for her to communicate with all of her customers on a first-name basis. Each of her communications can have the intimacy of a personal letter and, where appropriate, the urgency of a postcard. By establishing a pattern of communicating this way, she can create a very profitable, long-term relationship with all of her customers.

STEP THREE: A CRASH COURSE IN SALES AND MARKETING

Take an hour, right now, to study the following crash course in advanced marketing—and then study it again once a month for the next year. Each time you read through it, you will be surprised to discover that you have learned something new and useful that you can put to use to create more sales. When you have mastered all 20 of these lessons (plus one more major lesson that you will learn in Chapter 16), your business will be producing at least $10 million in sales each year.

Lesson 1: Your customers don't care about you or your business. They care about themselves.
- Do your marketing messages take this fundamental fact into account? Do they talk to your customers about their problems and desires, or do they talk about your company and your products?

- Are your customer-service people trained to be sensitive to your customers' needs? Do they see themselves as problem solvers, or just as data input clerks?
- Do your salespeople ask thoughtful, probing questions? Do they listen to what your customers are telling them? Do they see themselves as problem solvers or as peddlers?
- Do your top executives buy into this outwardly focused orientation? Do they understand that the reason the company exists is to serve your customers? If they understand that, do they teach it to their employees?
- What's the most common pronoun used by anyone in your company who deals with customers? Is it *I* or is it *you*?

Lesson 2: A small portion of your customer base is giving you the lion's share of your corporate profits.
- Have you identified the big spenders in your customer base?
- Do you communicate with them separately from your other customers?
- Do you communicate with them more frequently?
- Do you thank them for their business?
- Do they know how much you value their patronage?
- Have you given them an opportunity to up their status to VIP customer?
- When you go after new customers, are you targeting these big spenders?

Lesson 3: Understand why your customers buy from you.
- Jeffrey J. Fox, the author of *How to Become CEO* (Hyperion, 1998), says that customers buy for only two reasons: to feel good (about themselves) and/or to solve a problem.
- Are your marketing efforts doing those things? If not, why not? If so, how well? Going out to dinner, buying scuba equipment, and getting a new puppy are feel-good decisions, Fox says. Buying a home, a lawn mower, or car accessories are problem-solving decisions.
- If you sell feel-good products, make sure your advertising makes prospective customers believe they will feel better after they buy them.

- If you sell problem-solving products, express the value of those solutions in terms of dollars. For example, if you are selling rubber O-rings at 10 cents each, make sure your advertisements and your salespeople point out that purchasers will save 30 cents in reduced warranty claims for every O-ring they buy from you.

Lesson 4: Almost every sales transaction begins with the process of generating leads.

- Lead generation can be accomplished in many ways, but the most effective, by far, is with direct marketing.
- If your business doesn't use direct-marketing methods to generate leads, you are missing a great opportunity.
- Become a direct-marketing expert and double your sales.

Lesson 5: Learn multichannel marketing.

- In today's world, single-channel marketing is good for starting up, but not good for getting through the later stages of business growth.
- There is no reason why every business can't employ at least three or four separate sales and marketing media.
- Among those that you should try are direct mail, direct e-mail, radio, television, magazines, and newspapers for the purpose of generating leads.

Lesson 6: Follow the Golden Rule of Marketing Genius: Treat your customers the way you want to be treated.

- Many CEOs and marketing directors have condescending attitudes toward their customers. They even sometimes talk about marketing in warlike terms, with their customers as "the enemy." Unless you begin to view your customers with respect, you will never be able to build a large, self-sustaining business. You may develop a large company, but it will require an extraordinary amount of energy to keep it going.
- Develop the habit of thinking of, speaking to, and treating your customers the way you like being thought of, spoken about, and treated.

Lesson 7: Understand the Secret of the Four-Legged-Stool.

- Every great marketing campaign has four elements. If you make sure your creative team addresses all four in every advertisement and/or promotion, you won't have to worry about failures. Like a four-legged stool, it will be rock-solid.
- The first element (leg) is the Big Idea: Each individual advertisement should have, at its core, one engaging idea. It takes guts to go with one idea rather than half a dozen, but big breakthrough ads are always based on big, new, cutting-edge ideas.
- The second element (leg) is the Big Benefit: Remember that your customers are interested in themselves—in their own wants and needs and problems—not in you or your company. In all your marketing and sales efforts, make sure the customer stays at the center of attention. Express all of your product's features in terms of benefits, including one Big Benefit, and how they will benefit your customer.
- The third element (leg) is the Big Promise: Somewhere in each advertisement or sales pitch, a Big Promise should be stated. The Big Promise should be a succinct and compelling projection of the Big Idea and the Big Benefit, melded into one. Insist that your copywriters take the time they need to craft the perfect promise, and everything else will be easier.
- The fourth element (leg) is the Proof: Throughout your sales and advertising efforts, you will be making specific claims about product quality and performance. Be sure that every claim is backed up by solid proof. Claims and proof do not really sell products (promise and benefit do), but claims and proof allow customers who have already made an emotional decision to buy a product to rationalize that decision.

Lesson 8: Understand that customer complaints and objections are the key to better selling.

- Inferior businesspeople hate customer complaints and objections, because they feel like they are being criticized.
- Superior businesspeople understand that complaints and objections are the building blocks of better products and stronger sales pitches.
- Marketing geniuses encourage objections; they don't run from them.

Lesson 9: Maintain a "no dead end" policy regarding your products.

- Every sale should be seen as a link in a massive system of links that go on forever.
- There should be no limit to the number of things you sell.
- Each sale should lead to some other opportunity for you to solve a customer's problem or satisfy a desire.
- Figure out where each customer is after making any particular purchase, then figure out what he might want to buy at that point, and then sell it to him.

Lesson 10: Take advantage of customer inertia.

- Establish a "bill till forbid" relationship with as many of your customers as possible.
- Marketing geniuses understand that lethargy and apathy are the main reasons why customers stop buying.
- By making their additional purchases automatic, you can easily double the profits of your business and keep them at that higher profit level. Although each business is unique in terms of how customers need to be sold, almost every business can benefit from some sort of bill-till-forbid sales program.

Lesson 11: Understand the 80/20 Rule.

- Apply Pareto's Law to your marketing strategy. Since 20 percent of your customers will be giving you 80 percent of your profitable sales, be sure they are treated like the VIPs they are.
- Big spenders know they are big spenders. When they don't get treated like the good customers they are, they can become disillusioned with your company. You don't want that.

Lesson 12: Understand the unique selling proposition (USP) of every product.

- Before launching a product, ask, "How will this be different and better than the other products out there? And is that quality or characteristic meaningful to the customer?"
- Ask "Is it something that people really care about today? Or is it something that is no longer valued?"

- It is not sufficient to have a unique selling proposition. The USP must be desirable. Make sure every one of your products has a desirable USP, and then promote it like crazy.
- Make sure that when your customers think of the product, they think of that USP.

Lesson 13: Every product line needs its own branding.
- Just as every product needs a USP, every product line needs an identity.
- Be aware of how each of your product lines differs from the competition. Translate that difference into a benefit, and market that benefit as a brand.

Lesson 14: Never lose your marketing edge.
- Don't ever lose sight of the effectiveness of individual marketing and sales campaigns.
- As your business gets bigger, you will notice that many sales and marketing efforts go on simply because they have been going on for many years. Whether they are still profitable is a question nobody asks.
- Be sure that you are aware of the efficacy of all your company's major marketing and sales campaigns. Eliminate the weak ones and promote the strong ones.

Lesson 15: Understand the Secret of the Core Complex.
- To create breakthrough marketing campaigns, you need to be in touch with your customers' core worries and desires.
- What appears to be a desire for luxury on the outside may be a fear of embarrassment on the inside.
- Knowing the subtleties of how your customers think and feel will make you a much stronger salesperson.
- Think of a customer's personality as an onion. To really understand what is going on in his heart, you have to peel back many layers.

Lesson 16: Practice reciprocity with your customers.
- Giving your customers something valuable for free is the best way to start to establish a long-term, profitable relationship.

- By giving before you get, you will teach your customers that they are safe doing business with you.
- Once you have given, make sure you get something in return. This is the fundamental ethic of a commercial transaction. Honor it.

Lesson 17: Understand that intimacy is the key to a customer's lifetime value to your business.
- Familiarity is the soil in which sales grow. Intimacy makes easy sales even easier.
- Constantly speak to your customers about what they are interested in.
- Make your company "transparent." Let customers know about products you are developing and about which of your products are popular and which are not.
- Always be honest with them in your communications. They will appreciate it if you do, and know it if you don't.

Lesson 18: Be confident and enthusiastic when you sell.
- Never be afraid to make a sales pitch. Great home-run hitters seldom get a hit more than once out of every three times at bat. And they never, ever get a hit when they don't swing.

Lesson 19: Don't push or bribe your customers.
- Cold-calling and other forms of hard-core selling are fundamentally weak because they rely on bullying and, therefore, create imbalanced relationships.
- If your business relies on hard-core selling tactics, you will be doomed to all the troubles that accompany such tactics for as long as you are in business.
- By developing a benefit-oriented marketing strategy that prequalifies customers before you sell them, you will eliminate 80 percent of the hassles of selling and assure yourself of a steadily growing and more profitable business.

Lesson 20: Develop and nurture a marketing culture that emphasizes three sentiments.
- First, make sure that providing benefits to your customers is at the heart of all product development.

- Second, teach your employees that providing value should be at the heart of all your sales transactions.
- Third, put sincerity at the heart of all your communications with your customers.

There's one more lesson you need to learn in order to turn yourself into a marketing genius: Understand the buying frenzy. And this one is so important to Stage Two growth that it merits its own chapter . . . coming up next.

CHAPTER SIXTEEN

AIMING THE MARKETING, PART 2

Understanding the Buying Frenzy

What you learned in Chapter 15 about the difference between wants and needs will help you understand something very important about making sales: a phenomenon known as the buying frenzy.

Let's say you are a salesperson at an upscale accessories store for men. A customer comes in looking for a ballpoint pen. He is self-confident, well-spoken, and relaxed. You get the feeling that he is there to enjoy himself, to shop for something nice. He is not a businessman who has lost his pen and is just looking for another one to replace it.

You ask him if he has anything special in mind. He says, "Something different. Something nice." You notice that he's wearing Gucci loafers and a Patek Philippe wristwatch. You make a quick, intuitive decision. "I have something I think you may like," you tell him. "It just arrived."

You show him the most expensive pen in the store, a sterling silver, gold-trimmed Montblanc at $2,995. "Well, I wasn't planning to spend quite that much at this time," he tells you. And then, because you are good at what you do, you say nothing. The seconds tick away. "Oh, what the hell," he says. "I'll take it."

You are feeling good. You have just doubled your quota for the day. The store usually sells no more than one of these pens every week.

Question: What should you do now?

a. Thank the gentleman for the purchase and say good-bye.
b. Thank him, give him your card, and say good-bye.
c. Thank him, give him your card, put his name on your mailing
   list, and say good-bye.
d. None of the above.

The answer is "None of the above." Yes, you should thank him and give him your card and put him on your mailing list. But you should do all of that *after* you have done something else. What is that something else?

You should sell him something else. Yes, something else. And right away—before you ring up the first sale. As in:

"You have excellent taste, Mr. Jones. This is our finest pen. Did you know that there is a matching pencil?"

"Is that so?"

"Can I show it to you? I just want you to see how they look together!" You don't wait for an answer. You quickly select the pencil and place it on the display tray next to the pen he has just purchased. "Do you see how the silver and gold are symmetrically designed?"

"Yes, I do."

You pick up the pencil and hand it to him. "And feel how light that is, and yet it's very comfortable in your hand. Don't you think so?"

"Well, yes, but . . ."

"And look at this," you say, reaching for something behind the counter. "Look at this beautiful leather carrying case. It was made especially for this matching pen-and-pencil set. It's a limited edition. It normally sells for $295, but I can give it to you free if you would like to add the pencil to your collection."

"Well, I wasn't quite ready . . ."

You show him the pen and pencil together in the case. "Isn't that gorgeous?" You hand the case to him and stand back. "In my opinion, that is the finest set of writing implements in the world."

He is admiring it now. "Yes, it is very nice."

"Distinguished and beautiful. Yet not overdone."

"Yes."

"And if you think you'd like it, this is the perfect time. I can give you a 10 percent discount on both pieces, plus the case for free."

"Really?"

"It's a promotional discount that was supposed to end yesterday, but I can extend that special offer for you."

"And how much is the pencil?"

"It's only $1,995. Shall we do it?"

"Sure. Let's do it."

That's what you should do before you thank him for his purchase, give him your card, and put him on your mailing list.

Why?

There are three reasons:

1. It will make your business more profitable.
2. It will make you a better salesperson.
3. It is likely that buying another writing implement is exactly what your customer wanted to do the moment he finished buying the first one.

And why would that be?

Because the experience you provided him with is exactly what he was looking for when he walked into your shop. You said things he wanted to hear. You did things he wanted to have done. You then gave him an opportunity to repeat a buying experience that he has probably had many times before and will have many times again.

In this chapter, I will be talking about one of the most important secrets of developing a successful business: getting your customers to buy many more products from you than they have ever bought before.

But before I get into that, let me postulate another situation.

Let's say you are the branch manager of that same upscale accessories store for men. Every day, you get a printout of all the sales from the day before. What do you do with this information?

a. You keep it on file for future reference.
b. You transfer the names and addresses of the purchasers to a mailing list for your twice-yearly catalogs.
c. Something else.

The answer—yes, you are onto me—is "Something else." As the manager of a retail store selling quality merchandise, you should keep track of your customers in order to serve them better, and you certainly should send them catalogs when you have new products. But you should also try to stimulate additional purchases immediately, even if the customer has just bought an expensive pen and pencil, complete with a carrying case—more than he intended to buy when he walked into the store.

If you want to maximize the lifetime value of your new customer, you shouldn't let him cool off after that first sale. Instead, you should send him an immediate thank-you note, along with a bounce-back promotion that replicates the psychological trappings of the prior day's purchase and stimulates in him, once again, the desire to buy something from you.

That bounce-back promotion might be a brochure featuring some hot new pencil set, or a handwritten letter from the president of your company announcing a very limited edition pen that just arrived (with a photo of it enclosed). Since he is a customer in good standing, you might offer him a discount. And you should probably let him know that if he responds to this offer within 24 hours, he will be placed on your platinum list of VIP customers, which will give him access to the highest form of customer service you offer—essentially, he will have his own personal buyer.

Does this feel like too much selling to you?

If so, you are in good company. Most people feel that way. Nearly everybody, in fact, except for really good salespeople and really good customers.

This is not about high-pressure selling. High-pressure selling is stupid and counterproductive. High-pressure salespeople use psychological force to temporarily persuade customers to buy things they don't want to buy.

The scenarios I presented here are entirely different. They are about putting the customer in an environment where he can do what he wants to do: buy once and then keep buying!

How long will this customer want to buy?

That depends on two things: how much money he has and how good he feels when he makes a purchase. You have nothing to do with how much money he has. But you can control how good he feels when he buys something from you.

This chapter is about how some businesses get their customers to buy products repeatedly, while others sit back and content themselves with taking the easy, passive sales. It's about putting into place marketing and sales protocols that stimulate repeat buying. It's about turning occasional buyers into habitual buyers and single-item purchases into double- and triple-item purchases.

In other words, this chapter is about how to dramatically increase your profits by stimulating your customer's natural wants and turning them into a buying frenzy.

---

iPOD FRENZY

Have you noticed? Hardly anyone with an iPod is content with the basic white earphones that come in the box.

More than likely that trendy portable MP3 player from Apple is protected by a snug, specially fitted case, is docked in a desktop stereo system at home and at work, is connected to a car stereo via a special cable during the commute, or even hooked into a PA system at a local bar or dance club.

These products are usually not from Apple, but from other companies that have focused a large part, if not all, of their business on producing every iPod accessory imaginable to take advantage of the fervor that causes iPod fans to gobble up every little item with an "i" at the beginning. It is rare to see someone leave a store with just an iPod. More often than not their bag also contains several accessories. And if they don't buy those extras then, it will be soon enough, and often. It's classic buying frenzy behavior.

These iPod users feel they really need all those extra gadgets, even if they didn't know they needed them before they got an iPod. Forget about the radio or that old CD player; *this* is the hot new thing and they *must* use it as much as possible.

Apple hasn't been left out in the cold. For many iPod owners, one version is not enough. The large 60-gigabyte iPod with pictures and video is fine for long trips, but the lighter, smaller Nano is better for shorter jaunts. And don't forget the ultralightweight Shuffle for working out and jogging. And everybody needs the new iPhone, which connects to the Internet, is a cellphone, and—oh yeah—plays music. And while they're at it, why not one for the husband or wife, the kids, or the grandkids?

THE RAGGED, RATTY, 15-YEAR-OLD CARRY-ON BAG AND THE HUMAN ATM

One of my clients owns a $270 million international publishing business. His business responsibilities require him to travel all over the world. In the past 15 years, I have taken at least 50 trips with him. During that entire 15-year period, I have known him to have only one carry-on bag.

It is a ratty-looking nylon thing, shapeless and worn at the edges. The zipper barely works, and there is a tear forming at one of the corners. He stuffs his laptop and all the paperwork he can fit inside it, and then he slings it over his shoulder and carries it around the world with him, in first-class cabins and five-star hotels in London and Paris and Madrid.

In my view, he desperately *needs* a new bag. But he doesn't see it that way. As long as his pathetic little sack can transport his belongings, he will not buy another one because he feels he doesn't need one. And if he doesn't *need* one, he doesn't *want* one.

I, on the other hand, want a new bag almost every time I walk into a luggage store. I want one in black leather, another in brown suede, another that has many compartments, another that is plain. Outside the room where I am typing right now is a wall that is literally lined with bags and briefcases. There are 14 of them—in all shapes and sizes.

Even in this room, in my office, briefcases and bags abound. At my feet, there is a hand-stitched leather bag from Italy. On the chair across from me is a high-tech synthetic bag made in Japan. Next to my secretary's desk sits a canvas bag that was made in France. And in the trunk of my car is my latest purchase—a skinny portfolio that should be perfect for carrying manuscripts on my upcoming trip to New York.

Clearly, I don't need any more of these things. Yet I am sure that the next time I walk by a luggage store, I will want one.

The comparison between me and my client illustrates the difference between wants and needs and highlights something every budding business genius should know about selling. If you convince a customer to buy your product when he needs it, you will have a loyal customer. But if you can persuade him to buy a product from you every time he wants it, then you have a human ATM.

Often, when my client and I travel together, we pass a luggage or accessories store that has bags and briefcases in the window. I almost always stop to look at them . . . and then suggest that he step inside the store with me to get himself a new carry-on.

He usually obliges, but never with any enthusiasm. For him, a store that sells such things is about as interesting as a fabric store is to me. Surrounded by dozens of new bags, I find myself flushed with energy. "What about this one?" I say. "This is great, because there is a space to put a fresh shirt for an overnight stay." Or, "Look at this! It's got a place where you can put your newspaper!"

But everything that excites me about these bags bores him. Before 10 minutes have elapsed, he has wandered out of the store, his old bag still in his hand, and I have made my way to the counter with some new bag to add to my collection.

This is the routine we follow. He buys what he needs, while I buy what I want.

Question: If you were in the luggage business, who would you want as your customer—the guy who has one bag and really needs another? Or the guy who has umpteen bags and definitely *doesn't* need another?

It's interesting. When I ask that question at seminars *before* I tell my little story, most people say they would rather have my client as their customer because he clearly needs the product. But when I ask the same question *after* telling the story, they *get it*.

They understand that it's not about what customers need; it's about what they want. And that if you cater to their wants rather than their needs, you will have a much better (and by that I mean richer and more long-lasting) relationship with them.

This is a very important lesson to learn.

> **The Law:** The likelihood of a customer buying a particular product is inversely related to his need for it.
> **And Its Corollary:** The less a customer needs a product, the more likely he is to buy it.

Being a bit of a contrarian, I love making counterintuitive pronouncements in the strongest possible way. And I am guilty of doing that here (but just a little). As I will explain in a few minutes, these two rules aren't true for every commercial transaction. But they are true for most of them. And by applying them to your business—even if you are currently selling necessities—you will increase the long-term value of your average customer and, thus, increase the long-term profitability of your business.

AN APOLOGY FOR CONSUMERISM

Let's look at the psychological implications of these two rules by examining my penchant for bags and briefcases. Am I crazy to have so many?

Maybe. But I don't *feel* crazy. I feel kind of good about them. Like some (many? most?) women feel about their shoes. Or like some men feel about their cars. Or like many of us feel about books.

When I walk into a store that sells bags and briefcases, I am not thinking rationally—but I'm not irrational, either. In the back of my mind, I am fully cognizant of the fact that I don't need any more of what this store has to sell. But I am also aware that I get pleasure from owning these products, and I know that sometimes—if the store has the right inventory and the right sort of salespeople—I get a lot of pleasure from the buying experience itself. I rationally recognize that there is a reasonable chance that if I walk into that store and things go right for me in there, I will enjoy myself and then leave the store with something I can enjoy in the future.

That isn't so crazy, is it?

I think it's rather sane. Our first objective, as rational creatures, is to take care of our basic human needs: nourishment and shelter. The next objective, if we are smart, is to store valuables (or put money away) so we can feed and shelter ourselves when times are tough. After that, the working and the spending are directed toward providing ourselves with a better life, which means—when you stop to think about it—things we don't actually need.

Sane spenders recognize the difference between their wants and needs and treat their want-based buying accordingly. They will buy what gives them satisfaction, both immediately and afterward, and will not buy things that don't.

So long as I have my basic needs taken care of and I've put aside enough money for a rainy day, the only sane thing to do with the money I don't need is to spend it on things I don't need that give me pleasure. (And by that, I would include all forms of charitable giving. But that's another book.)

I have taken the time to defend my spending habits to make the point that you should never feel bad about selling people products they don't really need, because (a) there is very little selling that doesn't fall into that category, and (b) since buying things you don't really need is something you do all the time, then selling to wants and desires is very effectively following the Golden Rule of Marketing Genius: Treat your customers the way you want to be treated.

WHEN IS THE BUYING IMPULSE STRONGEST?

Let's get back to looking at my buying habits, because they reveal another worthy little business secret.

Understanding the Buying Frenzy

Although I am clearly a habitual luggage buyer and have rationalized my penchant for this kind of incessant consumerism, I don't buy bags and briefcases in a regular, rational way. If you charted my buying over the years, you might notice a pattern to my briefcase buying frenzies. (See Figure 16.1.)

What's going on here? Why the periods of inactivity and then the sudden buying sprees?

I have done a good deal of thinking about this over the years, and I have come to the conclusion that there are three factors that stimulate these buying frenzies:

1. Having the feeling that I have more money than I need.
2. Being exposed to psychologically effective selling signals.
3. The good feeling I get from buying.

Each of these reasons has important implications for the savvy businessperson.

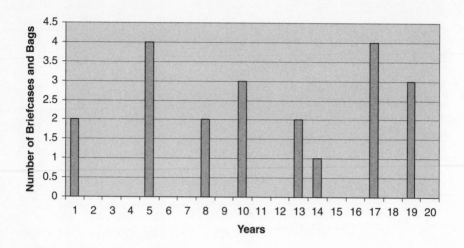

FIGURE 16.1   Michael Masterson's Briefcase Buying Frenzy

Generally speaking, the more money a person has, the more he will spend on any individual thing. Rich people spend more money than poor people on housing, food, clothing, entertainment—you name it.

A person with an income of $85,000, for example, might spend $350,000 on a home, whereas the person who makes 10 times that amount—$850,000 a year—might very well spend 10 times that much, or $3.5 million, for a home. Likewise, someone who waits tables for a living might spend, on average, $65 to $85 for shoes, whereas the owner of the restaurant is likely to spend considerably more.

The imaginary customer who walked into your imaginary men's accessories store at the beginning of this chapter spent almost $3,000 on a pen that is, from a practical point of view, no better than a pen he could have bought for $300. Yet he was happy to do so. Why? Because that's what he expects of himself. He expects to spend more money on discretionary purchases because he makes more money.

If you look at the world of consumer goods from this perspective, you can see that commerce is set up to accommodate this. For almost every sort of consumer goods, there is an astonishingly wide range of prices that can be paid for any given thing. Pens, to take our first example, can be purchased for as little as a dollar apiece up to as much as $3,000 at your local mall. Meanwhile, the pinnacle of collectible luxury pens is the jewel-encrusted Mystery, created by Montblanc and Van Cleef & Arpels, which retails for $730,000. There are only nine in the world.

Watches, too, are sold for as little as $10 apiece up to a quarter of a million dollars or more for limited-edition, hand-made timepieces. A $10,000 watch may have features you won't find in a $10 watch, but few if any of those features relate to needs. Titanium bolts? Diamond fittings? These things are clearly frivolous—except that they make the buyer feel good about the watch and about owning it.

I have been using watches and pens as examples because they are so easy to talk about. But this principle applies equally well to other, less obvious consumer products.

Investment newsletters, for example, routinely sell for as little as $39 a year to as much as $10,000. It can be argued (and it surely would be by the publishers of the expensive ones) that the higher-priced newsletters deliver better value. But when the performance histories of such publications are objectively tracked, the investment recommendations made by the lower-priced ones frequently deliver the highest average returns.

Yet the expensive publications are very popular and usually much more profitable to publish than their poor cousins. Why would that be? Perhaps it is because wealthy investors (or investors who feel wealthy) who are experiencing a buying frenzy feel like they need to spend a lot of money to get the psychological satisfaction they are craving.

That is what happens to me when I get into a bag/briefcase buying frenzy. Since I do have more discretionary income than most people, I am likely to spend a lot more money than most during a buying frenzy—as long as the business that is catering to me understands how I like to be stimulated.

In my case, I want to feel like I am making a smart choice, that the bag I am buying is of superior—nay, world-class—quality, and that this bag will accommodate some special need (with, for example, a pouch that can hold my plastic bag full of liquid items for airport security) that isn't already covered by one of my other bags.

THE 80/20 RULE OF BINGE BUYING

Twenty percent of your customers will be responsible for 80 percent of your profits. This is a business truism that no smart businessperson should ignore.

I believe that if you study the 20 percent of your customers who are giving you most of your profits, you will discover that their buying is consistent with the binge-buying pattern I identified in this chapter. So, to make sure your business gets all the profits it can get, you have to:

1. Identify the potential big spenders among your customers.
2. Market to them aggressively as soon as they make their first purchase.
3. Make sure your marketing stimulates their psychological desires, not their physical wants.
4. Keep selling to them until they spend themselves out of their frenzy.

If I'm feeling flush (and that is almost always a component of a buying frenzy), I will feel the need to spend a certain considerable sum of money before I am satisfied. Usually that is in the thousands of dollars. So if the wrong salesperson is dealing with me and sells me a perfectly good bag for $69, I will walk out of that store very unsatisfied, because my preprogrammed psychological spending threshold hasn't been crossed. And with his $69 price tags, I don't have the time or the closet space to satisfy my urge with this merchant.

Understanding the psychology of selling is essential to ensuring a long-lasting, profitable business. At least one aspect of the psychology of selling—how people think when they buy nonessential (discretionary) products—is especially important to learn early on because it is counterintuitive.

Take watches, for example. If we grant, for the moment, that a certain percentage of the population does indeed need a watch in order to tell time, then we can understand why there is so much competition at the lower end of the market, competition that keeps prices—and profit margins—down. But with the availability of cheap plastics and digital technology, very good and reliable watches can be manufactured for just a few dollars apiece. Add a few plastic bells and whistles, distribution and storage costs, and you can have a good-sized business selling watches in the $19 to $39 retail range.

As watches move up in price, profit margins increase. The higher up they go, the greater the profit margin. Thousand-dollar (and multithousand-dollar) watches can have huge profit margins.

But why would that be? Why would there be only, say, a $3 profit margin on a $19 watch, while there could easily be a $9,000 profit margin on a $12,000 chronograph? Shouldn't there be equal downward price pressure from the competition at all price levels? Don't rich people like bargains just as well as poorer folk?

The answer is that as watches move up in price, the public's perception of what the watches are changes from simple devices that tell you what time it is (which are, essentially, commodities) to luxury items. And the monetary value of a luxury item is dependent on all sorts of psychological things, such as status, beauty, exclusivity, and prestige. An intelligent watch seller who understands this will focus less on a watch's ability to keep time (which no longer has much value) and more on those subtler, more elusive things.

Thus the cost of owning a watch can range from the price of a screwdriver to the price of a piece of jewelry or even the price of a piece of fine art.

Once a customer has taken that psychological step—to seeing a watch as a piece of jewelry—it will be easier to sell him another expensive watch than it will be to sell him an inexpensive one—as long as you sell it as jewelry.

And if you've taken him to the next level—where he wants to buy your name on a watch—the next sale should be as easy as telling him that you have set aside the latest such and such just for him.

At the highest level—selling watches as works of art—you have the best customers. They won't buy everything from you. You have to know their taste. But when you get it right, they will spend hundreds of thousands of dollars on watches.

In short:

- What is good about selling commodities is that you are meeting a need. What is bad about it is that your customers won't be loyal to you, and will always try to pay as little as they have to for the kind of product you're selling.

- What is good about selling discretionary items—and especially luxury items—is that it is relatively easy to convince your customer that your particular products are unique, and that only by purchasing them can he get the psychological benefits they offer.
- What is also great about selling discretionary items is that your customers will never be satisfied with a single purchase. In fact, the more they buy, the more they will want to buy, because their purchases are stimulated not by need but by desire. And if there is one thing marketing geniuses know about desire, it is that it can be satisfied only temporarily.

THE "SHOES MAKE ME BEAUTIFUL" LOGIC BEHIND GETTING YOUR CUSTOMERS TO BUY

A marketing campaign that stimulates long-held and deeply held desires (such as the desire for acceptance, recognition, admiration, and even love) will create the best kind of customers: buyers who will buy repeatedly over a long period of time.

It may seem unrealistic or even absurd to think that the product you market (lawn sprinkling systems, for example) could achieve this sort of lofty psychological objective, but it isn't. Great advertising campaigns do just that.

To know how to develop these sorts of campaigns, you have to understand the logic behind discretionary purchases.

Let's take something as simple as selling shoes to women.

What do women think about shoes? Do they think that shoes are useful things to cover their feet?

If that were the case, their thinking about shoes would be something like this:

First thought: Shoes are useful for protecting the feet.
Second thought: I have a perfectly good pair of shoes. Therefore, I don't need to buy another pair until this pair wears out.

This is not, obviously, the way most women think. When it comes to shoes, their thought process is closer to this:

First thought: Gucci shoes are beautiful.

Second thought: Wearing Gucci shoes will help me look beautiful.

Third thought: When I look beautiful, I feel good.

Fourth thought: Every time I want to feel good, I should buy a pair of Gucci shoes.

Fifth thought: Or two.

If you understand this logic, you will never go too far astray in your marketing campaigns, because you will always have a fundamental sense of what your prospective customer wants to believe. Whether the challenge is writing the copy or figuring out which media to advertise in, decisions will always be easier if you understand the psychological trigger points that drive the purchase.

Here is something very important to understand about this type of buying: Once a customer has decided that buying a certain type of product will give him the psychological feeling he is looking for, the purchase itself will stimulate the desire to purchase again. The more he buys, therefore, the more willing he will be to buy again.

Most inexperienced businesspeople have a hard time grasping this concept. They figure that the more a customer buys now, the less he'll want to buy later. This fundamental mistake, which is based on confusing needs and wants, is the main reason why so many businesses start off well and then gradually deteriorate.

To satisfy a customer who has made a discretionary purchase, you must recognize that in buying one thing from you, he is stimulated and willing to buy another. If you don't meet that need, some other business will. And if that other business is better at keeping this customer than you are, you will lose his business.

It's all about the buying frenzy—that fascinating, nearly universal pattern of buying that takes place whenever a consumer equates psychological gratification with any sort of discretionary product.

My research assistant, Jason Holland, tells this story about his infatuation with alternative music.

> Park Avenue CDs is an independent record store down the street from where I used to live in Orlando, Florida. Until my recent move, I'd been a regular customer, probably too regular when you consider how many CDs and vinyl LPs I have stacked around the house (much to

the annoyance of my wife). I have so much music that I really haven't listened to everything, even months after purchase, and I'll probably buy more before I get through what I already have.

What kept me coming back, again and again, to that little shop—and helped it compete and thrive against larger music retailers in the area and online? Well, they have a great selection of stuff that I and other alternative-music aficionados love—world music, experimental rock, electronica, the list goes on. But they have also taken a bead on me and my music-collecting brethren.

Because we subscribe to the store's weekly e-mail newsletter that lists new releases, in-store performances, and exclusive, limited-edition, and imported merchandise, they know that we are in their grip. We are helpless. The frenzy has taken hold.

I'd tell my wife, "I am just going over to Park Avenue to browse, maybe pick up a CD if I find something I like." She'd usually refuse to go with me, knowing that despite what I just said, I'd spend hours in the aisles with a steadily growing pile in my arms and a big smile on my face.

Even though I no longer live in the neighborhood, I'm still a subscriber to Park Avenue's newsletter and check it often. Let's just say I can't wait for my next visit to Orlando.

In the 2005 documentary *Just for Kicks*, filmmakers Thibaut de Longeville and Lisa Leone investigated another subculture that is a prime example of the buying frenzy, though not very well known in the mainstream. In fact, you might be shocked by what this group is buying—literally spending a small fortune to obtain.

They are sneaker collectors.

The film profiles individuals, from famous and wealthy to barely scraping by, who have hundreds, even thousands, of sneakers in their collections.

Why do they have so many sneakers, many of which they never wear so as to preserve their just-out-of-the-box condition?

The collectors can barely contain themselves when describing the rush they feel when they buy every color combination (known as "colorway") of a new Nike or Adidas shoe, or finding a store that carries old stock of a favorite shoe from their childhood. They buy every single one they can get their hands on, even those not in their size.

In the most telling scene of the film, collectors camped for days outside a store that was set to sell a limited edition of Air Force Ones, a Nike shoe that is the Holy Grail of sneakers. Those lucky enough to get a pair (they were heart-wrenchingly limited to one pair per customer) had to brave armed thugs circling the block, waiting to pounce on them and either keep the sought-after sneakers for themselves or sell them to unscrupulous collectors.

WHAT TO DO WHEN YOUR CUSTOMERS ARE PRACTICALLY FROTHING AT THE MOUTH

The single fastest way to turn your ordinary business into a cash machine is to redesign your sales and marketing strategies to focus on stimulating buying frenzies among the top 20 percent of your customer base.

Here's how to do that:

- Market to your core customers' wants, not their needs. Figure out why your best customers buy your products. Don't ask them directly, because they won't tell you the truth. Study your best advertising campaigns and ask yourself, "What is the hidden promise here?" If you can figure that out—the deeper, embedded feelings and thoughts that are driving your best sales—then you can design another advertising campaign that will commence the moment you receive your first order and continue with regularity until the market has proven to you that it is exhausted. But until then, push on.
- When a marketing campaign works, keep using it (with modest changes) until it wears itself out. Don't assume that just because you are bored with it, your customers will be. Keep the main elements of the campaign (the tone, the offer, the type of promise) the same. Trust the market to tell you when it is sated.
- Know that every industry has its own unique buying frenzy. How long it lasts, how much the customer will spend, and what kind of messages will work best—these are all questions that vary from one industry to another.

I can't describe all the major industries here, but I can say that all frenzies are stimulated by the same three things:

1. New money to spend.
2. Effective marketing that appeals to the right desires.
3. The purchase itself—the stimulation of buying the product.

HOW TO STIMULATE A BUYING FRENZY

If you want to create superprofitable customers, you have to locate the customers who are capable of spending big and then stimulate their core desires in such a way that they will equate buying your product with satisfying those desires.

Is your customer a middle-aged man who wants to be attractive to younger women? Then create an ad campaign that will make your car (or watch, or cologne, or cigarette) feel like an aphrodisiac.

If you are selling expensive lock sets, you have to figure out what your target customers feel, think, and want with respect to locks and doors. Is security on the top of their list? Do they worry about someone breaking into their house and stealing their things? If so, then your advertising campaign should focus on that. Are they more concerned about prestige—about feeling like they have the nicest house in the neighborhood? If that's the feeling/thought/desire that is closest to their hearts, design your advertising campaign to appeal to those sentiments.

In making psychological promises in your advertising, it is usually better to make them subtly rather than overtly. If you come right out and say that your product will make your customer smarter or sexier than his neighbors, he will see your ad as pandering and derogatory and thus resist it. If your promises are strong, the ad might still work, but if you can make the psychological promises indirectly, they will generally be stronger.

Understand the Length, Strength, and Nature of Your Customer's Buying Frenzy

As I have suggested in this chapter, buying frenzies vary depending on the customer's socioeconomic bracket, his cultural belief system, his financial circumstances, and the advertising he is exposed to.

Low-end buyers, for example, usually have short buying frenzies with very short intervals between purchases. The frenzy begins when they get some cash in their pocket (on payday) and ends when they have depleted all their available cash. If your business depends on selling to customers like these, you will have to find out when they get paid and time your advertising to hit then or very soon thereafter ... and keep hitting them hard and often for the following few days.

High-end buyers tend to have long buying frenzies with moderate intervals between purchases. If you are in the business of selling bonds or financial advice, for example, you should know that your customers' buying frenzies will begin when they are near or at retirement age, and will continue for 10 or 20 years at monthly or semimonthly intervals. If you are not there to sell them something, someone else will.

CHAPTER SEVENTEEN

READY, FIRE, AIM
IN ACTION

I have been talking about *Ready, Fire, Aim* as a method for increasing the speed of product innovation for second-stage entrepreneurial businesses. In fact, it applies to every sort of innovation—from accounting procedures to customer-service protocols to every type of operational process.

It is also the best way—as you will soon see—to launch a new career or develop a little side business.

Ready, Fire, Aim means disregarding most of the obstacles and detours that waylay others. It means finding and following the fastest path to any objective you set for yourself so that time and all the problems time brings with it don't defeat you. *Ready, Fire, Aim* achieves more in less time because it puts the correct value on *action*. It is also a realistic approach, because it acknowledges human imperfection and failure in an intelligent way. In effect, *Ready, Fire, Aim* is a way of increasing the success you have in just about anything.

Following are several stories that illustrate how you could incorporate *Ready, Fire, Aim* into your life.

HOW TO BECOME A FILMMAKER THE *READY, FIRE, AIM* WAY

For most dreamers who want to become filmmakers, this would probably be the most sensible path for them to follow:

1. Spend six months to a year locating a film school that would accept you.
2. Invest tens of thousands of dollars to enroll in the best program you can find.
3. Spend two to six years studying film and developing a familiarity with all the major skills.
4. After you have gotten your degree, spend six months to a year looking for a job. If you don't find a job (and chances are you won't), get a nonpaid apprenticeship with a movie-related business and work at that until you get a shot at something better.
5. Keep at it for 10 or 20 years until you finally get a lucky break.

So that's one way to do it: Devote half your life to academia and internships and groveling and schlepping and kissing butt for an outside chance at stardom. Or you could take the *Ready, Fire, Aim* approach. That's what Marc Singer did.

Singer was an unemployed immigrant from England when he heard the rumor: Hundreds of homeless people were living beneath the ground in New York City.

There was something about the idea that struck his imagination. He couldn't stop thinking about it: a village of homeless men and women hidden in a subway tunnel. How did they live? What did they do? And where, exactly, were they?

He got his chance to find out when an article in an independent newspaper gave him a clue as to where this urban Atlantis might be—and it wasn't far from where he lived.

For several weeks, Singer poked around and talked to homeless people. Finally, he found what he was looking for: an otherwise unremarkable pile of rubbish in a tunnel stretching north from Penn Station.

For several days, he watched raggedy people disappear into the tunnel and come out again. Eventually, he approached them. He told them that he was interested in getting to know them. They thought he was crazy. But one of them finally invited him down.

It was an Alice in Wonderland experience for Singer. In the cavernous darkness, he discovered dozens and dozens of painstakingly constructed huts made from discarded plywood, plastic, and canvas that housed hundreds of squatters.

The property they were squatting on had been abandoned long ago when the subway stopped running along that route. There were still, however, electrical wires and water pipes running through it that the crafty squatters had tapped. Inside the shacks, radios played. Beneath a jimmy-rigged water line, the denizens of this dark city showered.

It was everything Singer had imagined ... and more. He built himself a little shelter among his new neighbors and for several months spent half his days there.

At one point, sitting around a makeshift campfire, playing cards and talking to several of the men, someone suggested that Singer make a film about it all. The moment he heard it, the idea struck him as exactly right. He'd always had a secret desire to make movies, and despite the fact that he had none of the necessary skills, he got started on this one immediately.

Singer spent the next several weeks hustling around the city, gathering up equipment, and reading books on filmmaking. He used his newfound (and equally inexperienced) friends as his crew and, relying mostly on instinct, directed the filming, lighting, and sound. As the weeks went by, he accumulated hundreds of hours of film. When he ran out of film, he borrowed money and shot more film.

After several months, Amtrak announced that they were going to clean up this abandoned tunnel to make way for some new project, and they contacted the police to force the squatters out. Singer went to Amtrak and asked for a deal. If they would give him just a month or two of leeway, he said, he would sell his film and use the money to find other places for the squatters to live.

It was a promise without a foundation, based entirely on faith. But, miraculously, he pulled it off. The second half of the amazing black-and-white film he produced down in the tunnel tells the story of how these people fought for their right to stay, and then, when that effort failed, worked with Singer until he found homes and jobs for all of them.

The film, a documentary called *Dark Days*, went on to win several awards at the 2000 Sundance Film Festival, and was even nominated for an Academy Award. Marc Singer became an instantly credible and credited filmmaker, and his career has been flourishing ever since.

Rent the film and enjoy it. But then watch the extra feature that describes how Singer made it. You will be impressed by his ingenuity and the tenacity he showed, given the obstacles that faced him. For me, the big lesson was that he went full speed ahead with his goal of making the film the moment the idea was presented—*Ready, Fire, Aim.*

After spending all that time and effort getting integrated into this unusual community, he recognized on a gut level that making the documentary was the right thing for him to do. He didn't let anything stand in his way: not his complete ignorance of filmmaking, nor his lack of money to fund the movie, nor the fact that he didn't know anybody in the business.

The only thing he knew was what he had to do right away—and that was to take immediate action. In his heart, Singer knew that if he didn't get going immediately, the opportunity would be lost or something else would take his attention and his dream of making a movie would never materialize. So he jumped in and learned along the way, making mistakes and fixing them.

It happens to be a very good film, and that certainly had to be gratifying to him. But, as he explains, his goal was simply to get it done—and accomplishing that goal gave him his greatest satisfaction.

Singer's objective was simple: He wanted to make a particular film to tell a particular story. He had no intentions of winning any prizes or making any money on it. He was smart enough to know that the odds of doing either were next to nothing.

Personal goals like this lend themselves perfectly to a *Ready, Fire, Aim* approach, because they are uncomplicated by the profit objective that must always be a factor in an entrepreneurial business. Personal goals usually fall into one of two types: (1) doing something (like making a movie or swimming across the English Channel) or (2) becoming something (like a filmmaker or a writer or a painter).

Singer's story illustrates how you can do what you have always wanted to do or become what you always wanted to become by jumping into the process and going forward until you have finished.

Singer was lucky in that although he wasn't rich enough to finance his film on his own, he had enough money to support himself for the year it took to complete it.

Most people can't take a year off of work in order to pursue a dream. But you can still take a *Ready, Fire, Aim* approach to something that you have always wanted to do—as long as your goal is straightforward and not complicated by secondary objectives like prizes or profits.

IF YOU HAVE A PERSONAL GOAL...

If you want to become something like a filmmaker or a writer or a painter, you should begin filming or writing or painting the moment you feel ready. You don't want to wait until you know a lot about how to film or write or paint, because if you do, chances are you will never be what you want to be.

The main reason that otherwise intelligent and accomplished people never achieve personal goals like this is because they are afraid to begin seriously working on them until they are good at the filming or the writing or the painting. The effectiveness of the *Ready, Fire, Aim* approach to getting things done is based on the willingness to start doing something when you are not especially good at it.

Think about the lifelong personal goals you have had but never accomplished. What is it that stopped you?

It may feel like you never had the time or the resources—but if you think about it honestly, you may find that the fear of not being good enough was lingering there in your subconscious, prompting you to delay action until a "better or more convenient time."

Do this now. Write down a list of everything you have ever wanted to do or become. Arrange that list according to what is most important to you (or will be most important to you in a few years). Narrow your choices to three. Then pick one of the three.

Promise yourself that that goal, and only that goal, will be your top priority for the next 365 days. Acknowledge that everything else will be secondary. (This may be scary at first. Get used to it.) Communicate this decision to those people who will be affected by it. Tell them how you think things might change and how you intend to handle the responsibilities that affect them.

Then make an outline of exactly what you have to do to become what you want to become. Don't worry about being good at it. Don't worry about being recognized. A filmmaker is someone who makes films. A writer is someone who writes. A painter is someone who paints. A guitar player is someone who plays a guitar. A gardener is someone who tends a garden.

(continues)

IF YOU HAVE A PERSONAL GOAL... (*Continued*)

Make a plan, today, to begin doing what you need to do as soon as possible. In most cases, you will be able to begin today. Again, don't worry about being good, and don't think about getting any recognition for what you're going to do. Do it because you have always wanted to do it and because time is running out. Start immediately.

MY FIRST *READY*, *FIRE*, *AIM* ATTEMPTS AT FILMMAKING

Like Singer, I always wanted to make movies. For many years, I did nothing but talk about that dream. But soon after I started writing articles for *Early to Rise*, I decided to start practicing what I was preaching in them.

For openers, I wanted to make a 30-minute documentary related to my experience with Jiu Jitsu. I also had an idea in the back of my head for a feature-length film.

From experience, I had learned that the best way to accomplish these kinds of personal goals is to:

- Find a partner who can cut your work in half.
- Carve out a single block of time to get the work done.

So I was ready. And I fired.

For the documentary, I partnered with a friend who, like me, was a Jiu Jitsu enthusiast and also had a desire to make movies. Paul had more free time than I had, so the deal was that he would do the groundwork, I would put up the money, and we'd hire a professional production company to do the actual shooting.

I remember the day the project began. It was a Saturday morning. I came by the office, because Paul told me that he was conducting a casting call for three people who would participate in our movie. There were 150 people waiting to be interviewed. It took us most of the day to select our three "actors," and the following Monday Paul was working with the production company we'd hired, following a quick-and-dirty story line I had written on Sunday.

For two weeks, I spent every evening with Paul, reviewing the footage that had been shot and tweaking our plans as we went. At the end of that time, we had a documentary in the can. It was not, I admit, of the caliber of Marc Singer's film, but it was done. And I could check off one more item on my list of lifelong fantasies.

About a year later, Paul and I got together to turn my more ambitious dream into reality: writing, producing, directing, and editing a feature-length film. We didn't have a definitive plot in mind. We were inspired by Robert Rodriguez, who had made a critically acclaimed action film in Mexico on a budget of only $7,000.

We had learned something about filmmaking from our documentary experience, but this time we were going to do all the production work ourselves. The sensible approach would have taken several years of planning and preparation. But we both knew we couldn't commit several years to this goal. So instead we used the *Ready, Fire, Aim* approach.

Again, Paul did all the preliminary work, setting up casting calls, arranging for equipment, and figuring out—very roughly—what our needs would be in terms of people and money. I had hoped to have the script written and edited by the time shooting began, but my business life kept me from completely finishing it. And so, when that first day of shooting arrived, I still had a few hours of work to do on the scene we were about to shoot.

For two weeks, we worked that way. I awoke at 5:30 and started working on the script at 6:30, and we began shooting at 9:30. Paul and I took turns directing the actors. One of my sons did the camera work. Another son did the lighting. Two other young people—Ben, a friend of one of my sons, and Annabelle, the daughter of one of my friends—took care of such things such as sets, costumes, and charting continuity.

We shot half of the movie outdoors and the other half in a friend's apartment, cleaning up at the end of every day so the place wouldn't be in shambles when she got home from work at 6:30.

The truth was that none of us—except for some of the actors—knew what the hell we were doing. I remember seeing my son and his friend Ben sitting in the back of my pickup truck on a break during the first day of shooting and reading a book titled *How to Make a Movie*. "That's how to get something done *Ready, Fire, Aim* style," I thought.

We didn't know how to make a feature-length film, but that didn't stop us from doing it. Paul got us ready, and then we fired even before we knew how to aim. But had we not been willing to do that, I am 100 percent sure the movie would never have been made.

When we finally got the filming done, Paul set to work editing it. When the rough cut was done, I held a very private screening—just my youngest son and two of his cousins. They watched it intently for 90 minutes. When it was over, I asked them what they thought—and I got the following three pithy critiques:

My son: "On a scale of 1 to 10, Dad, I'd have to give that a zero."

His cousin Eaman: "Let me put it to you this way, Uncle Michael: You will never be able to call another movie bad."

His brother Justin: "That's not true. You will be able to say other films are bad. You'll just have to say that your movie was worse."

Clearly, I wouldn't be entering my movie in the Sundance Film Festival. It almost certainly would have been better after sound effects and music were added, but it wasn't going to make me or Paul the next Robert Rodriguez.

Oh well, I thought, who cares? I made a movie—a bad movie—and that's something only one out of a thousand people who have that dream can say.

Since then, I have been considering other small-budget movie projects that will almost certainly be better than my first two—and that level of progress is perfectly satisfactory to me. I like to think of myself as a part-time filmmaker. *Ready, Fire, Aim* has made it possible.

MY FIRST *READY, FIRE, AIM* ATTEMPT TO PRODUCE AN ALBUM

Just this year, I applied *Ready, Fire, Aim* to a new project: producing an album. I got this idea after meeting Joselito, a guitarist and singer who entertains people at a resort development I consult with in Nicaragua. (In my untutored opinion, Joselito sings Spanish ballads better than anybody on the planet.) After having a few too many margaritas at the bar one night, I promised to bring him to New York and make a recording of his music. When I came back a few days later, sober and preoccupied with property-development issues, he reminded me of my promise.

It took six months to secure a visa for Joselito to come to New York. Finding a partner for the project was easy: My son was starting his career in New York as a producer and composer of music.

I blocked out four days on my calendar, and then flew Joselito first-class from Managua to the Big Apple. He had never been on an airplane before, had never been in a high-rise hotel, had never been outside his country, and had never made a recording. Spending those four days with him and my son was a great and memorable experience. And because my son actually knew how to make a good recording, we succeeded in producing what I believe will turn out to be a truly great and beautiful product.

The final work on the album—the aiming of it—is being done as I write this. As with my two films, I am happy to have completed the project, and have no personal need for it to be good or profitable. But from what people are telling me, it may be both.

That's the great thing about using *Ready*, *Fire*, *Aim* to achieve personal goals. You get your reward—the satisfaction—in the doing of the project, not in its outcome. This is how all experiences should be, of course, but it is more difficult to achieve when you have to put profits first, as you do when starting a business.

READY, *FIRE*, *AIM* TO CREATE A SECOND INCOME

I have taken a *Ready*, *Fire*, *Aim* approach with just about every new business I have ever been involved in. For 25 years, I have been either the key person or part of the start-up team of more than a hundred separate enterprises.

I know that it is perfectly possible to start and grow a business by aiming before you fire. And I acknowledge that there are some sorts of businesses where this approach is necessary. But for the great majority of entrepreneurial businesses, *Ready*, *Fire*, *Aim* is the way to go, even when it's a side business intended to produce a second income.

Let me give you one example.

About 12 years ago, I got interested in the rental real estate market. At that time, I had no knowledge of how the business of rental real estate works, but I had a strong feeling that property was about to appreciate in my neck of the woods (South Florida), and I wanted to take advantage of it.

I knew that the smart thing would be to spend many hours studying this industry and then gradually immerse myself in it.

But I didn't have the patience for that, nor did I feel I had the time. The longer I waited, the higher prices were rising, and I knew enough to understand that prices wouldn't escalate forever. The sooner I got in, I figured, the better my investments would be.

I announced to friends and family members that I was looking for property (in case they knew of anything) and promised to pay them finder's fees if they came up with anything.

Next, I made a deal with a real estate broker that would make it easy for me to accomplish my investment goals. She would get paid for her time doing due diligence and would get a split commission on the properties I bought. And then, if she wanted to do it, she would get a fee for managing them.

It took me about two months to get all this going. I started by making phone calls the day I had the idea, and for the next 60 days I talked to everyone I knew in the real estate business and read everything I could about what I was (already) doing.

During that initial period, I bought three properties. All three seemed good on paper. In reality, they were a mixed bag. I made several big mistakes in assessing their value (that I won't make again). I also learned things that I'll never forget about how to write a contract and how to screen rental applications.

What I learned from books and conversations was enough to get me started. But what I learned from experience was the good stuff—true inside stuff that you can pick up only when you are actively involved in a particular business on a day-to-day basis. You can't know it any other way.

Today, I have dozens of rental properties all over the world, ranging from single condominiums to 30-unit apartment complexes, office buildings, and commercial properties. Looking back, I am sure that if I hadn't gotten started right away, I never would have gotten involved in rental real estate at all—and it has turned into a significant source of income for me.

READY, FIRE, AIM ON THE FIRING RANGE

A friend of mine, a successful builder and entrepreneur, told me that when he recently took up skeet shooting as a hobby, he was surprised to discover that "ready, fire, aim"—not "ready, aim, fire"—is the new method of teaching this skill.

"The way they used to teach you was to ready the gun and then aim it a little ahead of the object so you could hit it on the run," he explained. "But now they teach you to take the rifle, ready it against your shoulder, and then bring it up to your eye and shoot. They don't want you to aim. They found that aiming actually decreases accuracy, because the brain is already programmed to make the adjustment for movement. And by trying to aim, you are trying to manually replicate what the brain does automatically." People who are learning this new method are becoming better shooters more quickly.

I found out that Bob Knopf, an instructor with the National Wing and Clay Shooting School, advises students to "focus on the target and not the gun barrel or bead. Point, don't aim." He says that "aiming slows your swing and causes you to shoot behind."[1]

I asked Jason, my research assistant, to see if there is any good supporting science behind this notion. Here's what he learned:

> If the "no aim" approach to skeet shooting seems counterintuitive, it might be easier to understand if you look at some other activities you do every day that require speed and accuracy, but don't require much concentration.
>
> Think about it. You can pour liquid into a glass without consciously "aiming." You can change channels on your TV remote without "aiming" your finger.
>
> You can do these things because human beings have a sense of "proprioception," which involves the flow of information between sensory organs—such as the eyes, inner ears, and skin—and the brain.
>
> You are not conscious of it, but your mind, since the day you were born, has been storing all the complex coordinations made between your mind and body that allow you to interact with the world around you. Without this sense, you couldn't write, hold things, walk . . . do anything.
>
> Catching a ball, riding a bike, or shooting a rifle might take more practice to get right—but it still has everything to do with establishing and strengthening the appropriate connections between the brain, the body, and the eyes.

The idea of investing in rental real estate was part of a bigger idea: creating additional streams of income so I would never be completely dependent on my main consulting business.

Since I was devoting most of my time to my consulting, I couldn't do the groundwork myself. So, in every case, I found a partner to work with—usually a friend or colleague whose business acumen (or potential) I admired—and gave my partner a very attractive deal: "I will take care of funding the business and provide advice to help you run and grow it, and you will earn equity in it by doing all the work."

And that's how it worked.

I created the game plan—usually a four-page business proposal much like the one outlined at the end of Chapter 12. My partner did almost everything else. I would meet with my various partners relatively frequently at first (usually weekly), and I would answer their questions and give them suggestions and contacts. As things moved along, we would meet less frequently. Seldom did these meetings last more than two or three hours. Most of them were done during lunch.

Right now, I have an interest in about a dozen income-producing businesses, including EarlytoRise.com, which has grown from zero to more than $20 million in less than seven years. These side businesses provide me with an income that is greater than I need and equity that I will probably never tap into. Moreover, they are independent businesses that have their own unique economic characteristics. Together, they provide my business-investment portfolio with the kind of diversification that I could never expect from a single business, even though my main consulting business is now, in itself, very large and reasonably well balanced.

CHAPTER EIGHTEEN

A QUICK REVIEW OF THE PROBLEMS, CHALLENGES, AND OPPORTUNITIES FACED BY THE STAGE TWO ENTREPRENEUR

Starting a business is great fun and very rewarding. But only a very small percentage of the population of dreamers ever accomplishes it.

Getting a business beyond that first million—to Stage Two (with revenues from $1 million to $10 million)—is an even rarer achievement. But if you follow the program I outlined for Stage One entrepreneurs earlier in this book, you will be able to do it. And if you follow the program for Stage Two entrepreneurs that I just outlined, you will be able to get your business to the next level—Stage Three (with revenues from $10 million to $50 million)—relatively quickly.

Growing your business from $1 million to $10 million as a Stage Two entrepreneur is enriching from every perspective. You will make more income. You will start to acquire equity. And you will be able to share your growing wealth with key employees.

And if you know a few secrets and learn a few tricks, Stage Two will also be easier. Being faster and more enriching and easier, it can't help but be more fun too—which makes this stage of entrepreneurial growth in many ways the best of all of them.

Here are some of the most important ideas about Stage Two entrepreneurship:

- Stage Two begins when the growth you have been enjoying from selling your first lead product ends. Some entrepreneurs make the mistake of assuming their first great success will go on forever. Accepting the fact that it won't early on while sales are still strong gives you a planning advantage.
- Let your key people know that when sales slow, things will change. The business will no longer be as simple as it was. The big difference will be in the number of products you will be marketing. Stage Two growth is stimulated by the development and marketing of a profusion of products.
- Don't make the mistake of shifting into Stage Two until you are ready for it. Stage One is about selling a single product as aggressively as possible in the market that is available to you. Take full advantage of this opportunity. Become an expert at selling. Make sure your key employees understand the process too, because when you get to Stage Two you will want to delegate much of this responsibility to them.
- When you have exhausted the potential of your first product, call your people together and announce your next major company-wide goal: becoming very good at creating, testing, and marketing lots of new products. Explain how this growth will benefit them. Don't make specific promises, because they may be impossible to fulfill. But persuade them that growth means the opportunity for a better, more interesting work life and more income for them.
- The transition between Stage One and Stage Two is a chance for you to become a better, more sophisticated leader. Being able to visualize the future and communicate that vision will no longer be optional. During Stage Two, it is a necessary skill.
- Learn how to create efficient four-page business plans. Teach your key employees how to create them too.
- Introduce your employees to innovation and speed as the two essential skills of Stage Two growth. Discuss why they are

necessary. Explore how they will change the way you do business. Establish them as corporate values.

- Organize your business to deal with both front-end and back-end product development. If appropriate, identify two separate creative teams. Put your strongest marketers to work on the front-end products. Establish a corporate culture that values both front-end and back-end efforts.
- Teach your front-end creative team the concept of tipping-point marketing. Require them to keep track of trends and think forward, always focusing on the customer's needs, wants, and desires. Set high creative standards. Challenge the team to develop at least one breakthrough promotion per marketing season.
- Understand the difference between reinventing good ideas and slavishly knocking off successful products. Instill a sense of intellectual pride among your creative players.
- Rid your business of the idea that being second or third in the market is bad. Focus everyone's attention on developing good and useful products. Stay profitable, but generate growth through a proliferation of first-rate ideas.
- Understand how to run effective brainstorming sessions. Establish time limits. Set standards, rules, and specific goals. Establish a culture of creative equality.
- Understand how the "magic product cube" works. Use it to quickly identify all the many ways you can create new products. Incorporate price, product type, and the idea of a unique selling proposition (USP) in your calculations.
- Use the magic product cube to establish the potential for new product types, but don't follow it slavishly. Instead, respect the experience you have gained. Encourage your creative people to think intuitively.
- Become an advocate of innovation. Teach your people that the natural law of business is to grow or die.
- Understand the difference between distress and eustress. Diminish the first. Enjoy the latter.
- To preserve moments of genius during product-development sessions, use a tape recorder and insist on the 24-hour rule.
- Learn the danger of going too far afield with new-product development. Stick with the "one step removed" rule.

- Teach your people what *80% of G = IV²* means. Make it an indelible part of their thinking.
- Learn to love new ideas and hate sluggishness. Teach your key people to have the same feelings.
- Understand why your existing customer base will always be your best market.
- Take advantage of the relationships you have with your customers by pummeling them with back-end offers.
- Figure out how to test your ideas as cheaply and quickly as possible.
- Make direct marketing an integral part of your back-end strategy.
- Deepen the relationships you have with your customers by communicating with them more frequently and in more depth. Use the Internet to make that economically feasible.
- Make your people feel comfortable as innovators by establishing the concept of accelerating acceptable failures.
- Understand the effectiveness and efficiency of *Ready, Fire, Aim.* Make it a regular part of everything you do.
- Understand what a good idea is. Teach your people to be humble and let the market dictate what is good, bad, and indifferent.
- Know how to make ordinary ideas good and good ideas great.
- Rid yourself of the desire for perfection.
- Teach yourself how to avoid getting bogged down by little chores.
- Understand that taking action, even incorrect action, is often better than doing nothing and waiting. Make the process of taking quick action ubiquitous, especially among your product-development people.
- Remember, it's *Ready, Fire, Aim*, not *Fire at Will.* There are skills involved in getting a good idea ready for action. Learn them. Practice them.
- Do you know why only fools stay positive in the face of serious doubt? If not, find out.
- Before launching a new product, ask and answer the following seven critical questions:
  1. Is it a good idea?
  2. Does it feel like a good idea?
  3. Is it economically feasible?

4. Can I afford to test it?

5. Do I know what has to be done?

6. Do I have the people to do it?

7. Do I have a Plan B or an exit strategy?

- Learn how to create a *Ready, Fire, Aim* business plan. Use it every time you create a new product. Make sure your plan:
  - Is no longer than four pages.
  - Includes rough financial projections.
  - Identifies critical tasks.
  - Identifies key people.
  - Ties tasks to dates.
  - Answers each of the seven critical questions.
- Does your marketing team understand the importance of brevity? If not, teach them.
- Learn the trick of contriving realistic projections quickly. Teach it to your top marketing protégés.
- Know how to locate and manage champions, workhorses, and superstars. To be effective in Stage Two growth, you will need them all.
- Understand the signs of procrastination. Don't fall victim to it yourself, and don't allow others to.
- Don't waste your time trying to hoard your good ideas. Recognize that if they are good, someone else is already onto them, not just you. Putting good ideas into action will make the difference. Make speed a priority.
- Read the story about incremental degradation in the candy company. Tell it to your people. When they have a full comprehension of it, introduce them to the idea of incremental augmentation.
- Do you know why you can't really measure the value of incremental improvements? If not, find out.
- Become an expert at assessing success quickly. Know when to play your cards and when to fold them.
- Understand when it pays to reduce product costs and when you shouldn't try.
- Become skillful at reducing costs while increasing quality.
- Do you know the difference between the Golden Rule and the Rule of Gold? Do you know which one to follow?

- Cultivate a sharing culture in your business, especially among your product-development and marketing people. Teach them why hoarding doesn't pay.
- Make sure your salespeople understand the foolishness of going for short-term money. Teach them to believe in lifetime value.
- Learn to recognize hoarders and avoid doing business with them.
- Adopt the maxim "If it ain't broke, fix it." Teach your employees why that works in business.
- Be aware of the costs of incremental augmentation, especially the strain it puts on your best production people. Find ways to relieve that strain without lessening your commitment to quality.
- Determine how often improvements should be made for each of your products. Set up a schedule and keep to it.
- Make it a habit to speak to your customers about the improvements you make. If at all possible, take full advantage of the Internet to communicate with them.
- Figure out how sales-oriented you are. Make a commitment to change your thinking if it needs changing. In particular, learn the truth behind the three most common myths about sales and marketing:
  1. Wants and needs.
  2. Fair value.
  3. What good businesspeople really do.
- Develop and execute a three-part marketing plan:
  1. Selling your product to more people.
  2. Selling more products to your customers.
  3. Charging more for your products.
- Take my *Ready, Fire, Aim* crash course in marketing, including all of the following lessons:
  - Your customers don't care about you or your business. They care about themselves.
  - A small portion of your customer base is giving you the lion's share of your corporate profits.
  - Understand why your customers buy from you.
  - Almost every sales transaction begins with the process of generating leads.
  - Learn multichannel marketing.
  - Always follow the Golden Rule of Marketing.

- Understand the Secret of the Four-Legged Stool.
- Understand that customer complaints and objections are the key to better selling.
- Maintain a "no dead ends" policy regarding your products.
- Take advantage of customer inertia.
- Learn how to intelligently apply the 80/20 Rule.
- Understand the unique selling proposition (USP) of every product.
- Never lose your marketing edge.
- Understand the Secret of the "Core Complex."
- Practice reciprocity with your customers.
- Be confident and enthusiastic when you sell.
- Don't push or bribe your customers.
- Become a master of the buying frenzy. Understand why customers really buy your products, and let them enjoy most what they truly like about the buying experience.
- For every product line, determine:
  - How strong the buying frenzy will be.
  - How long it will last.
- Understand how to apply the *Ready, Fire, Aim* methodology to any goal you have in life—business or personal.

PART FOUR

STAGE THREE:

ADOLESCENCE

CHAPTER NINETEEN

MAKING THE STAGE THREE TRANSFORMATION

If you are successful in taking your company to or near the $10 million mark, you may one day feel that it has somehow gotten beyond you.

It has been growing by leaps and bounds, but so have the problems. So far, ingenuity and determination have kept things together, but now the entrepreneurial skills that helped you start the business no longer serve you. Despite everything you know and everything you do, problems are mounting. You may sometimes feel that the market itself has changed and you have been left behind.

Your key people, who were so helpful in getting your business started and pushing it through the second stage, are now too busy to handle this proliferation of problems. When you ask them for explanations, they get frustrated. "We are neck deep in marketing challenges," they tell you. "We will get to these problems, but there are things we have to do first."

You may find you have trouble getting the reports you ask for. The routine numbers—the numbers you've been asking for since day one—are still coming to you regularly, but you can't get any new data.

> **STAGE THREE: ADOLESCENCE—$10 MILLION TO $50 MILLION IN REVENUE**
>
> Main Problem: Your systems are strained, and customers are noticing.
> Main Challenge: Turning the chaos into order.
> Main Opportunity: Learning how to establish useful protocols and manage processes and procedures.
> **Additional Skill Needed: Running your business with just three or four simple management reports.**

And you need that data to analyze the lifetime value of your customers and assess future opportunities.

Lacking those reports, you are pushing ahead, flying by the seat of your pants. Because you have built a company that is good at innovation, some of your new-product launches are working. But an increasing number of them are failing, and you have neither the data nor the intuition to figure out why.

In other parts of the business, things are getting out of hand. Customer service problems are mounting. Product development is slowing down. And profit opportunities are being discarded because nobody has any spare time.

You have the sense that everything is moving too fast and that if you don't do something significant quickly, things will fall apart. Like an engineer whose train is running at full pressure, you are looking at the gauges and wondering how much longer the frame will hold.

THE SECOND MAJOR TRANSFORMATION

All the vibrations you are feeling are real. And you are right to be worried about them. But they are also normal for a business that has been growing as quickly as yours has. Speeding up the process of innovation has accelerated your growth and changed your business into something it has never been before. Unless you respond to these changes, the problems will only increase.

But the good news is that it is relatively easy to get the train running smoothly again.

To get through this second transition, you need to introduce more structure to the way you do things. The *Ready, Fire, Aim* approach that got you this far so fast needs some modifications.

Specifically, you need to create stronger controls. Better accounting procedures. More rigid customer service protocols. And more efficient operations. To develop and implement these controls, you will need to retrain your key people. You may also need to hire outside executives for the first time in a long while—perhaps even a few MBAs.

During its first stage of development, your business had one primary product and one primary function: selling that product. As founder and CEO, you drove those sales. Everyone around you, however capable they were, understood that their job was to support you in that effort. If there were people who couldn't support your goal, you replaced them with people who did.

During its second stage of development, your business became a production machine. By being quick and flexible, you were able to develop and sell more products in a month than you used to be able to sell in a year. This stressed everything to the limit—and now it is time for a change.

Stage Two is usually a period when lots of new employees are added to the payroll. A few of those people report to you, but most are directed by others. This has created, for the first time, a serious communication gap in your company. Some of your employees understand what you understand and want what you want, but many have totally different ideas.

Twice removed from your influence, protocols and procedures are changing in ways that do not always mesh with your desires. But because you understand the danger of trying to micromanage your subordinates, you learn to tolerate these inconsistencies. You continue to communicate as well and as clearly as you can to the six or eight people who report directly to you, but you notice an increasing disconnect between your intentions and what happens.

The most important disconnect has to do with the priority you had established to make sure every customer would be handled with the utmost of care and consideration. (And that includes giving your customers the best possible chance to buy as many of your back-end products as they might want to.) But because of the communication gaps and the growing complexity of operations, customer service problems are mounting faster than you, or any of your key people, can seem to manage them.

Walking Through the Looking Glass

So it's time for a change. And this one, like the last one, will challenge you to learn new secrets and develop new skills. It will also challenge your emotional flexibility, because the kind of transformation that's needed now is one that runs contrary to the instinct that has made you so successful to this point.

I'm talking about a transformation into a business that looks and feels a little more *corporate* than the business you have now. As a successful entrepreneur, you may feel uncomfortable with that kind of change, but you will have to get used to it if you want those problems to go away. It is also possible that you will have to bring in some professional managers—people who understand conventional corporate structures and know how to organize employees and processes to produce an efficient organization.

Yes, it's time to redo the company's organizational chart and establish functions and functionaries, just like all the Fortune 500 companies have. Much has been written in business magazines about the need to keep big companies small. Maintaining your capacity to develop new products and marketing campaigns is and always will be first on your leadership agenda. But right now, at least until you get the engine reconfigured, you will have to give lots of attention to having your business managed professionally—even if the sound of it gives you the creeps.

I have spent my entire career in small business. The largest business I have ever been associated with has revenues of less than $500 million a year. I have all the typical entrepreneurial aversions to corporate culture. I don't like people telling me what to do, and that's especially true when I've hired those people.

But I've learned that when a business I'm growing reaches a certain level, I make much better decisions when I work with corporate types. The corporate executive is always wondering what can go wrong with a good idea. I don't want to spend any time thinking that way. It's much easier and better to have someone else do that for me, to listen to what they say, and then to move ahead.

Making your business more organized will not slow it down as long as you develop your communication skills so you can convey your vision to everyone in the business, including all those people you will never get to speak to except at holiday parties.

HOW TO CHANGE YOUR BUSINESS THE RIGHT WAY

Corporate executives are good at solving problems. But they are bad at creating growth. Give them the latitude and support they need to do their jobs. But make sure they understand that your job is to keep them busy by creating new problems.

Don't allow your professional managers to dictate policy to you. Ask them to help you achieve your goals. If you see that they are bent on implementing foolish, counterproductive ideas, fire them—but don't put "yes" people or marketing mavens in their place. They are called managers for a reason. Let them do the managing.

Understand and accept your differing personalities.

- You like selling, innovation, and speed. They don't.
- You like *Ready, Fire, Aim.* They like planning and preparation.
- You like cocktail-napkin guesstimates. They like 500-line budgets.
- You believe in accelerating failure. They believe in avoiding it.
- You like your freedom. They want to control you.
- They love consistency. You think it's the "hobgoblin of little minds."

In short, professional managers have ideas and instincts that are contrary to yours. So why am I suggesting that you bring them in? Because your business can't continue to grow without them.

To get to the next level, you have to solve the big problems you've been having. And the solutions need to be foundational, not temporary patches that will fall off over time. To be able to handle this third stage of your company's growth—from $10 million to $50 million in revenues—you need to have all of your operational activities running smoothly. That can be done pretty easily if you are willing to let these people help you. That's what they are trained to do. Give them the tools they need, and let them go to work.

WHAT YOU NEED TO DO

A good place to start is to create an organizational chart; but you can't do that properly until you figure out how things are running now. If your business is like most entrepreneurial businesses that are bordering on Stage Three, it is likely that—regardless of what the specific job titles may be—your current organization looks something like Figure 19.1.

This very busy way of arranging things has worked for you so far—or so you think. But it is clear from the stress you are feeling that you have become your company's major production bottleneck rather than its main instigator. The traditional way to change that is by establishing a traditional corporate structure that looks something like Figure 19.2.

Putting this new structure up on the wall will not make any difference if you don't respect it. Respecting it means letting your managers run their areas of responsibility. A sure sign that you are violating this structure: One of *their* subordinates is regularly speaking to you.

In addition to giving your managers authority that is equal to their responsibility, you should be spending 80 percent of your time with your marketing manager and only 20 percent with all the others. There are two reasons for this:

1. Marketing is and always will be your main job.
2. You know—and should always know—much more about marketing than anything else.

Sit down with your corporate managers and explain your objectives. Tell them that you will give them all the support you can, so long as

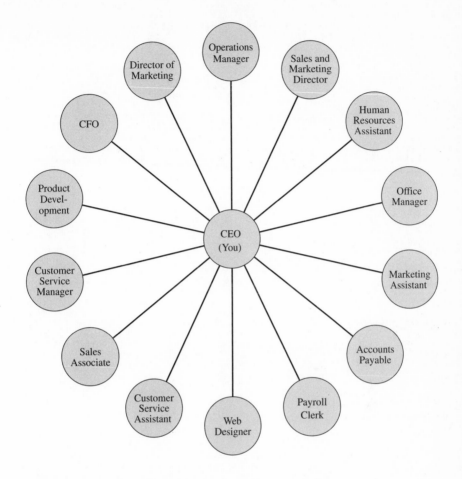

FIGURE 19.1 Structure of Many Businesses Bordering on Stage Three

Source: Richard Schefren.

they support your goals. Meet with each one individually to work out how often you should meet and what kind of reporting you would like from them. Except for the marketing manager, you shouldn't be meeting with any of them more than once a week, and those meetings shouldn't last more than 30 minutes.

You may find that you have strong instincts about operations and accounting. Give those instincts less credit than you do your marketing ideas. Remember that you have no experience whatsoever managing a business of this size. The person you hired to be your chief operating officer (COO) has that experience, so let it be used.

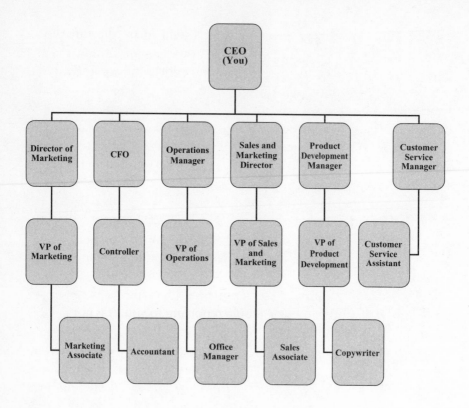

FIGURE 19.2 Traditional Corporate Structure

Set objectives with your operations managers that dovetail with your goals. Discuss what information you need and what information might be needed by others. Design reports, but err on the side of economy. You don't want to waste their valuable and expensive time running calculations that will never be studied. If they are going to go to the trouble of providing you with information, read it and respond.

The Rule of Three

After years of getting both too few and too many reports from operational managers, I have settled on what I think is the right number. That number is three.

The idea is that each manager should be required to give you only three numbers every month. He may give other people more information, if that is needed, but should send only three numbers to you.

These three numbers represent what I believe are the three most important indicators of a manager's work, the three measurements that best indicate his department's progress toward its ultimate goals.

When you speak to a profit center manager, for example, you will want to know revenues, profits, and—depending on the business— deferred income or inventory. From customer service managers, you will want to know the number of problems addressed, the percentage that were solved, and the amount of time it took to solve them. When you get a report from a fulfillment manager, you will want to know how many products were delivered, how long it took to deliver each one, and how much it cost. And from a marketing manager, you will want to know how many new customers they have acquired, how much those customers are spending with you, and how many refunds they've had to process.

I recommend limiting these reports to three apiece, because you will probably have six or seven people reporting to you. It is not feasible to pay attention to more than 21 numbers each month, so why try?

If you want to dig deeper than that, you can simply call them up and ask them more questions. You're likely to want to get into more detail with your marketing manager, because you will understand his numbers better and can often push the conversation further by asking for more data. But for the operational aspects of the business, your concise, three-number reports are usually all you'll need. They'll give you the vital statistics—and those will be enough to stimulate the conversations you'll want to have.

Reading six or seven reports, however short, each month is not my idea of fun, but I don't believe it's possible to lead a business through Stage Three unless you do. I have had partners—many partners—who felt it was okay to ask for operational reports and never read them. But doing that sends a very bad, very destructive message. It tells your operational managers that the work they do isn't as important as the work you do—that their work is so unimportant, in fact, you don't need to pay attention to it.

If I were an operational manager reporting to someone who felt that way, I'd have a hard time caring much about the business. I might try to ignore the insult and carry on, but I would find it increasingly difficult to care about achieving the company's goals. If the owner of the company didn't think my work mattered, why shouldn't I just ease up and take it easy? What would be the worst thing that could happen? That things would go south and he would realize he was wrong?

The only thing worse than an entrepreneur who neglects his managing executives is one who pays attention to them only when they err. Again, I have known many business owners who behaved this way—and what usually happened was that their neglected and abused managers became very good at covering up mistakes or blaming them on others.

Are You a "Big Idea" Person?

Entrepreneurs who make these mistakes usually rationalize them by telling you that they are Big Idea people. What they mean is that they see themselves as creative geniuses and all their operational executives as drones.

In my role as a consultant, I have their same inclination to focus on marketing ideas, but I make an effort to give operational issues equal treatment. I don't give those issues equal time—and I've explained the reason for that—but I do accord them the same level of respect. And when I talk about them, I make sure that everybody listening knows I care.

To get your business through and beyond the $50 million barrier, you need a well-balanced organization that is not hamstrung by chronic and acute operational problems. To eliminate those problems after they have arisen and keep them in check, you need a staff of very competent, very experienced professionals.

All of the professionals who are working in accounting, data management, and customer service determine how outsiders feel about your business. Many of them are the only human contact your customers or vendors have with your company. Unless their departments are well managed, your business is at risk.

HOW TO MANAGE A $100 MILLION BUSINESS

I defined Stage Three as the level at which a business grows from $10 million to $50 million in revenues. But the management structures and systems you put in place now will carry your business to $100 million and beyond. Essentially, I am talking about developing an operational core for your business that is rationally organized and professionally managed. The marketing and product-development aspects of your business should still be run entrepreneurially—with innovation and speed as core values, and *Ready, Fire, Aim* as the primary growth methodology.

It's for that reason that I recommend you organize your growing business accordingly, with your operational functions grouped together under a single chief operating officer (COO) and your marketing and product-development activities organized by product lines as separate profit centers. Refer to Figure 19.3 for an example of this recommended organizational chart and structure.

When you are doing only $10 million in sales, you will probably have far fewer executives than this chart would indicate. Many of those roles will be taken up by the same people. But as the business grows, the

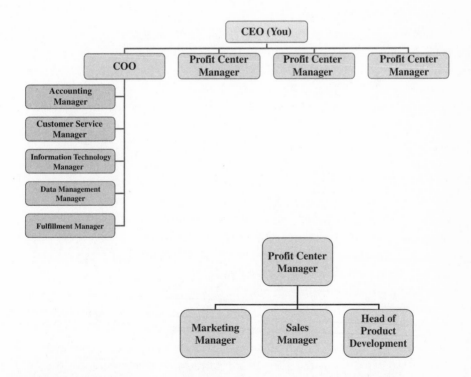

FIGURE 19.3 Recommended Organizational Structure for Businesses at Stage Three and Beyond

responsibilities will probably break down this way. Having the skeleton of your future business established now will make things easier later.

One advantage of this type of structure is that no one person—including you—has more than six people reporting to him. A second benefit is that 80 percent of your time can still be devoted to marketing and product development. A third benefit is that the operational part of the business will be run by operational pros. A fourth benefit is that the future growth of the company will be unimpeded by operations, because profit center managers will be reporting to the CEO (you), not the COO.

I have used this structure, more or less, with every entrepreneurial business I have worked with in the past 10 or 15 years. What I like about it is its flexibility: Once put into place, it can accommodate continued growth. So long as they communicate with the COO, the profit center managers are free to pump out new products and create new sales. Given fair warning, the COO can staff up the operational divisions to accommodate that growth.

Sometimes profit center managers are not happy with the support they are getting from the centralized core. Usually, the complaint is that they believe they can get better, faster, or cheaper service from an outside vendor. In the most successful businesses that I work with, we deal with such questions by following a free-market-based management style—which is to say, we tell them, "Except for cash controls and legal review, you are free to move outside if you want."

We tell them that, but we also warn them that they will probably be better off relying on corporate services for their operational needs. New vendors may fill their heads with happy ideas about cutting costs and speeding up transactions, but such changes generally result in more expense, more wasted time, and a big increase in stress for everybody.

There are exceptions, and that is why we prefer not to dictate policy, except for cash flow and legal review. But as a general rule I've found that a well-managed internal staff is the way to go for anything and everything that affects the service the customer receives.

There are other structures that would work. This is just one that has worked for me. The important point is that Stage Three is the time when you have to restructure your entrepreneurial company into a professional corporation. Those changes will contradict much of what you have been doing to stimulate growth, so you must find some way to (1) separate the growth side of your business from the control side of your business and (2) connect the two so they can both function to support one another as you grow.

Of course, no structure or system can possibly be better than the person who is in charge of it. To change your business for Stage Three growth, you have to:

1. Change yourself.
2. And then change or hire great people to run your business operations.

I'll tell you how in the next two chapters.

CHAPTER TWENTY

CHANGING INTO A
CORPORATE LEADER

Many businesses never get beyond Stage Two because the entrepreneurs who grew them refuse to make the personal changes needed to accommodate the next level of growth.

Steve Carter, my first boss in the publishing industry, was that way. A true entrepreneur, he made his first fortune selling tractors to the Russians during the height of the Cold War. When I went to work for him, he had two businesses: a trading company that was selling American technology overseas and a publishing business that was reporting on international commerce.

I worked for the publishing company. (I told you a little bit about that experience in Chapter 4.) And it was apparent, right from the beginning, that Steve was a persistent entrepreneur. I remember how he would worm our way into international meetings and embassy functions and, once inside, force me to walk around with him, interrupting clusters of important businesspeople and diplomats, pushing our newsletters—literally pushing them at those people—to garner subscriptions.

Steve loved selling. And almost every conversation I had with him was about selling. This was very effective in getting our business to a certain level; but we had trouble growing it beyond that point, because we were spending money as fast as we were bringing it in. Steve wasn't interested in managing the business. He left that up to me. But I was an English literature major just back from two years in Africa with the Peace Corps. What did I know about managing a growing business?

Eventually, all of Steve's businesses failed because he was not able to make that personal transition. He liked owning his companies, but he could have made much more money over the long run if he had continued doing what he did best—selling.

Steve was good at starting companies, but he could not lead them through their growth stages because he refused to grow himself. He hated big corporations and disdained the executives who worked for them. "They work for well-known companies, but they've never done what I've done," he told me one evening after being snubbed by a clutch of Fortune 500 vice presidents at an embassy party.

He was right—and that made me both proud of and sorry for him.

I have worked with dozens of entrepreneurs since then, and many of them share Steve's disdain for corporate culture. I share their loathing for bureaucracy, but I have learned from experience how necessary corporate structure is once a business reaches a certain level.

In other words, if you want your business to grow beyond being a $10 million entrepreneurial candy store, you have to learn to love both numbers and also the people who love numbers.

You have to do that and a whole lot more.

FROM ENTREPRENEUR TO *INC.* 500 CEO: WHAT IT TAKES

Running a growing Stage Three business takes at least six skills that are not needed to start and grow a modest-sized entrepreneurial business. Those are:

1. Controlling operations
2. Managing your managers
3. Communicating your vision
4. Networking for joint ventures
5. Negotiating deals
6. Being good at hiring

CONTROLLING OPERATIONS

I covered much of this topic in the preceding chapter. The secret to controlling operations as your business continues to grow is to (1) structure it for growth and (2) hire professional managers.

My preferred structure, as I said, is one that keeps you at the helm but frees you up from micromanaging operations so you can focus on product development and marketing. The best way to do that is to break your business into two parts: an operations core that is controlled by a chief operating officer (COO) and a group of profit centers run by salaried "intrapreneurs" who report to you.

What's an intrapreneur?

Entrepreneurs do not make good employees. They don't like working for other people. They don't like following directions. And they are unhappy with their compensation, no matter what it is, because they believe they could be making more if they were on their own, running their own businesses.

If you manage to hire an entrepreneur, he will eventually leave you. Usually, it will be when the profit center he is in charge of is doing very well. And if he can possibly get away with it, he will take that business with him.

Intrapreneurs are an entirely different type of person. Like entrepreneurs, they like being in charge. But, unlike entrepreneurs, they don't mind taking direction (as long as it is suggested and not dictated), and they are reluctant to go off on their own so long as they feel that they are being reasonably compensated.

The only chance you have of hiring entrepreneurs is when they are down on their luck. Often, that is because they have lost touch with the market. In other words, if you do manage to persuade an entrepreneur to work for you, you will be hiring someone who may not be able to do what you are hiring him to do. And if he does do it, he will eventually take it away from you.

Intrapreneurs are easy to find. They are entry-level and middle-level people whom you hire as employees. When they start working for you, they don't realize that they have what it takes to build your business. They are simply happy to have a good job, and they distinguish themselves immediately by their positive attitude and work ethic.

In the next chapter, I will show you how to find these natural superstars, how to mentor them so they become capable of growing your business for you, and how to treat and compensate them so they stay with you.

The thing to remember is that you need two kinds of people to take your business from $10 million to $50 million to $100 million and beyond: professional managers to run your operations, and intrapreneurs to run your profit centers.

MANAGING YOUR MANAGERS

To head up your operational group, you must find a very competent, very professional person who will be both flexible enough to embrace your vision for growth and also strict enough to institute and manage the systems needed to run all your operations. Individuals who are capable of doing this are hard to come by, but they can be found if you look in the right places. The best COO types that I have found have been working successfully as business managers—often in accounting, but also in other operational areas—for mostly larger, established corporations. You can find them through the conventional routes: placing ads in trade magazines, working with executive brokerages, and putting the word out at trade shows and conferences.

Because you want flexibility and loyalty from your COO, you have to take time during the hiring process to find out whether you have a good rapport with the candidate. Don't make the mistake of thinking that because you need someone strong you should hire someone who likes to say no to you. The best personality is someone flexible enough to say yes on the big issues and no on the small ones.

This brings up the subject of your own flexibility. Having been the chief cook and bottle washer since your company's inception, you may have gotten away with dictating the details. And you may have done a good job of it so far. But as your business grows to $50 million and then to $75 million and then to $100 million and beyond, you won't want to be dealing with the hundreds of smaller decisions that continuously crop up. To run a business that has 100 or 500 or more employees, you have to be willing to let your managers make the management decisions. You tell them what you ultimately want done . . . but let them figure out how to do it.

If you stick to the simplified reports I suggested in the preceding chapter and limit your meetings with each manager to once a month (or once a week in the beginning), it will be difficult for you to micromanage. But you also have to develop the mental flexibility to accept the fact that there are many ways to skin a cat. Just because it's not your way doesn't mean it is not a good way.

It is also important to curb your instinct to correct mistakes. And *never* correct your managers in front of their people. If you discover a mistake during a group meeting, resist the temptation to express your dismay then and there. Ask the responsible manager to stay behind and talk about it in person, just the two of you.

I've found that criticism is more effective when it is expressed after something positive has been said, and when it is phrased as a question rather than a declaration. Instead of saying, "I think it was wrong to spend $16 on that cog," it is better to ask, "Why did you think it was necessary to spend $16 on that cog?" Phrasing your concern as a question does not obscure its clarity or diminish its force, but it does allow the other person to respond positively rather than defensively. And, occasionally, you will avoid embarrassing yourself because, occasionally, you will get a good answer.

COMMUNICATING YOUR VISION

Because you are so far removed from the rank and file during Stage Three of your business's development, it is highly likely that your most important ideas about how the business should be run will be muted or blunted or distorted as they work their way down the communication chain. Since it is imperative for everyone to understand your main ideas about the business, you must develop good corporate communication skills. These, like corporate management skills, are different from the skills needed when the business was smaller.

One way to get your messages across is to spend a lot of time walking around your offices and talking to people. This is a practice that is highly recommended by some keep-it-small business gurus. It is not, however, something that I would recommend.

Having conversations with your subordinates' subordinates is likely to cause more confusion than clarity. And it might also undermine your managers' authority, especially if rank-and-file employees feel they can skip over their bosses to talk to you.

I recommend a more formal approach: sending out regular letters to all your employees to update them on major changes in the business and upcoming plans, and explaining how these changes and plans reflect your overall vision.

This was recently done by a client of mine, and the results were immediate and impressive. After about 10 years of speaking to employees only once a year at the company's annual holiday party, he began writing monthly memos that were 80 percent upbeat information and 20 percent articulations of core corporate beliefs.

Each of his memos is ostensibly an update of some of the company's recent accomplishments, but he also makes some "observations" about "how our business works" and how it shouldn't. By expressing his thoughts and feelings so abstractly and benignly, he gets his message across without offending anyone or creating controversy or resentment.

With your profit-center teams, you can (and should) communicate more frequently and more directly. Establish regular (weekly or monthly) marketing and product-development brainstorming sessions, and use them to teach principles and practices that you have been thinking about lately.

Again, you must leave the management of the profit centers to the profit-center managers. Your role is to act as a sort of expert consultant. Make suggestions. Point out problems, but let the team figure out the answers.

Never use interoffice e-mail to criticize, condemn, or complain. Those difficult conversations must be had in person. E-mail is an excellent vehicle for good news, though, because it is fast and can be widely disseminated. And every once in a while, try a personal, handwritten note to your key people, reminding them of why you trust them and are counting on them to continue to build your business.

HOW TO WRITE A GREAT BUSINESS MEMO

When writing memos, there are certain basic rules, which, if followed, will make your communications clearer and stronger. These include:

- Before you begin writing, figure out what you want to say.
- Don't try to say too much. Each memo should focus on one and only one topic.
- Begin each memo with a statement that identifies why it is important. Explain why the memo matters to the business, and also explain, if at all possible, how it will benefit the reader.
- Keep your paragraphs short, and limit each paragraph to a single idea.
- Write clear, concise sentences, and make sure each one expresses a single thought.
- End the memo with a recap of why your message is important to the company and how it will benefit those reading it.

For all of your written business communications, the bottom line is this: Good writing is good thinking clearly expressed. Think well. Write simply. Avoid ornamentation.

NETWORKING FOR JOINT VENTURES

When your business reaches a certain size, you will find that you will be doing lots of networking with colleagues—and even competitors—that could lead to joint-venture opportunities. Some of these opportunities will be substantial, and some will be small. Some will dovetail well with what you are already doing, and some will not.

The most important consideration when considering a joint venture is not what your partner might be bringing to the table or how much your company will benefit, but what the long-term potential of the relationship is.

When I meet with a new colleague who is bright and ambitious, I usually ask, "How can we work together?" even if I have doubts about whether there is any chance we can. My goal is not to make an immediately profitable deal. It is to start a relationship with a good person who might, at some time, provide me and/or a business I'm involved in with a substantial opportunity to profit.

I feel this way because my personal business goal is always to work less and gain more in the future. Taking a long-term view of business deals is a smart strategy, because it results in long-term growth. I am happy to make less on a deal—or even make nothing at all—so long as I think something good may be coming to me later.

Lots of businesspeople I know don't agree with this point of view. They believe that good business deals are those where they make more than their joint-venture partners. In making deals, they like to push for the best deal they can. They think that proves they are superior negotiators, but all it really does is plant a bad seed in fertile ground.

My rule for joint-venture deals is that I'd rather be the screwee than the screwer. I don't make deals that put me in a position to lose money—but I am happy to break even if it makes my joint-venture partner happy, because I know that the more happy partners I have, the more good deals will come to me.

NEGOTIATING DEALS

Tons have been written about the art of negotiating, and when I was a young man, I read those books and was impressed with the many tough and clever ways there are to get what you want. I was never very good at using those techniques, though, because I never liked the way I felt when I was doing it. But I did admire them. And I admired people who were natural negotiators, because they seemed capable of getting just about anything they wanted out of life. I, on the other hand, felt like I was taking what was given.

That's the way I felt then. Now I'm glad I never mastered those techniques, because I have discovered a much simpler, more elegant, and immensely more effective negotiating tactic that anyone, even a timid person like me, can quickly master.

I learned how to do it by watching BB, the founder and CEO of the biggest company I currently work with, do it dozens of times over many years. It has two very simple parts. It goes like this:

Business colleague: "So, what do you think it's worth?"
BB: "I don't know, what do you think it's worth?"
Business colleague: "I was thinking maybe $500,000."

At this point, BB responds in one of two ways. Either he says, "That seems fair to me," or he says, "Gee, I don't think I can afford that."

That's it. Nothing more. He has been making deals like this for as long as I've known him, and I have to say he is the best negotiator I have ever met.

Let me tell you why.

BB understands some very important truths about the art of making a good deal:

- A good deal is one that lasts.
- Once a deal goes bad for one partner, it goes bad for the other one.
- It is almost impossible to hold a partner in a bad deal if he really doesn't want to stay with it.
- Legal words on paper have their value—but that value lies in protecting you from getting screwed, not permitting you to screw your partner.
- What is fair isn't a single point; it's a range. Trying to get exactly what you want is a childish game.
- Situations change over time. Partners do too. Fairness shifts accordingly.

Because he understands these truths, BB knows he doesn't have to fight for position. He goes into a negotiation with a good idea of what is acceptable to him. He knows what he'd like to get (i.e., the upper limit of the range of what is fair, from his point of view) and what he would accept (i.e., the lower limit of that range). If his negotiating partner suggests a deal that falls somewhere within that range, he doesn't haggle. He accepts it.

By quickly accepting the offered deal, BB recognizes that his future partner might think he initially offered too much and try to come back with a less generous offer. But that would tell BB something very important: that the person doesn't have character. And he can simply say to that lesser offer, "No, I don't think I can afford that," and be done with what would have turned out to be a bad relationship.

In getting the other person to put a dollar amount on the deal, BB puts himself in the position of being happily surprised. The offered deal might be at the top of the range that BB had already decided would be acceptable to him. Or it might be above it. If it is above BB's predetermined range, he can choose to accept it or to offer to take less. Why would he offer to take less? Because when he does, he astonishes his partner with his sense of fairness and instantly wins his partner's trust.

Another great benefit of this simple approach is that nobody ever thinks of BB as a good negotiator. Because he has a reputation for being so easy to deal with, people come to him frequently with deals. And when they agree on terms, BB's partners feel very confident that they haven't been fleeced—because BB is not, after all, a "good negotiator."

And if all that weren't enough, BB enjoys one final benefit from his technique: As far as I know, nobody who has ever made a deal with him has ever said anything bad about him.

This is in stark contrast to JSN, my first business partner, who was an extremely bright man and an amazingly powerful negotiator. JSN's intelligence and sophistication at negotiating landed him many favorable deals. And because of his skills, he was known, industry-wide, as the toughest negotiator in the business.

But his objective was always to make the best deal possible for *him*. The more he got, the better he liked it. As a consequence, he made many deals that turned out to be lopsided in his favor. Not only were the benefits he derived from these deals short-term, but his tactics eventually backfired because there were just too many people in our industry who felt like he had taken them for a ride.

The interesting thing about JSN was that he never treated me or his friends like that. Whenever it came time to negotiate with him for my compensation, for example, he took an approach that was much closer to BB's. As a result, I was always loyal to him. (And I made him a ton of money.) In the long run, JSN's best negotiations were when he negotiated the least. I think that is true for everybody.

In making the case for BB's negotiating method, I have to remind you that it will not work for you unless you prepare, beforehand, by figuring out a range of what would be acceptable to you. Too often, I see my colleagues going into negotiations with no idea of what they want or what they think is fair. They just jump in and see where the conversation takes them.

If you want to incorporate BB's beautiful little negotiating technique into your bag of business tricks, you will have to develop the discipline to do your homework.

Doing your homework, by the way, includes getting the advice of your key people. And if you have one or more partners, it may include getting their consent. BB now does this. And so, when he goes into a negotiation these days, he takes with him settlement options that everyone has already agreed are within the range of what is fair.

By the way, I don't want to imply that BB always makes what I consider to be a good deal. Sometimes, when he is buying something for himself, he will pay an amount that I think is too much or too little. But that's my point of view, not his. It is BB who has to live with BB's deals. If he is happy with them, that's what counts.

BEING GOOD AT HIRING

Almost every difficult business problem is at some level a problem with people. And almost every great business achievement is at almost every level an achievement of people. Being good at hiring may be the single most important skill you will need to develop if you want the rest of your business career to be successful and enjoyable. In the next chapter, that's what I'll be talking about.

CHAPTER TWENTY-ONE

FILLING YOUR STAGE THREE BUSINESS WITH STARS AND SUPERSTARS

You've had the experience. After struggling for years with a good but problematic employee, he quits and you replace him with someone who does a much better job, pleasantly and in half the time. You shake your head, thinking: "Why didn't I just dump that jerk years ago?"

Every businessperson I know has the same complaint: "I need more really good people!" And every great employee hears the same bad joke repeated endlessly: "Do you know how I could clone you?"

The people you hire make such a difference.

In this chapter, I am going to talk about how to fill your business with great people. I will talk about how to find them, how to hire them, how to train them, and how to keep them.

If that sounds like a lot, don't fret. If you find the right people, hiring and training and motivating them is almost no work at all!

WHERE ARE THE GOOD ONES?

As I said, every businessperson I know complains about the dearth of good people. But when I ask them how much time they spend on finding good people, they look at me like I'm asking a stupid question. "I spend the normal amount of time," they say.

And that's the problem.

There are plenty of great and supergreat employees out there in the workforce. But you won't get to them if you do the normal things—like asking someone to place an ad in a local paper or on the Internet, then sorting through resumes, and then doing some interviews.

That process is designed to usher mediocre people into your company. To find extraordinary people to fill your top management positions, you have to take extraordinary measures.

First, you need to accept overseeing the process of hiring extraordinary people as one of your two most important jobs as a Stage Three entrepreneur. Overseeing the development of new-product ideas and new ways to market them has to come first—but finding great people to help your business grow is right behind it.

A single great person, properly situated, can easily be worth $10 million or $20 million or even $50 million to you. Off the top of my head, I can name a dozen people who have been worth at least $10 million to me: Myles Norin, Julia Guth, Porter Stansberry, Christoph Amberger, Sandy Franks, Alex Green, Steve Sjuggerud, Katie Yeakle, Brian Sodi, Addison Wiggin, Will Bonner, Erika Nolan, Rebecca McEldowney, Greg Grillot, Jenny Thompson, Karen Redell, Shannon Couch, and MaryEllen Tribby.

Bad employees, on the other hand, can cost you millions. (I do have a short list of people who have cost me millions, but I think it's better to keep it to myself.) Great employees can make your job feel effortless. Bad employees can make you want to quit.

If you want to enjoy the financial and personal benefits of being surrounded with great employees, you have to be willing to devote some serious time and attention to finding them. They are out there waiting. They just don't know anything about your business.

Recruiting great people is not unlike running a successful direct-response advertising campaign. You have to identify your target audience, figure out what benefits you can provide them, and then express those benefits to them in an overwhelmingly convincing way.

You can't just place some standard help-wanted ads and hope for the best.

A well-designed recruitment plan for great employees includes a great sales pitch, aggressive ad placement, and lots of personal canvassing at professional events.

Let's take a look at three recruitment efforts.

A Conventional Ad

Copywriter Wanted

South Florida–based alternative-health doctor looking for talented advertising copywriter to assist in promoting Internet newsletter and natural supplement line. Qualified candidate should have at least two years' experience writing successful direct-response packages. Salary and benefits competitive. Send resume to XXXX.

A Much Better Ad

Your Dream Job Is Waiting for You

This is what you have been looking for—an exciting, relaxed atmosphere to develop your writing talents and rise to the top of the world's best career: direct-response copywriting. It's a dream job for anyone who's ever thought about writing for a living—with great pay, unlimited upside potential, and a chance to show the world how good you are. Plus, you'll be working with attractive, intelligent people who are all committed to creating better health through natural medicine. I am a South Florida–based practitioner of natural medicine with an exciting side business in Internet publishing and the direct marketing of natural supplements. I am looking for a talented person to develop into my top creative person as the business grows. Experience helps, but what I am most interested in is intelligence, a strong work ethic, and a talent for writing. Great jobs like this come along once in a lifetime. Don't let this one slip by. Send me a two-page letter telling me why you would be good for this job.

Note several differences between the conventional ad and the much better one.

- The first ad is short. The second one is somewhat long. A longer ad will get noticed more easily. Longer ad copy has also been proven to be more effective in persuading qualified people to respond.

- The first ad talks about what the business is looking for. The second one talks about what the job offers the candidate (a powerful persuasion technique based on a well-established principle of direct marketing). That's a big difference.
- The first ad makes lack of experience a limiting factor. The better ad makes it less important—and, in fact, character is much more important than experience for most jobs. By not making experience a requirement, you widen the net and increase your chances of catching really good people.
- The first ad asks for a resume. The better ad asks for a letter. This has several benefits. First, and most important, it weeds out the ordinary people who are too lazy or unimaginative to write a letter. Second, it gives you a chance to get a sense of the candidate's personality—something you can't possibly get from a resume. Finally, it gets the candidate excited and thinking about the job in a more serious way. That means a greater likelihood that he will take the job if it's offered.

The Ideal Recruitment Effort

Writing a persuasive ad is not enough. You have to be assertive about how you place it, treating it as you would a direct-response ad. By that I mean you would test it in as many places as you could, take note of which ones produce the most interesting (note I did not say "qualified") candidates, and re-place your ad multiple times. Your goal is to establish a significant pool of potential candidates—as many as 50 or 100 for each job opening.

Now the work begins: reading all those letters. Yes, it would be so much easier to scan resumes for experience and qualifications. But that is exactly what everyone else is doing. And that's exactly why everyone else is getting such disappointing results.

By putting in the time to read the letters you are getting in response to your ad, you will be able to get an immediate feeling for the personality of each candidate. You'll have a sense of an applicant's character, ability to communicate, vision, ambition, and intelligence.

Those qualities are what determine a person's potential greatness as an employee.

After reading all those letters, you're going to have to make some phone calls—10 or 20 or 30 of them. Speaking to the job candidates at this point may seem preliminary, but it is the best way of determining whether the hunches you have about them, based on their letters, are valid.

Get the candidates to talk about themselves as much as you can. But if you notice one who keeps turning the conversation back to you and how he can help you . . . then you know you've found a winner. Great employees understand that their main concern should be how much they can do for the business, not how the business can take care of them.

Eventually, you will interview a handful of finalists in person. These interviews should be more substantial than the usual half-hour conversation and handshake. Put aside several hours to get to know each prospect. Introduce them to other members of the team. If possible, go out to lunch or dinner together.

If you use this approach, you will find that anyone who gets to the personal interview stage is already a very qualified candidate. You will almost certainly feel that you'd be perfectly happy with any of the final five or six. And you probably would be. So just pick one and put him to work on a trial basis. In the unlikely event that you made a mistake, you can replace him quickly and easily with one of the other potential superstars you have put on hold.

TAKING YOUR SEARCH FOR SUPERSTARS ONE STEP FURTHER

What I've just outlined is a superstar search on steroids. But it is by no means the only thing you should be doing to fill your business with extraordinary people. You should also be going to lots of trade shows and other industry events and getting to know lots and lots of people.

By becoming a regular attendee of such events, you will pick up all sorts of ideas about how to reorganize and improve your business. You will also make connections that will end up as joint-venture deals. Most important, if you handle yourself right, you will recruit a lot of really great employees.

In the investment-newsletter industry, the master of this was the president of a major publishing company. He had a great business and plenty of executives working for him who could go to the trade shows. He really didn't need to go himself. But he saw these events as networking opportunities—and the networking he liked best was meeting bright young people who could possibly work for him one day.

He seemed to be everywhere at these events, smiling and shaking hands and making friends. He had an ability to make you feel both impressed and flattered by him at the same time. You knew he was wealthy and powerful, but he seemed so interested in *you*. This combination was a very effective recruiting tool. I never heard Tom make an outright offer to anyone to come to work for him, but the message was somehow conveyed that he would be pleased to make a deal.

CREATING YOUR OWN SUPERSTARS

Your goal should be to have only two kinds of employees: stars and *superstars*. Stars are workers who show up on time, ready to get going and enthusiastically put in a full day of work for you, always putting your customers' interests first. Superstars have all the good qualities of stars, but they also possess the rare ability to create corporate growth.

Everyone who is answering your phones, configuring your data, making your products, handling customer problems, and processing and fulfilling orders should be a star employee. And everyone who is managing all those stars should be a star, too.

The growth side of your business should be manned by superstars, for only superstars are capable of creating and marketing innovative ideas. You also need superstars to create and manage your profits.

You won't find many stars and superstars in the job market. That's because they are already working happily for other people. You might be able to poach a few, but for the most part you will have to create your own. The way to create stars and superstars is by hiring their untrained counterparts: *very good* and *great* people.

Very good people turn into stars, and great people turn into superstars, as long as you provide them with the training and mentoring they deserve.

WHAT ABOUT BAD EMPLOYEES?

When you get to Stage Three of business growth, you can't expect to have nothing but good and great employees. With so many new people coming on every year, there will surely be a few bad ones. But just because the chances of having clunkers increase as your payroll grows doesn't mean you have to accept them.

Jack Welch, the legendary CEO of General Electric, is famous for having said that he routinely fires 10 percent of his workforce every year. I don't know if that is the right approach, because I think it's possible to have a bad-employee percentage of less than 10 percent. That said, I do believe that when you spot bad employees you should do everything you can to make them good fast. And if that fails, you should fire them—because their behavior will be contagious.

But don't worry too much about firing bad people. If you conduct a solid recruitment campaign and manage your employees correctly, the bad apples will drop off the tree themselves.

THE CARE AND FEEDING OF CELESTIAL EMPLOYEES

One of the great things about hiring nothing but very good and great people is that you can dispense with about 90 percent of what conventional corporations do to train, motivate, and mentor their employees.

Very good employees are happy to train themselves. Just give them some training materials and show them where they can get their questions answered. They will do the rest.

Very good employees don't need to be motivated. They come to you hardwired with all the motivation they will ever need. All you have to do is provide them with a goal and step out of the way.

Mentoring, too, is easy with very good and great people. For one thing, you do not need to seek them out. They will come to you. Very good and great employees are intellectual sponges, absorbing everything you tell them even when you think you may have given them too much information. They also understand the deal with mentoring. They know that they are receiving something very valuable from you, and they repay you with long-standing loyalty.

Seven Myths about Training, Motivating, and Mentoring
Employees

**Myth #1: Employees need job descriptions in order to know
the scope of their responsibilities.** This is a popular belief among
corporate types—even the best of them—because they are usually
operations people accustomed to working with formal standards and
complicated processes where precision matters and mistakes can be
costly.

   Reality: Job descriptions aren't necessary. For lower-level operational jobs, it makes sense to spell out responsibilities and procedures.
But for operations managers and almost everyone on the innovation
and marketing side of your business, job descriptions are unneeded
and can be counterproductive because they are, by their very nature,
limiting. My philosophy about responsibility is simple: If you are responsible for growth or the management of operations, there is nothing
you shouldn't be willing to do. Saying "That's not my job" is equiv-
alent to saying "I don't want to work here." Great people don't want
limits to their work, because they see limits as boundaries. The most
motivating thing you can tell a future star or superstar is this: "You can
do anything you want to do here, so long as it contributes to our goals
and objectives."

   **Myth #2: Employees are always motivated by money. It's
naive to think differently.** This oft-refuted myth is still common
among CEOs and entrepreneurs, especially younger ones who have
limited experience leading people. Just yesterday, I heard it from a
young man who had taken his business to Stage Three in less than six
years. He was looking to hit the $50 million mark, and felt he could
do so only by locking in his superstars. But he mistakenly felt that the
way to do that was to throw more money at them.

   **Reality: Money is not even the second most important mo-
tivating force for very good people.** Sleazy salespeople and offi-
cious managers are motivated by money, but very good and great employees are motivated primarily by the opportunity to become more
than they are. Next on their list is recognition. Very good people thrive
on being recognized as good and appreciated. There have been countless studies on what motivates employees, and money is never among
the top three factors. That doesn't mean money doesn't count. You
can't expect to underpay good people and get away with it. Pay your

employees just a little bit more than the going rate so they don't ever feel like you're taking advantage of them—but keep in mind that the main reason they'll stay with you is because of the challenge of their jobs.

Myth #3: To win loyalty from your employees, make them all owners. This, I admit, was a myth that I held near and dear for many years. It always seemed to me that if we could make our employees feel like they had a vested stake in the future of the business, they would work harder and smarter and stay longer.

Reality: Most employees don't want to be business owners. That's why they are employees. In the preceding chapter, I talked about the difference between entrepreneurs and intrapreneurs. Intrapreneurs, I said, are people who have the ability to grow businesses but don't feel comfortable going out on their own. They feel better being a part of something that is larger than they are. They thrive as leaders among leaders, building divisions rather than starting and growing their own companies. This attitude is even stronger among nonintrapreneurial employees, which is to say 90 percent of the very good people who will ever work for you. In my younger days, I tried various ways to motivate employees through stock incentive plans—even creating a cooperative-like structure where every employee had actual stock in the company. None of those strategies ever made a positive difference. The good employees worked no harder. The superstars were no more common. The bad employees were just as bad, and groused because they felt their stock shares were too few. The only substantial difference was that because the people at the top owned only a small percentage of the business, they lacked the motivation needed to grow it. That was bad for everybody. I learned my lesson and promised myself I'd never make that mistake again.

Myth #4: Flat organizations create happier and more efficient employees. The idea here is that employees work more effectively when you eliminate tiers of management. The ideal is to run a business of peers, where every employee can go directly to the CEO to ask questions or get directions.

Reality: Employees like hierarchy. Hierarchy gives them a sense of structure. They know who they report to and who reports to them. Our working lives are confusing enough. It makes it worse, not better, to seek some phony egalitarian flatness by demolishing hierarchy, which is entirely natural and ubiquitous in any form of human enterprise.

Myth #5: The way to make work fun is to fill the workplace with amusements. This was a popular myth during the Internet boom. Every company featured in *Inc.* magazine boasted about its basketball court or Frisbee field or pinball arcade. The idea was that if you allow employees to have fun at work they will work longer and harder.

Reality: Fun comes from doing good work, not from distractions. Turning your office into an amusement park is foolish and counterproductive. Your stars and superstars will not bother with the toys, because they find their satisfaction in their work. Your laggards and goof-offs will use the games—but those people should be working for someone else, not you. I have seen good results from sponsoring workout classes for employees during lunch hours. Other than that, the only "toys" that are helpful are new tools that help people work better and faster.

Myth #6: A good boss is a sensitive boss, one who is willing to respond to employees' personal problems. This is the management philosophy of Michael Scott in the wonderful sitcom *The Office*. The concept, in a nutshell, is that a boss who is also your friend is a boss you will work harder for.

Reality: Mixing business with friendship is always a bad idea. You shouldn't do it as an employee. And you shouldn't do it as a boss. When you treat an employee like a friend, you are giving him the wrong message: that in the business environment, his personal life comes first. Every enterprise can have only one primary purpose, and the purpose of every business should be to improve the lives of its customers, not its employees. When you put your employees' interests above those of the business, you put them above those of your customers. That is a violation of your primary reason for being in business. That doesn't mean you have to be insensitive to your employees on a personal level. You can, if you like, extend all the charity you want to them. But if you do so, you should do so outside of the business environment and with your own resources. Doing otherwise is unfair to the other employees and especially unfair to your customers.

Myth #7: A good boss listens to employee complaints and responds to them. The idea is that employees work better when their job problems are quickly solved.

Reality: Some complaints are better off ignored. If the complaint is related to a problem in getting a job done, by all means listen to it and solve it. But when it has to do with personal feelings ("I'm not getting enough recognition" or "Sally doesn't like me"), it is generally best to listen briefly and then redirect the conversation to the work at hand, as in: "Ah, so you feel like your work on the Mendelson project was not given sufficient praise? Okay, now how are you progressing on the Brown project?" If necessary, remind the employee that you both have the same objective, and that is to make your customers' lives better. Say, "Let's talk about that, shall we?" And then end the discussion as soon as possible. Most of the time this is all you will have to do. If the problem persists, you may have to get rid of the employee.

The bottom line is this: The best and easiest way to grow your business from $10 million to $50 million to $100 million and beyond is to fill it with very good and great employees and to turn those very good and great employees into stars and superstars.

The way to create stars and superstars is to create as much upward mobility as possible in your business so that your employees can achieve what all good employees really want: to exercise their talents as fully as they can, doing something that matters.

Happiness comes from working hard and well at something we care about. If you want your employees to work happily (and you should), you have to communicate your vision of growth and customer service, and then give them the chance to realize that vision by working hard and well in an environment of limitless responsibility.

SOMETHING ELSE TO THINK ABOUT

Back in Chapter 3, I briefly mentioned Elliott Jaques, a Harvard-educated psychologist who had a long and distinguished career studying corporate culture.*

---

*Tom Foster (Foster Learning Corporation, www.managementblog.org) is the colleague who put me onto Elliott Jaques. At the same time, he showed me a chart created by a man named Ichak Adizes, who had a theory about how corporations grow and die that was similar to, but more complicated than, the four-stage theory I have presented in this book. Adizes' idea was that there are 10 stages of corporate growth and decline, beginning with courtship (getting ready to launch the business)

Jaques had a fascinating and persuasive take on how people operate in business. His theory was that in every sizable business there are five levels (he called them strata) of work. At the bottom, stratum one, is what I would call the rank-and-file work—routine physical and rote mental work that often involves simple tools or machinery. Machine-shop workers and data-input operators would fall into this category. In stratum two are jobs that make sure this routine and rote work gets done—what I would call first-level managers. The next stratum is comprised of jobs intended to create the work that stratum one workers do and stratum two workers manage. We might call these people directors or middle managers. In stratum four are the higher-level supervisory jobs—making sure that the people responsible for creating work create it and that the work they create is useful. And, finally, in stratum five, you have the people who manage the supervisors of the work creators—the CEOs.

Each stratum, Jaques argued, has not just different roles, but different tools, learning styles, problem-solving strategies, and values.

A stratum-one employee, for example, might use a hammer or a keyboard, learns best by rote teaching methods, solves problems best by following established protocols, and provides the business with the fundamental value of getting the physical work done. Stratum-two employees use schedules and checklists as their primary tools, rely on charts and projections and plans to do their jobs, and provide the business with the values of accuracy and completeness. Stratum-three people use flowcharts and time schematics to do their jobs and solve problems, can learn well theoretically, and add consistency to the corporate mission.

Underlying all these differences, Jaques said, is a fundamental difference in the span of time workers in each stratum employ when they think about work. The lower the stratum, the shorter the time

---

and then moving to infancy (my Stage One) and then to the go-go stage (my Stage Two) and then to adolescence (my Stage Three) and then to prime (my Stage Four) and then to stable (a later period of my Stage Four) and then on to the declining stages of aristocracy, early bureaucracy, bureaucracy, and finally death. Since my focus in this book has been on entrepreneurial businesses and not on big corporations, I have omitted any reference to those declining stages. But if your business grows bigger than $500 million and becomes stifled by bureaucracy, I would recommend Adizes to you, as well as Jaques.

span. Stratum-one workers, for example, typically think in terms of days, whereas stratum-three workers think in terms of months and stratum-four workers think in terms of years.

This certainly makes a lot of sense. For employees who are filling pill bottles for you, for example, every day is more or less the same. They go into work with the expectation of filling up a certain number of bottles. If they make their quota, they can feel comfortable knowing that the following day their work will be pretty much the same. They don't have any need to think more than a day ahead at any time. And if they did, it wouldn't make them any better at their jobs.

Their managers, however, must think ahead—at least a little bit. They have to schedule all those workdays according to their demand sheets. They must plan to hire more workers or extend hours when they see that larger orders are around the corner.

The vice president in charge of product development must think months ahead, because he is creating the deals that create the demand. And, finally, the guy at the top—the CEO—must think years ahead if he is going to be able to guide the business through its inevitable stages.

Jaques was not just a theorist, he was a clinician. He tested his ideas against carefully observed evidence and found, over the years, that these time-span mental frameworks were not the result of the work—a conclusion I would have drawn—but a result of the inborn nature of the individual employees.

In other words, people are hardwired to think in differing time spans. Most feel comfortable looking forward only a day or two. Some can look months ahead. But those who can see years into the future are very few.

You can't change people's hardwiring, Jaques believed. The secret to putting the right people in the right jobs is to identify potential employees' time-span wiring at the hiring stage, and then place them in jobs that match their natural inclinations. And to get the best out of every employee, you must train them according to their ability to learn and assign them tasks they are capable of.

Pushing employees to perform in a stratum that is above their nature is asking for failure, Jaques believed.

To man your organization according to this theory, you would make sure that you hired stratum-one personalities to do your labor, inspect your products, take orders, conduct research, do filing, do billing, and so on. For jobs like payroll compliance, research director, account manager, and project manager, you would hire stratum-two personalities. Your vice presidents would come from a pool of stratum-three thinkers, and your CFOs and COOs would come from the very tiny group of people who think years in advance, the stratum-four personalities.

Though I have never tested this theory against my experience, it does seem to make some sense. I am not convinced that people can't be trained to think in longer time spans, but I do believe that some people naturally think in shorter periods and that those people probably do need to be trained and managed differently.

In looking for stars and superstars in the future, I intend to keep Jaques' theory in mind. When conducting interviews, I will attempt to discern such time-span proclivities and avoid placing people in positions they are not mentally geared to handle.

Ultimately, you will recognize your potential superstars by the way they respond to challenges, tackle obstacles, and deal with problems. The really good people will perform very well. The great people will astound you.

If you have 100 people working for you, you need about 92 stars and 8 superstars. Finding great people and converting them to superstars is the single most powerful way to solve all your business problems and continue your company's growth.

CHAPTER TWENTY-TWO

BOTTLENECKS, BUREAUCRACY, AND POLITICS

You know how to sell. You are great at producing new products. You have staffed your business with superstars to stimulate further growth, and with other stars and superstars to manage that growth. Everything is in place to grow your revenues to $100 million and beyond.

Yes, the sky's the limit now. But sometime during this third stage of business growth, between $10 million and $50 million in revenues, the structures and systems that you set up to promote and allow growth may begin to grind against one another. So although you've hired a COO to run the operational side of the business, you will have to stay involved on an as-needed basis to readjust the cogs when you hear that grinding noise and ensure that the machine is running smoothly.

During the first two stages of your business's growth, you sped things up. Using the *Ready, Fire, Aim* approach, you discovered how to break into a new market and sell a front-end product successfully. You also changed your business so that it could pump out new products as fast as the market could take them. All that innovation and speed created pressure. And you relieved that pressure by making your business more structured. You created an operational core. You groomed and/or hired professional managers. You urged those new managers to implement new procedures, protocols, and processes, and you stepped back and let them do their thing.

And you have noticed the difference. The chaos that was such a normal part of the day-to-day environment for some years has gradually disappeared. Orders are now processed more quickly. Products are delivered on time. Customer complaints have decreased. The business is humming.

But watch out, because the pendulum is now swinging the other way. And if you don't intervene, your business may swing off balance.

Yes, establishing all the organizational systems and procedures was necessary to provide a basis for further growth. But now that they are in place, there is also in place a corporate tendency toward bottlenecks, bureaucracy, and politics.

These are the primary viruses that affect Stage Three businesses. Yours will probably experience them too—however unlikely that seems to you now. I remember very well how surprised I was each time one of the businesses I was involved with developed these bugs. During the first two stages, everything was always so *Ready, Fire, Aim* and everybody was so gung ho. It seemed impossible that we could succumb to those typical corporate diseases.

But we did, time and time again. Finally, I had to accept it as a natural and inevitable phase of growth. They are destructive bugs, to be sure, but they can be exterminated.

Let's define our terms:

- Bottlenecks are people or procedures that slow things down.
- Bureaucracy is any system or protocol that exists independent of the core purpose of the business.
- Politics is the destructive dynamic that results when people pay more attention to power than profit.

LEGAL COMPLIANCE

The most obvious example of bottlenecking is in the legal compliance area. Many entrepreneurial businesses go through their first two stages with nary a nod to regulatory formalities. Somewhere along the line, legal questions arise. Then, as the organization becomes more corporate, vetting procedures are instituted to ensure that its products and marketing are not problematic. This is all good. As your business grows, it becomes more valuable. The more valuable it is, the more protection it needs.

The easiest and most common way to handle compliance issues is for you, as the CEO, to send out a short memo saying, "From now on all new products and marketing have to be approved by the legal department."

But if that's all you do, the bottlenecking will begin almost immediately. To remedy that situation, you will have to speak to your legal counsel about streamlining the process by educating your marketers, developers, and salespeople—and by training legal associates, if necessary, to handle the traffic.

Compliance is not always a cut-and-dried, black-or-white process. Every industry is plagued by regulations that are obscure, overlapping, and even contradictory. And the regulations themselves don't matter nearly as much as the current practice of enforcement. If the dangers of regulatory sanctions in your industry are significant, you will have to get personally involved in the process, at least in the beginning.

You'll have to become very familiar with the issues and you'll have to monitor your compliance team in action. You may be upset to find that the process is stricter than it needs to be, or you may be alarmed because it seems too liberal. Your job will be to steer everybody along a sensible course that provides the protection you need without slowing down the process too much.

If you can think on your feet, you can make regulations work in your favor. Remember that every restriction you face is also limiting your direct competition. If you can figure out a clever way to follow the regulation without diminishing your production and sales capacity, you will be that much ahead.

That's how I look at legal obstacles—as nothing more than opportunities to make products and promotions more creative.

OTHER BOTTLENECKS

There are many other areas of your business where you can experience bottlenecks. They can, in fact, occur almost anywhere—and that is what is so troublesome about them. You can have bottlenecks in the accounting department that slow down project development or inhibit sales operations. You can have bottlenecks in the data input department that will result in all kinds of subsequent delays. Information technology is, next to legal compliance, probably the most notorious place for bottlenecks. But you can also have bottlenecks within the *Ready, Fire, Aim* side of your business—usually in the quality control functions for product development or the editing and amending functions of marketing.

All bottlenecks are bad for business, and they should all be eliminated. Like legal compliance bottlenecks, the rest of them can be fixed by your intervention. You have the financial power to approve additional technical support if necessary. You also have the leadership power to demand that your teams work together and come up with creative solutions.

Whatever you do, don't accept the argument that bottlenecks can't be fixed.

THE INVISIBLE BOTTLENECK

The good thing about bottlenecks is that you usually hear about them pretty quickly. The employees who are frustrated by them will find a way to let you know what's going on. If you are smart, you will jump in and get things going, and that will be that.

But there is one kind of bottleneck you may not hear about, because everyone's afraid to tell you or because everyone is so accustomed to it. That bottleneck is you.

Just a few months before I sat down to write this book, I led an exclusive business-building retreat where 30 entrepreneurs from all over the world spent four days with me talking about strategies to get their businesses to the next level. (I told you a little bit about it in Chapter 1.) To set the program off, I explained my theory of how entrepreneurial businesses grow—an abbreviated version of what you have learned in some depth by reading this book.

Of the 30 entrepreneurs who attended, 27 had businesses that were squarely in one of the first stages of growth. Three had more substantial businesses, at or around the $25 million mark.

These three had lots of valuable experiences and ideas to contribute to our group discussions. And two of them were happy to explain their businesses to us in some detail and submit themselves to a lot of pointed questions.

Those two entrepreneurs had accomplished most of what all the other attendees were still trying to accomplish. Yet they were there to learn as well as teach, because their businesses weren't growing anymore and they were looking for ideas to jump-start them again.

When I started the interview session with them, I had no idea how it would go. I had been confident that the sessions with most of the other attendees would be helpful, because I had so often been in their shoes, and so had so many of the others. So I was sure that, as a group, we'd come up with a lot of good and useful ideas for them. And we did. But now we were interviewing two men who had stable, highly profitable, Stage Three businesses. Could we come up with anything that would be helpful for them?

Yes. In fact, we had the same recommendation for both of them— one suggestion that could easily have been the most valuable of all that were given at the retreat. And it was as simple as it was powerful: Get out of the way!

Get Out of the Way?

Listening to these two entrepreneurs was inspiring. They had each started with nothing but an idea, struggled in the early years, and then hit on a product that sold well. They then built their businesses on that success by care and worry and lots of attention. They were early risers and hard workers, and they were proud of the products they were providing to their customers.

But although they had both surrounded themselves with superstars and had developed a structure that could accommodate growth, they were so involved in some day-to-day aspect of their businesses that growth was being bottlenecked through them!

One was insistent on inspecting and refining the quality of every product. The other was determined to have all the advertising and sales efforts cleared through his office. The fact that their businesses had grown as large as they had was a testament to how much work these two men could do. But, by their own admission, it was clear that they could do no more.

It took courage for the other attendees, entrepreneurs who hadn't yet done what these two had done, to point out the fatal problem with their businesses. But after the first person made the observation, the others followed. By the time we were finished talking, these two strong-minded businessmen could not deny what was evident: They were interfering with their own businesses' growth.

Since it is unlikely that your employees will tell you if you are the bottleneck in your company, you will have to find out for yourself. There are two simple ways to do that.

The first way is to take a look at how you spend your time and see if you are doing any quality-control sort of activities. As CEO of a Stage Three business, you will certainly want to have some final say over some things, but you should by now have in place qualified and capable people to do most of that work for you. If you are spending more than an hour a day doing that kind of work, you are probably bottlenecking progress. Figure out who could take on some of that work for you, and train that person to do it. Remember that you are not looking for someone to do it the same as you do it. You are looking for someone to do it better than you do it, even if he does it differently.

The other way you can find out if you are bottlenecking your business is to ask. But ask in a way that is likely to get a response. Call a meeting of your top people, tell them that you are committed to eliminating all bottlenecks, and say that you suspect you may be acting as a bottleneck somewhere. Ask them: "What can I delegate or stop doing entirely that would make your lives easier or our business run faster?"

You might hear some surprising suggestions.

BUREAUCRACY

Bottlenecks are pretty easy to spot. Bureaucracy is not. Bottlenecks will frustrate your best people, and they will tell you about them. Bureaucracy is often invisible to them. The problem with bureaucracy and the reason it is so prevalent is that it creeps over an organization slowly, in tiny, incremental degradations.

If bottlenecks are blood clots, bureaucracy is hardening of the arteries. Both can kill you, but one is treated after it occurs, the other by preventive medicine.

To prevent bureaucracy from clogging up the arteries of your business, you should establish a business fitness program almost as soon as

you install your professional managers. Start by establishing and promoting a culture of efficiency. Remind your managers that you are
all working in the service of your customers. Ask them to help the
business do a better job.

Explain that every unnecessary action that is performed in the
business is taking away something good that could be given to the
customer. Tell them that the systems and procedures that have been set
in place are there to speed up and improve things, but that sometimes
systems and procedures become obsolete. Ask them to help you identify
obsolete practices so you can replace them with more efficient ones.

Be on the alert for bureaucracy buffs—managers who have an un-
healthy attraction to formalities—and help them understand the mission or let them go.

Buddy X, a senior manager from the newspaper industry, was hired
by one of my partners to act as chief operations officer for what was
then a $10 million business. The first thing Buddy did, after looking
around the business to see what it needed, was to send out a memo
dictating how all future memos would be written. He was very specific
about how memos would be formatted, and about the type font and
point size of the boilerplate copy. Buddy was particularly insistent on
all employees observing standards regarding the size of their names.
Regular employees should print their names in 10-point type, lower-
level managers in 11-point type, middle managers in 12-point type,
and so forth.

I actually loved Buddy, and during the time I knew him he taught
me a lot about personal productivity and organizational systems. But
his penchant for protocol was over the top. Issuing that first memo on
memos was a bad omen. Several weeks later, when he sent out another
memo insisting on a uniform desktop code (all desks were to have only
four things on top of them: an in-box, an out-box, a nameplate—all
company issued—and the one piece of paper that was being worked
on at the time), his tenure as COO came to an end.

OFFICE POLITICS

Bureaucrats can be mean-spirited sometimes, but usually they are
just overly enthusiastic organizers who lose sight of their role in the

business. Office politicians are much worse. They are people who harbor very bad and destructive ideas about how to get ahead. If you don't root them out of your business, they will destroy it.

If bottlenecks are blood clots and bureaucracy is hardening of the arteries, then office politics is cancer.

I have difficultly liking any political activity, because it is fundamentally flawed. Politics is based on power. And power, as we know, corrupts.

Not all politicians are evil. Some are just plain naive. When your idea of doing good in the world is based on the presumption that you need to have power over other people so you can do it—well, to think that way, you have to be either naive or fundamentally evil.

Politics is, in many ways, the opposite of business. And in almost every comparison, it is inferior.

Ostensibly, politics and business have the same purpose: to make the world a better place. But their methodology is different. Politicians can't start doing good until they get their power. Businesspeople can't get their profits until they do their good.*

This is a big difference. Many politicians, driven to do the good thing, would be willing to deceive voters (if necessary) in order to acquire the power they need to enable citizens to experience that good. It is an inevitable outgrowth of the political system. So long as you believe you know what is best for the world, you can't be a politician and avoid this sort of methodology. You can go into it naively, but sooner or later you are going to be given a choice: Lie now and do good later, or be honest now and lose the power to do good. You choose to do good, and thus you are corrupted.

This is why some of our founding fathers sought to limit the power of the federal government. They understood the fatal flaw of politics. They knew that the best government is that which governs least.

Business is fundamentally better than politics because of this basic difference. In business, you don't pretend to know what is good for the world. You may have an idea about what people might want. You

---

*In making this argument, I am taking a nonjudgmental view of good. It would be fun to compare the merits of a higher minimum-wage law versus a more efficient carburetor, but that is not a fit subject for this book.

create that idea first, and then you sell it to them. They are not forced to buy your idea of what is good. They are free to ignore it. If you are wrong, you realize (unless you are a foolish businessperson) that the idea you thought was good is actually bad. So you stop it. And the world goes on.

If you happen to be right about your idea about making the world a better place—your iPhone or Harry Potter story—the world rewards you by paying you money for it. And all that money makes its way through your business, paying off all the operating and production expenses and eventually settling below the bottom line as profit.

That profit—assuming it is honestly delivered—is the measure of the good you've done. And that's why profit is so important in a business. It forces everybody to pay attention to the ultimate purpose of the business, which is providing benefit to its customers.*

HOW POLITICAL EMPLOYEES WILL HURT YOU

What does this have to do with office politics?

Just this: People who think politically believe in power. They don't feel comfortable operating in a free market, because they don't have the confidence to compete in it. Lacking that confidence, they want to control it. They seek to gain that control by political maneuvers.

Political employees will corrupt your business in two ways. Internally, they will screw things up by setting agendas that are about their amassing personal power rather than about generating benefits for your customers. Externally, they will hurt your business by trying to control the competition. They will spend their time fighting to control things

---

*In saying this, I acknowledge that there are more bad businesses than good ones. Bad businesses are of two kinds: those that deceive their customers and those that try to control markets. The first is based on avarice and stupidity. It is a strategy that may work to make short-term money, but it is not a good strategy for building a business. The second is based on foolishness and greed. Such a business is just like politics, because its aim is to acquire control over customers rather than engage them in commerce.

they cannot ultimately control, and worrying about market share when what they should be doing is helping you create and sell new ideas to benefit your customers.

To prevent political employees from damaging your business, you should recognize who they are (they will often be managers who seem very good to you precisely because they are political), and reform them or get rid of them. I have had very good success reforming former politicians, I am happy to say. I think that is because, fundamentally, the political life is an unhappy one. If you can show them a better way, they will be grateful to take it.

Here are some signs of the political personality:

- They come to you to complain about people, rather than discuss problems.
- They jealously guard their titles, their prestige, and the products they are in charge of. They want you to prevent other managers from encroaching on them.
- They play favorites, and their favorites are those who support them.
- They want their employees to be loyal to them, not to the customer.
- They punish perceived acts of disloyalty, usually by firing or permanently freezing out the offending party.
- They are extremely supportive of you—to your face. But you sometimes wonder if they really embrace your ideas about the business.
- They get into frequent squabbles with their peers over territorial issues.
- They tend to hire employees who are good at following orders.
- They almost never hire people who are better than they are.

THE SOLUTION TO POLITICS

The best way to rid your business of the corrupting effect of politics is to eradicate power mongering wherever you find it.

You can do that by intervention—but that is messy and difficult, because politicians are very good at rationalizing their power plays.

A better way to destroy the spread of this cancer is to destroy the environment in which it operates. That environment is control. The opposite of control is freedom.

The ultimate solution to politics is freedom. The more freedom you establish in your business, the more difficult it will be for politics to thrive and spread.

Freedom means giving your profit center managers and creative people the opportunity to compete with one another in an environment where information is shared and restrictions on product development and marketing are limited. Rather than using your time and intelligence to try to separate and regulate product line barriers, teach your people that, over the long run, they are all better off if they are free to learn from one another and compete with each other freely.

What I'm suggesting is that you take a laissez-faire attitude toward product development and marketing. Some business gurus call this free-market management. When your stronger profit center executives complain that weaker ones are not contributing their fair share, tell them not to worry about fair. Tell them to worry about coming up with the next great idea for your customers.

As your Stage Three business grows, you will find that your stronger profit centers will thrive in this environment while the weaker ones will fail. That shouldn't worry you. It is exactly what you want. You want the growth side of your business to be evolutionary, where the strong survive and the weak extinguish themselves.

In promoting competition, watch out for any effort to curb or control information. Production leaders will naturally want to protect their positions by keeping secrets and setting up barriers to make it difficult for their internal competitors to catch up. Your job will be to make sure those secrets are widely known and to reduce or eliminate those barriers.

This isn't something that can be done once and then forgotten about. It requires constant maintenance so long as you are CEO. When promoting freedom and cooperation in your business, remind your superstars that protecting what they have already done is counterproductive. To continue to lead, they must be focusing on the next great product idea or marketing strategy, not the last one.

At the same time, you have to limit abuses from the weaker profit centers. They shouldn't be allowed to steal trademarks or plagiarize marketing copy. Free-market-based management doesn't mean there are no rules or standards. It means that you apply the common standards that exist in all free markets.

The main thing you can do is keep preaching the gospel: "Our mission is to create new and better products for our customers." Everything your people do, internally or externally, must achieve that end.

CHAPTER TWENTY-THREE

A QUICK REVIEW OF THE PROBLEMS, CHALLENGES, AND OPPORTUNITIES FACED BY THE STAGE THREE ENTREPRENEUR

Getting a business to Stage Three, in which revenue goes beyond $10 million and approaches $50 million, is a great accomplishment.

You've tried and tested ideas, learned from failures, and cheered triumphs. You've taken your initial idea and grown it into an organization that is generating substantial profits by offering quality, market-tested goods to customers. You've had to go from an unruly start-up to a more organized system with well-oiled processes and procedures, but that doesn't mean you aren't still innovative and reacting to the market.

You've learned that at this stage you can no longer do everything yourself. That was fine when you had just a handful of employees, but now you need professional management to run the ship and its crew of superstars, with you as captain.

Most entrepreneurs never even get close to this level. But it's not a time to rest on your laurels. A variety of challenges and problems will crop up during this stage that you will have to face and overcome if you hope to move your company forward to the next level, just as you did when you were going through Stage One and Stage Two.

Using the skills and techniques I taught you in Chapters 19 through 22, you will be able to move your company to the next level, Stage Four, where you can expect revenues of $50 million to $100 million and beyond.

Here are some of the important ideas from this section:

- Can you recognize the signs that your Stage Two business is ready for a change? Do you know what to do if these warning signs appear?
- If more than six people are reporting to you—or coming to you with questions on a regular basis—you have a problem.
- If customer service is falling behind and your operations and fulfillment people are frustrated and overworked, you have a problem.
- Do you understand why you should never have more than six or seven people reporting to you?
- Going from Stage Two to Stage Three is a big change. You are transforming your business from a fast-growing entrepreneurial enterprise to a fully fledged growth-oriented corporation.
- The stronger the entrepreneur, the more he needs the help of professional managers when the business starts straining from too much growth too fast.
- Professional managers should be given lots of freedom, but they must be responsible for achieving your overall corporate goals.
- Don't overdo the amount of information you keep track of. For most departments (and even divisions) of your company, it will be sufficient to keep track of only three important numbers.
- Some entrepreneurs can't bring themselves to pay attention to the operational side of their business. This is a big mistake. Treat your operations managers with the same respect and interest that you give your creative people.
- Don't go around telling people that you are a Big Idea person and you don't like to get caught up in the details. It sends the wrong message to the people who are working on the details.

- To make the transition to Stage Three, you have to change the way you think about corporate culture and introduce both structure and systems into your business.
- There's a difference between an entrepreneur and an intrapreneur. The secret to growing your business from $10 million to $50 million to $100 million and beyond is to make joint-venture deals with entrepreneurs, and to develop superstar employees into intrapreneurs and then let them run your business.
- Do you know how to find, hire, and keep superstar employees? These are the key people who will play a major role in the growth of your business—and one of them could eventually become your business partner and even successor.
- Remember that standard hiring practices are designed to stock your roster with mediocre employees. Finding extraordinary people to work for you requires extraordinary measures. You must dedicate time and attention to the search, and forget about simply posting an ad online or in the newspaper.
- Hiring the right people is one of the most important jobs of any Stage Three entrepreneur.
- Don't become your employees' friend. When you do, your personal life can interfere with business.
- To maximize their potential, for themselves and the company, put employees in the right job, the one most appropriate for their skills.
- You will inevitably hire a few bad employees. Do what you can to help them improve—but then, if there is no improvement, don't hesitate to fire them.
- There are at least six skills you need to develop to be able to manage an entrepreneurial business as it grows into a more substantial company. Do you know what they are?
- There are two secrets for maintaining control of the operational side of your business. The first is creating a core structure that can be centrally managed and sustain growth. The second is to staff it with people who are capable of managing operations in a professional way.
- You may be able to convert some of your key people into executives capable of running some of the operational parts of your business, but you will likely have to import some professional managers too. You need to know where to find them, how

to hire them, and how to compensate them so they stay with you.

- There are many ways to restructure your business to accommo- date growth. On the operational side, departments are usually organized around such functions as accounting and data man- agement. The marketing and product-development side of your business can also be set up functionally, in which case you will have a vice president of marketing, a vice president of product development, and so on. Another way to organize the growth side of your business is to break it into discrete profit centers, each run by a separate intrapreneur.
- Do you understand the advantages of organizing the growth side of your business around profit centers? Do you know the risks?
- If you divide your company into two halves—operations on one side and marketing and product development on the other—it is usually a good idea to hire someone competent to run the oper- ational side of the business and have the profit center managers report to you.
- At this stage of your business's growth, beware of the tendency toward bottlenecks (people and/or procedures that slow things down), bureaucracy (systems outside the core purpose of the business), and politics that can hobble any large company.
- Legal compliance will become an issue during Stage Three. How you react and deal with this potential bottleneck will determine whether it becomes a minor irritation or a major, and expensive, problem.
- As you look for bottlenecks in your company, remember to look in the mirror. As CEO, you should have final say in some matters, but you should have the right people in place to make most decisions in your place.
- Bureaucracy can take over a business, but it is hard to notice because it does so incrementally, over a long period of time. Pre- vention—instilling a strong corporate culture based on efficiency and service to customers from the beginning—is the remedy.
- Don't be obsessed with formalities and protocol.
- Office politics is a cancer that will kill your business. It shifts focus away from your true purpose: creating and selling new ideas

to benefit your customers. Personal agendas, playing favorites, whining, complaining, and backstabbing are poison.

- Watch out for managers who covet power to the detriment of the bottom line, who hire people who just follow orders, or who are more concerned with personal prestige than profits.
- Destroy the environment that breeds office politics. It's too time-consuming and difficult to sort out on a case-by-case basis.
- Freedom for your employees through a laissez-faire management style is the best antidote to office politics. It sets the stage for your brightest to generate the best ideas, and creates an incentive for the weak to improve their contributions.
- Teach your managers and employees to compete in an environment where they cooperate for the greater good. This system will generate the best ideas.
- Instill in your staff that their first priority is creating value for the customer. This should be the basis of any business.

PART FIVE

STAGE FOUR:

ADULTHOOD

CHAPTER TWENTY-FOUR

THE LAST
BIG CHANGE

Very few people are capable of starting businesses. And fewer still ever get their businesses to the third level, where revenues reach $50 million. Anyone who has done that deserves a great deal of credit. Statistically speaking, they are in the top one-one-hundredth of the top one-one-hundredth of the world's population.

So, congratulations. You have achieved the entrepreneurial dream.

If you have developed your business according to the principles outlined in this book, it is highly likely that it will continue to grow to its natural potential. It may grow quickly for a while—perhaps doubling annual revenues to $100 million and then to $200 million

> **STAGE FOUR: ADULTHOOD—$50 MILLION TO $100 MILLION IN REVENUE AND BEYOND**
>
> Main Problem: Sales slow down and may even stall.
> Main Challenge: Becoming entrepreneurial again.
> Main Opportunity: Getting the business to run itself.
> **Additional Skill Needed: Determining the role you will play in the business's future.**

and even to $400 million. But by that time, the natural forces of the universe will slow it down.

You have become a very big small business. Actually, a small big business. You will no longer be featured in *Inc.* magazine. *Forbes* and *Fortune* will be covering you.

This is a great stage. I hope you fully enjoy it.

Because of the nature of this final transition, you will have opportunities that you never had before. There are three in particular I'd like to talk about:

1. Selling your business privately.
2. Bringing it public.
3. Stepping back and becoming chairman of the board.

Richard Schefren, a colleague of mine, has a speech he gives that's titled "Entrepreneurial Roles and How They Change."

The premise of the speech, which he attributes partly to Robert Kiyosaki's *Cashflow Quadrant*[1] and Michael Gerber's *The E-Myth*,[2] is that there are basically four different roles that entrepreneurs must play, depending on the stage of development their businesses are in. The first three are similar to the roles Elliott Jaques identified in his book *Requisite Organization*[3] (which I discussed in Chapter 21).

ROLE 1: THE EMPLOYEE

When you began your business, you had to do many of the routine jobs yourself. You may have dug the holes or written the books or crafted the innovations. You almost certainly created the advertising and placed the ads and then collected the orders when they came in. When customers had questions, they would call you on the phone and you'd solve them. You were the chief cook and bottle washer because you had to be.

You may have enjoyed this role, and that is good—because it put you in a better mood to play the other roles you've had to play since then. But some entrepreneurs continue to play this role beyond Stage One. That is a mistake, because it creates bottlenecks and steals time from other, more productive work.

ROLE 2: THE MANAGER

During the start-up and early growth of your business, you were often, at least initially, the manager of everything. You had to create the structure to get work done and develop systems that were efficient and profit-oriented. You played this role when you first developed procedures to ensure that tasks got done on time. You played this role when you developed your first product and created your first marketing plan and arranged for orders to be taken and products to be shipped and bills to be paid.

What you were doing in the role of manager should have been largely eliminated when you restructured your business as a corporation during Stage Three. At that stage, the only people you should have been managing were the profit center managers, and you shouldn't have been managing their tasks for them. You should have been meeting with them and challenging them to do their jobs.

ROLE 3: THE BUSINESS BUILDER

As the entrepreneur responsible for your business, you have always played the role of business builder—and now that your business is bigger and more sophisticated, this is your primary responsibility. The first duty of the business builder is to articulate the company's core values, business philosophy, and vision for the future. This you may have been doing on an informal basis since the beginning. But back then it was easier. You were working person-to-person with a handful of people. They knew your thinking as well as you did. Expressing your vision was a simple matter of informal and even impulsive comments randomly put.

Now you can't do that. To make sure your ideas are understood, you've had to become adept at formal communication modes. You may not need to be an expert at public speaking, but you certainly have to know how to write a persuasive memo and express yourself forcefully at meetings.

Working with your chief operations officer and profit center managers, you must establish budgets, determine reporting requirements, review financials, negotiate disputes between divisions, and provide incentives for your star and superstar employees.

ROLE 4: THE WEALTH BUILDER

Being your company's primary business builder is a big job. But as it moves into its last stage of entrepreneurial growth, you will be required to play another role—stepping back from the fray and treating your company like a valuable asset. You will look at it not as a conglomeration of working parts but as a single entity: a product in and of itself.

You will have to look at your company the way an outside investor would. You will have to determine what the company is worth now and whether that worth is increasing. As the major shareholder of a Stage Four business, you will have to figure out the return you get on the time and money you put into it and compare it to the return you are getting on your other investments.

As a wealth builder responsible for the increasing wealth of your employees and vendors too, you will have to occasionally ask yourself frank questions about the value of the business. What is it worth today? And what is it likely to be worth five years from now? What can you do to increase that value? What is the greatest danger in its continued growth?

As a wealth builder, you will be less passionate about your business. At least, when you are having these wealth-building conversations with yourself, you will have to discipline yourself to see your business as others might see it, from the outside in. Many entrepreneurs have distorted (usually on the upside) views about what their companies are worth. This does nobody any good, and can be damaging and costly if you are contemplating going public or selling your business privately.

When you began your business, you may have spent half your time as an employee, 30 percent of it as a manager, and only 20 percent as a business builder. When sales kicked in and your business moved into Stage Two, your role as an employee should have been eliminated, and you should have been spending perhaps 60 percent of your time as a manager, 30 percent as a business builder, and 10 percent as a wealth builder. In Stage Three, you should have been spending no more than 30 percent of your time as a manager, at least 50 percent as a business builder, and about 20 percent as a wealth builder. And now that you're in Stage Four, you should make another shift and spend even more of your time as a wealth builder. The amount of time you spend on managing or business building is entirely up to you.

NOW IS THE TIME TO REASSESS THE ROLE YOU WANT TO PLAY

While a business is growing, there is always too much to do. If you are flexible enough to change roles when you need to, you will always enjoy your work, because it will be new and challenging and—most important—meaningful to your business.

When I first retired at 39, I swore that I would never get involved in another start-up business. My heart's desire was to settle into the life of a writer and art gallery owner—and, in fact, that's exactly what I did for a year and a half. That was a very educational time for me. As I explained in Chapter 4, I learned a lot about retirement and retirement businesses during that period of my life.

I learned that I could be very happy writing short stories and having them published. But the measly $900 I earned doing it was barely enough to pay one month's utility bills. I knew that typical extra-money retirement jobs like working as a retail salesperson weren't for me. But I also discovered that the art gallery business wasn't what I expected. I learned that all businesses are fundamentally the same, and that (for me, at least) the fun of a business is building it. Making my art gallery into a retirement career would involve just as much work as I had been doing before I retired. The only difference was that I was entering an industry I knew nothing about.

Luckily for me, I got invited back into an industry I knew a lot about (publishing) by BB, who is still my main client, 18 months after I had left it. Had I waited on the sidelines for another year, it might have been too late. In agreeing to go back to work, I insisted on all sorts of limitations—for example, I would work only as a consultant and no more than 20 hours a week. What I was really doing was trying to protect myself from the work I subconsciously understood I was going to have to do.

I was afraid to get back into business because I was afraid of working hard again. But the moment I started, I was back to my old work hours. I laugh now, thinking of that 20-hour limitation. Who was I trying to kid? BB, who agreed to it at the time, wasn't fooled. He would never have taken me on if he really believed I was going to give his business a part-time effort. Obviously, I was fooling only myself.

The important thing is that I love my working life. There have been moments of frustration and fear and irritation. There have been times when I was worried or upset. But most of my working life since getting back into business has been intellectually and emotionally rewarding.

WORKING EASY

I am telling you this because it plays into this discussion of roles and because you may have some of the same fears I had about being a Stage Four entrepreneur: that you don't want to work so hard, and that maybe your dislike for hard work means you are not really capable of doing it.

If you feel that way, don't worry. I am living proof that you can do very well as a business builder, even if you hate hard work.

I hate hard work, and I almost never do it. The work I do is easy—easy and fun. Because it is easy and fun, I don't mind doing a lot of it.

As a Stage Four business owner, you should be in charge of the work you do. You should not feel compelled to do any of the hard work. You should be able to do pretty much anything you want to do.

Avoiding hard work starts with understanding what kind of work seems hard to you. For me, hard work boils down to one of two things:

1. Doing something that bores me.
2. Doing something I don't care about.

Notice that "working hard" is not one of those things.

Hard work isn't working hard. Put differently, work doesn't become *hard* simply because I work hard at it. On the contrary, anytime I'm involved in something I like and find interesting, I get really into it. I'm fully involved, and time flies—and the next thing I know, my time for work is over. "If only I had more hours in the day," I think. And I mean more hours to work.

If working hard is doing something boring that you don't care about, then working easy is:

- Doing something that interests you.
- Doing something you care about.

One of the best things about owning your own business is that you can make it into anything you want. That means you're doing something that interests you at every stage of its development. And since you have control over your company's future direction, you can't help but care about it.

How do you keep your work interesting?

The answer, for me, is simple: What is new and challenging is always interesting. It's the old, routine work that is dull and boring.

I don't think I am unusual in that respect. I think almost everybody feels the same way. Yes, routines are comfortable and relaxing. But it's the new and challenging work that makes life exciting and fun.

By changing your role from primarily employee to primarily manager, and then to primarily business builder and wealth builder, you have filled your business life with interesting challenges. At every stage of your company's growth, you've had to overcome new obstacles. To do so, you've had to learn new skills . . . and work hard.

You may feel, as I did seven years ago, that you don't want to work harder; you want to work easier. That's good, because that's exactly what you should be doing as a Stage Four entrepreneur.

In fact, looking back at my career, I see a pattern of starting work and then trying to make it easy. I get an idea. It seems very exciting. I work with someone to help me launch the business. And from then on, I'm trying to get our employees to take over my work so I can do something more interesting.

HOW TO MAKE YOUR STAGE FOUR WORK FUN AND EASY

As a Stage Four business owner, you are in the catbird seat. You have a big, valuable business that is giving you more income than you need, and you have a very competent COO running its operations and a group of superstars creating new growth.

So long as you stay on as CEO, you can't abandon your role as the company's visionary. But this job should take you only an hour or two a week at most. How do you want to spend the rest of your time?

- *Employee work.* You shouldn't be doing any work as your own employee. But if there is something you love to do, figure out how to do it on the side—outside of the flow of production so you don't bottleneck business growth. Understand exactly what you are doing: You are not setting a good example for others; you are indulging yourself.

- *Management work.* You shouldn't be doing any management work at all, although you may still be managing the time and productivity of your profit center managers. This is a job that can, and should, be delegated to one of them. Select the one who has the best ability to promote sharing and cooperation. Give that person the reins, and step aside.

- *Business-building work.* The business-building work can be done by meeting with your profit center managers (who, at some point in time, will become vice presidents) and their marketing and product-development teams. If you have developed the skill of stimulating innovative new ideas, you might want to retain that role. But by the time you are doing $50 million or $100 million in sales, you should be able to do it very adequately in just a few hours a week, or a week every two or three months if you have five or six separate profit centers. Playing the business-building role for a business that is well-developed and running smoothly is no more than a part-time job.

- *Wealth-building work.* As your business's primary investor, you have to step back periodically and assess its current and future worth. This is something that needs to be done once or twice a year. It should take no more than a day or two. That still leaves you lots of time for working—if working is what you want to do.

The biggest question you face as a Stage Four entrepreneur is whether you want to continue to work full-time. If you don't, you should select one of your two top people, either the head of operations or the head of the profit centers, to act as CEO. You can still play an important role as wealth builder—and you'll have plenty of time to pursue personal interests without worrying about your business's health.

If you decide that you want to be more actively involved in your business, then you can spend your time as wealth builder, seeking out joint ventures, making acquisitions, and/or planning for divestiture. This can be a very worthwhile way to spend your time—and a lot of fun.

I'll give you my thoughts on that in the next chapter.

CHAPTER TWENTY-FIVE

ACTING AS YOUR COMPANY'S MAIN INVESTOR

I directed the development of two businesses that grew to more than $100 million—one in South Florida and one based in Baltimore. Both were moving along slowly for a while before we made a change. And then they shot upward.

The first was at around $135 million in sales when my partner, JSN, had a heart attack and wanted to stop working and retire. We didn't feel we could sell the business, because it was too dependent on us. So he suggested that we simply close up shop, take the cash, and retire.

That plan would have left me a pretty wealthy young guy. But because my spending habits were inflated, I wasn't sure the millions I'd be getting would be enough to carry me though another 40 years. I was only 37 years old at the time, and still had plenty of energy. Business was fun. And he was the one who had the heart attack, not me!

JSN was the controlling partner—and so I spent a weekend wondering how I could persuade him to keep the business open. My first thought was that he should simply give it to me and let me run it. But then I had a better idea. What if there was a way for us to work only five or 10 hours a week and keep the business open—to keep making money, but do only what we wanted to do?

"Well, if you could make that happen, I'd do it," he told me. So I explained my plan. Rather than shut the business down and take the cash, we'd break it up into five separately incorporated profit centers and provide each with its fair share of cash. We would hire people—mostly current employees—to head up those companies. They would be entirely in charge of their respective businesses, and we would spend only a half-day with each of them once a month, providing guidance and reviewing financials.

We would provide incentives by giving them all profit-based bonuses and shares in the new entities. They would have complete authority to run the businesses as they wished.

JSN was doubtful that the people I recommended as CEOs were fully capable of taking on this challenge. "They probably aren't," I told him, "but I think they are ready."

We talked about it for a week, and then agreed that it was a feasible strategy. If only one out of the five businesses worked, we would end up with more cash than we would be getting by shutting our business down. So we broke up our company and gave the pieces to these young people. And in the next 24 months, revenues went through the roof.

That was a life-changing experience. I discovered how much faster our business could grow when we stepped out of the way. Breaking it up into pieces was a good idea, since the one company that failed was headed up by the person we might have chosen to run the whole thing. More important, by stepping back and acting as consultants, we were able to be more helpful in stimulating growth than we had been when everything was centralized.

What we did was pretty simple: We figured out what one company was doing well and poorly, and used that information to advise the next. When knowledge was passed from one company to another like that, each one was able to advance more quickly than it could have advanced on its own.

That was the first time I felt the immense advantage of sharing and cooperation over hoarding and competition. As I said, it changed my thinking forever.

Ten years later, I found myself in a similar situation. The publishing business I was working in with BB had been hovering around $90 million for several years. Then, almost on a whim, he decided to move to England to try to shore up a fledgling publishing business he had recently purchased there. He had been playing the CEO role at his headquarters in Baltimore until then, so that was a big change. My role had been primarily that of business builder. I was able to do that, with his help, commuting back and forth to Baltimore from my hometown in Florida. But now, with him out of the picture, that was going to be more difficult.

Still, because of the experience I'd had with JSN, I was optimistic that things would work out. BB and I had already arranged the business into separate profit centers that we called franchises.* So with me in Florida and him in England, it was time to let someone else come in and play the CEO role. We promoted the CFO to that position—because we could see that he was ambitious and because we trusted him—and then we let each of the franchise groups know that we would be meeting with them less frequently now, probably only twice a year.

BB spent most of his time building the business in England, and I set about growing a new business (EarlytoRise.com) near my home in South Florida. I was pleased to discover that working with a new business was just as much fun this time as it had been the first few times I did it—maybe more so. Having been operating so long as a business builder, it was fun to do some managing for a while.

Naturally, BB and I were concerned that the core business would shrink because we were paying less attention to it. But something very different happened—the same thing that happened when JSN and I stepped away from our business. The business started growing more quickly now that the profit center managers were free of our constant attention. The new CEO provided some guidance for them, and his associate took over as COO.

What BB and I did was basically walk away from our roles as business builders. Or, rather, we did what we could as consultants—meeting with our profit center managers every quarter for a while, and then just twice a year. And we devoted the rest of our business-building efforts to the new fledgling companies we were developing in England and Florida.

---

*BB had made a big improvement to the simple system JSN and I used by making each profit center a franchise. By "franchise," we meant that it would have its distinct line of products. Our customers could easily understand how one franchise differed from another.

The results were very satisfactory. The core business grew from $90 million to $150 million to $200 million to $250 million, and it's on its way to $300 million. And the Stage One and Stage Two businesses in Florida and England grew and became profitable, too.

These two experiences have convinced me that the most important change you can make when your business gets to Stage Four is to gradually remove yourself from the CEO role and spend your time, if you want to, acting as both an adviser to your company and as its primary wealth builder.

PLAYING THE ADVISER ROLE

Being an adviser to your own business is a very rewarding experience if you can do it the way I've described—breaking the company into separate profit centers and devoting your consulting time with them to passing along secrets from one to another. By the time the business is in Stage Four, because your experience and knowledge of it are long and deep, you will be able to discover secrets about how your profit centers are working that perhaps even their own leaders don't understand. And because you care about their success, you will enjoy teaching those secrets.

As an adviser, you should never expect your profit center executives to do what you say. Their responsibility is to listen to your advice and make their own decisions. If they decide to take a course of action that is contrary to your best advice, you have to let them. If they are good—and they should be good—you will find that their decisions are more right than they are wrong.

By giving your profit centers autonomy, you free yourself from the responsibility to make everything work. It may take some getting used to, but once you have seen how well it works, you will never want to take that burden back.

As an adviser, you (and your partner, if you are lucky enough to have one) will be able to provide enormous value to your Stage Four business while working only a few hours a week. The rest of your time can be spent as a sort of investment manager, acting as the company's Warren Buffett.

PLAYING THE WARREN BUFFETT ROLE

Warren Buffett doesn't play the CEO role. He has made his billions by making wise decisions about how his company, Berkshire Hathaway, invests its assets. That's a very valuable role you can play for your Stage Four business—helping to increase its future value by guiding its most important investment decisions.

When JSN and I broke up our business, stepping back and acting as advisers, we didn't have a strategy for managing its assets because we really didn't believe we could ever sell it. The reason we couldn't sell it, I realize now, was because we weren't willing to treat it like Warren Buffett would have treated it: like a basket of assets. We thought of it as a vehicle to create income, and we pulled 90 percent of the income out of it every year with no thought of reinvestment.

BB didn't think that way at all. He's very frugal with his money. His interest in building a business had nothing to do with buying estates and driving luxury cars. He made it a habit to reinvest 90 percent of the profits back into the business every year. I must say, this took some getting used to at first; but because of him, I learned what Warren Buffett knew when he started out—that wealth building is about adding value over time, not taking it away as quickly as you can.

In my second experience with stepping aside and letting a business run itself, BB and I acted both as advisers and also as investment managers. We formed a committee of six people—the two of us, the CEO, the COO, our corporate counsel, and a senior consultant—and this group has been making the key investment decisions ever since.

Those investment decisions include:

- *Profit distributions.* Shareholders generally get 10 percent of the profits each year.
- *Leadership.* Division heads can be fired only by the investment committee.
- *Senior compensation and profit shares.* Since these decisions can amount to a lot of money, they are made by the investment committee.

- *Major new launches.* Most new products are created without our approval, but entirely new product lines must be run by us before they are funded.
- *Acquisitions.* Any profit center that is interested in buying a competitor can do so, but only after we have approved the purchase and the price.
- *Divestitures.* We have the right to control where the rights to a particular product will go, and how much its new owner will sell it for.

All these issues are regularly discussed by the committee at ad hoc meetings and through telephone conversations. We meet formally only twice a year. All told, our total time commitment is very modest compared to the benefits.

The major benefit we have gotten from playing this role is that there is now much more stability to the company's revenues and growth. We have seen far fewer costly mistakes (million-dollar mistakes) and many more successful new launches. Our profit center leaders understand that our long-term objective is to build long-term value. This makes many minor decisions—such as buying products or starting joint ventures—easier to evaluate, since we have a way to measure their value.

During the past five or six years, we have toyed with the idea of selling the company or taking it public. These ideas were suggested by circumstances. We did not seek them out. In the course of my personal career, I have bought, sold, or gone public with a company several times. So, when we have these conversations today, I make the following points.

Buying Other Businesses

Good businesses—those that are worth buying—are few and far between. But you can find them if you look for them.

A good practice is to tell every business owner you admire that you would like to buy his company. Make that offer as soon as you understand the company's value. Don't name a price, because he's unlikely to take you up on your offer. Still, making the offer will benefit you in two ways. First, it will endear you to him, because he will think of you as smart for recognizing his genius. Second, it will plant a seed that may flower years in the future.

I have been a part of about a dozen successful acquisitions. Almost every one of them happened as a result of this kind of casual suggestion, made years earlier.

Here are a few quick thoughts on buying a business:

- *Buy what you know.* Acquire a business that is, at most, one step removed from the business you are in. If you don't know how it works (if you don't know the optimum selling strategy, for one thing), stay away from it.
- *Don't chase profits.* You should be buying businesses that you can add something to—that you can grow. You should never buy a business because you see that its profits are growing and you'd like to own them.
- *Have a Plan B.* Your Plan A is your growth plan. But what do you do if the business doesn't develop the way you expect? Figure out a liquidation strategy before you buy in. Figure out which assets you could sell and to whom.

Going Public

Most entrepreneurs go public because they want to cash in their stock and earn the big public multiples. In other words, they want to retire rich.

I think that is pretty stupid and shortsighted thinking. If you are a principal of a profitable Stage Four company, you are making more money than you can reasonably spend each year, and you are richer—or will soon be richer—than you will ever need to be. You should never take your business public for a payday.

The only reason to go public is if it gives you a bank account that you can use to invest in the company's growth. If you have such a business, then look into going public. But be forewarned: The reporting requirements and regulations for public companies these days are extensive. The experience of running a public company—especially for an entrepreneur—is not nearly as much fun as running a private business.

Go public only if there is no other way for the company to grow.

Selling Your Business Privately

Why would you want to sell your company if you could simply step back and act as its business and investment adviser?

Again, you don't need the income and you don't need the wealth. Six months after you sell and pocket the cash, you will be tired of golf and looking around for something to do.

Bottom line: Don't sell your business and/or take it public except as a last resort. It's much more fun to own it and enjoy it, playing the roles that you want to play.

Starting and owning your own business is—and always will be—the best job in the world. Don't settle for any other.

AFTERWORD

I am writing this from the deck of a ship at the port of Seattle. We're about to embark on a 10-day journey up and down the Alaskan coast. I have brought my computer, but I will not use the Internet on board. Nor will I activate my cellphone.

My consulting business? I'm not worried about it, because all of my clients' businesses are being run very well without me. I am going to spend a few hours a day writing fiction or poetry or something for my next book on business . . . but when I do that, I'll be doing it because I want to.

I don't have to work hard anymore. I work only when it's fun and easy.

Like I said in the Introduction to this book, you, too, can have the world's best job. You can work . . .

- When you want.
- Where you want.
- With whom you want.
- Doing what you want.

That's what having your own business can give you.

Since I'm on my way to Alaska, let me tell you a story about Alaska.

In 1896, a huge hoard of gold was discovered on the Klondike River. Within a year, more than 100,000 Americans, fueled by the desire to get rich, set off for Alaska to stake their claims.

Of this stampeding 100,000, only 40,000 ever reached the Klondike River basin. The rest were incapable of completing the arduous journey. And of the 40,000 who got there, only half actively searched for gold. The rest were discouraged by the number of claims that were already filed and all the work and paperwork needed to set up a new claim.

Out of the 20,000 who did actively mine for gold, only 300 became rich. The rest eked out a living, always hoping that the next useless claim they staked would be the big one.

Not Belinda Mulrooney. She, too, went to Alaska to make her fortune—but she never intended to pan for gold. The odds of finding it were too long. Her plan was to become wealthy by selling products and services to the gold seekers. To learn about the retail business, she got a job in a women's clothing store in Juneau, and soaked up every trade secret she could while collecting a weekly paycheck.*

Belinda's first entrepreneurial venture was a restaurant that she built in the new town of Grand Forks in 1897. It was an immediate and substantial success. She did not spend the money she made there, however. Rather, she invested it in a hotel in Dawson City (which is now in Canada's Yukon Territory).

Legend has it that when she arrived there in 1897, she threw her last half-dollar into the Yukon River, vowing she would soon be wealthy enough not to miss it.

For her Dawson City hotel, Belinda had collected many fancy furnishings, and had paid a packer named Joe Brooks in Skagway $4,000 to ferry those goods over the pass.

Figuring he could get away with cheating a woman, Brooks dumped Belinda's shipment on the road. When she found out what he'd done, she went back to Skagway and seized Brooks' pack train, retrieved her goods, and brought them all back with her, riding Brooks' own horse.

---

*This account is taken from *Gold Rush Women* by Claire Rudolf Murphy and Jane G. Haigh (Alaska Northwest Books, 2003).

While tending her hotel's bar, Belinda heard the miners talking about which claims were good and which were not. She used this information to quietly make investments in promising claims—sometimes trading hotel and bar bills for shares, and sometimes lending money to gold panners and securing those loans with liens on their claims.

Most of the claims Belinda invested in turned out to be worthless, but a few of them paid off. She used those paydays to invest in a second hotel in 1898, the Fairmont, with cut-glass chandeliers, linen-covered tables, and brass bedsteads, all of which allowed her to charge $6.50 a night for a room and an extra $5 a day for meals.

Providing room and board was a good front-end business, but it was her back-end business—the saloon—that brought in the most profitable dollars. On its first day of business, Belinda's Fairmont bar brought in $6,000!

Belinda was now a successful Stage Two entrepreneur. To grow her business, she improved it—expanding the square footage, upgrading the decor, and adding services. To make it more professional, she hired a manager from Los Angeles and a chef from a famous restaurant in San Francisco.

At the same time, she put her mining businesses under the care of her mining partners.

By 1900, Belinda Mulrooney was the best-known woman in the Klondike, and one of its wealthiest and most admired businesspeople.

The only thing she was missing was a love life. She found that the following year with Charles Eugene Carbonneau, a charismatic Champagne salesman from Quebec who modeled himself in the style of a European count, attired in kid gloves, spats, and a monocle. He wooed Belinda, it is said, with smooth talk and roses, and married her in October of 1901.

The upwardly mobile couple honeymooned in Paris, where Carbonneau introduced his entrepreneur wife to the high life, visiting museums, galleries, and retail stores during the day and fine restaurants at night, traveling frequently in a red coach drawn by white horses. The Carbonneaus began spending winters in Paris and summers in Dawson City. But after a few years, Belinda's mining businesses began to falter. To turn things around, she fired her managers and went back to running them herself.

While all this was going on, her husband was conning people and embezzling money. He got caught and skipped town, taking Belinda's furs and jewels with him. He left behind a mountain of legal problems for Belinda, which she set about trying to resolve. In 1904, when a new gold strike in Fairbanks was announced, Belinda got on the last boat out of Dawson City and, within months, had options on three of the richest claims in the district.

She prospected and mined throughout that summer, and then returned the next spring with her two sisters. The three women set up housekeeping in Dome City, a mining camp 16 miles from the craziness of Fairbanks. Two years later, with profits from her mines, Belinda opened the Dome City Bank, naming her sister Margaret and a man named Jesse Noble as partners. Servicing the booming community, the bank became very successful—and Belinda became wealthy for a second time.

She left Dome City and the North Country for good in 1908 and bought property in Yakima, Washington, where she built a beautiful mansion, a local landmark that became known as Carbonneau's Castle.

She lived a long life, dying in Seattle in 1967 at the age of 95.

Born in Ireland, Belinda Mulrooney had spent her childhood as the daughter of a poor coal miner in Pennsylvania. She left home at the age of 18, and made her way to the booming city of Chicago. There are no detailed accounts of her life there. What is known is that when she arrived in Chicago, she was broke and uneducated. Six years later, she had scraped together enough money to open her first restaurant in Grand Forks.

Entrepreneurs are a rare and wonderful species. Spurred on by the hope of fortune, they make sacrifices and endure hardships that most will not contemplate. Of those who succeed in starting businesses, few develop them beyond what is essentially a self-employment job.

Yet... it can be done. In fact, it is easier to do it today than at any time in history. Thanks to the science of direct marketing and the global reach of the Internet, anyone can start and grow a substantial and highly profitable business. You don't need a gold rush in Alaska—just some experienced advice to guide you... and a bit of the spirit that was so alive in Belinda Mulrooney.

NOTES

CHAPTER 3   BECOMING A FIVE-STAR BUSINESS GENIUS

1. Elliott Jaques, *Requisite Organization* (Green Cove Springs, FL: Cason Hall and Co., 1998).
2. Seth Godin, *If You're Clueless About Starting Your Own Business* (Chicago: Dearborn, A Kaplan Professional Company, 1998), 2.
3. Ibid., 4.
4. Ibid., 12.

CHAPTER 4   THE SUPREMACY OF SELLING

1. James Koch, "Portrait of a CEO as Salesman," *Inc.com*, March 1988, www.inc.com/magazine/19880301/5901.html (accessed February 3, 2007), 1.
2. Ibid.
3. Ted Ciuba, *Mail and Grow Rich* (Nashville, TN: Parthenon Marketing, 2000).
4. Jill Andresky Fraser, "Start Me Up," *More*, February 2003.

CHAPTER 6 MASTERING THE COPY SIDE OF SELLING

1. Al Ries and Jack Trout, *Positioning* (New York: McGraw-Hill, 2001), 24.
2. Seth Godin, *If You're Clueless About Starting Your Own Business* (Chicago: Dearborn, A Kaplan Professional Company, 1998), 36.
3. Ibid., 34.
4. Jay Abraham, *Getting Everything You Can Out of All You've Got* (New York: Truman Talley Books/St. Martin's Griffin, 2001).
5. Ibid., 81–84.

CHAPTER 9 FROM $1 MILLION TO $10 MILLION AND BEYOND: HOW TO BREAK THROUGH THE ONE-PRODUCT-COMPANY SYNDROME

1. Number of Businesses by Revenue Size 2007, www.bizstats.com/businessesbyrevenue.htm.

CHAPTER 10 INNOVATION—THE KEY TO SECOND-STAGE GROWTH

1. Malcolm Gladwell, *The Tipping Point* (New York: Little, Brown and Company, 2000).

CHAPTER 11 SPEED: PUTTING *READY, FIRE, AIM* INTO YOUR BUSINESS

1. Robert Cialdini, *Influence: The Psychology of Persuasion* (New York: William Morrow and Company, 1984).

CHAPTER 12 GETTING READY

1. Rifka Rosenwein, "At Their Knee," *Inc.*, October 2001.

CHAPTER 17 *READY, FIRE, AIM* IN ACTION

1. Bob Knopf, "Ten Tips to Better Wing & Clay Shooting," *America Outdoors*, www.americaoutdoors.com/shooting/features/ten_tips.htm (accessed January 22, 2007).

CHAPTER 24   THE LAST BIG CHANGE

1. Robert Kiyosaki and Sharon Lechter, *Rich Dad's Cashflow Quadrant: Rich Dad's Guide to Financial Freedom* (New York: Warner Books, 2000).
2. Michael Gerber, *The E-Myth* (New York: HarperBusiness, 1986).
3. Elliott Jaques, *Requisite Organization* (Green Cove Springs, FL: Cason Hall and Co., 1998).

INDEX

SPECIAL for Readers of *Ready, Fire, Aim*

Discover Even More of Michael Masterson's Entrepreneurial and Business Building Secrets

Congratulations! You've just learned dozens of unique and powerful techniques for starting and growing a successful business in *Ready, Fire, Aim: Zero to $100 Million in No Time Flat.*

That's a great start, but experts agree that success is a continuous process. And that's exactly what inspired Michael Masterson to found what has now become the Internet's most popular daily success e-zine, *Early to Rise.*

Delivered to your in-box bright and early each morning, *Early to Rise (ETR)* is your daily dose of actionable information on wealth building, entrepreneurship, marketing, advertising, copywriting, and key success topics whose proper understanding and execution is essential to taking your business to the next level.

Different from so much of the "conventional wisdom" you'll read elsewhere, *Early to Rise* goes beyond the mass media to report the cutting-edge and contrarian business ideas that are actually working in the marketplace right now—not hackneyed ideas from months or years ago.

In *Early to Rise*, Michael Masterson and an extraordinary team of experienced entrepreneurs, marketers, copywriters, and industry leaders will be in your in-box every morning with constant encouragement and smart new ideas you can use to augment the business-building wisdom you've just acquired in *Ready, Fire, Aim.*

Like *Ready, Fire, Aim, Early to Rise* will provide you with tools you can use to take your entrepreneurial venture to the next level, no matter where you are at now. It's put together in an easy-to-understand format that will quickly become the most productive part of your morning routine. Reading *ETR* will take just five minutes, but what you learn will last a lifetime!

As a reader of *Ready, Fire, Aim*, you are eligible to immediately sign up for a complimentary subscription to *Early to Rise*. You can unsubscribe at any time with no obligation. So why not try it out? Please visit www.earlytorise.com/ReadyFireAim.htm right now and you'll receive your first issue tomorrow.